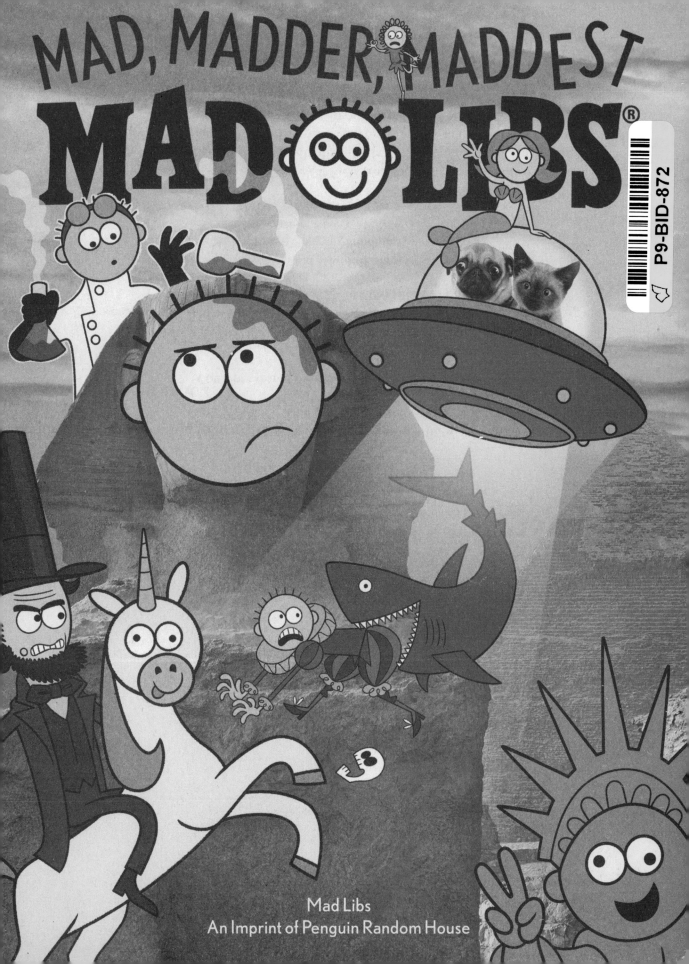

MAD, MADDER, MADDEST
MAD LIBS®

Mad Libs
An Imprint of Penguin Random House

MAD LIBS
Penguin Young Readers Group
An Imprint of Penguin Random House LLC

Mad Libs format and text copyright © 2014, 2015, 2016, 2017, 2018 by Penguin Random House LLC.
All rights reserved.

Concept created by Roger Price & Leonard Stern

Cover illustration by Scott Brooks

Photo credits: *Dog Ate My Mad Libs*: Eric Isselée/Thinkstock, *History of the World Mad Libs*:
Niko Guido/Getty Images, *Meow Libs*: GlobalP/Thinkstock

Mad, Madder, Maddest Mad Libs published in 2018 by Mad Libs,
an imprint of Penguin Random House LLC,
345 Hudson Street, New York, New York 10014.
Printed in the USA.

Mad, Madder, Maddest Mad Libs ISBN 9781524791520

1 3 5 7 9 10 8 6 4 2

MAD LIBS®
UNICORNS, MERMAIDS, AND MAD LIBS

by Billy Merrell

Mad Libs
An Imprint of Penguin Random House

INSTRUCTIONS

MAD LIBS® is a game for people who don't like games!
It can be played by one, two, three, four, or forty.

• RIDICULOUSLY SIMPLE DIRECTIONS

In this tablet you will find stories containing blank spaces where words are left out. One player, the READER, selects one of these stories. The READER does not tell anyone what the story is about. Instead, he/she asks the other players, the WRITERS, to give him/her words. These words are used to fill in the blank spaces in the story.

• TO PLAY

The READER asks each WRITER in turn to call out a word—an adjective or a noun or whatever the space calls for—and uses them to fill in the blank spaces in the story. The result is a MAD LIBS® game.

When the READER then reads the completed MAD LIBS® game to the other players, they will discover that they have written a story that is fantastic, screamingly funny, shocking, silly, crazy, or just plain dumb—depending upon which words each WRITER called out.

• EXAMPLE (*Before* and *After*)

"_____!" he said _____
    EXCLAMATION   ADVERB

as he jumped into his convertible _____ and
               NOUN

drove off with his _____ wife.
      ADJECTIVE

"_____OUCH_____!" he said _____STUPIDLY_____
    EXCLAMATION   ADVERB

as he jumped into his convertible _____CAT_____ and
               NOUN

drove off with his _____BRAVE_____ wife.
      ADJECTIVE

MAD LIBS®

QUICK REVIEW

In case you have forgotten what adjectives, adverbs, nouns, and verbs are, here is a quick review:

An ADJECTIVE describes something or somebody. *Lumpy, soft, ugly, messy,* and *short* are adjectives.

An ADVERB tells how something is done. It modifies a verb and usually ends in "ly." *Modestly, stupidly, greedily,* and *carefully* are adverbs.

A NOUN is the name of a person, place, or thing. *Sidewalk, umbrella, bridle, bathtub,* and *nose* are nouns.

A VERB is an action word. *Run, pitch, jump,* and *swim* are verbs. Put the verbs in past tense if the directions say PAST TENSE. *Ran, pitched, jumped,* and *swam* are verbs in the past tense.

When we ask for A PLACE, we mean any sort of place: a country or city *(Spain, Cleveland)* or a room *(bathroom, kitchen).*

An EXCLAMATION or SILLY WORD is any sort of funny sound, gasp, grunt, or outcry, like *Wow!, Ouch!, Whomp!, Ick!,* and *Gadzooks!*

When we ask for specific words, like a NUMBER, a COLOR, an ANIMAL, or a PART OF THE BODY, we mean a word that is one of those things, like *seven, blue, horse,* or *head.*

When we ask for a PLURAL, it means more than one. For example, *cat* pluralized is *cats.*

MAD LIBS® is fun to play with friends, but you can also play it by yourself! To begin with, DO NOT look at the story on the page below. Fill in the blanks on this page with the words called for. Then, using the words you have selected, fill in the blank spaces in the story.

Now you've created your own hilarious MAD LIBS® game!

HOW TO HATCH A DRAGON EGG

ADJECTIVE _____

PLURAL NOUN _____

PLURAL NOUN _____

COLOR _____

NUMBER _____

VERB _____

TYPE OF LIQUID _____

ADJECTIVE _____

PLURAL NOUN _____

NUMBER _____

ADJECTIVE _____

NOUN _____

SILLY WORD _____

A PLACE _____

ADJECTIVE _____

NOUN _____

VERB ENDING IN "ING" _____

PART OF THE BODY (PLURAL) _____

While most eggs need _____ love and care for the _____
ADJECTIVE   PLURAL NOUN

inside to survive, dragon eggs thrive on danger! In fact, the _____
PLURAL NOUN

of _____ dragons *require* a/an _____-foot drop in order to
COLOR   NUMBER

_____ open. Eggs of _____ dragons depend on
VERB   TYPE OF LIQUID

_____ lava from underwater _____ to heat the shells to
ADJECTIVE   PLURAL NOUN

temperatures of _____ degrees or more. Only then can the _____
NUMBER   ADJECTIVE

dragonets inside finally hatch. But the _____ of the skies,
NOUN

the _____ dragon of (the) _____, is the most _____
SILLY WORD   A PLACE   ADJECTIVE

_____-layer of them all! They have been spotted
NOUN

_____ into the _____ of hungry predators,
VERB ENDING IN "ING"   PART OF THE BODY (PLURAL)

hoping to be swallowed. Once they hatch, they cause quite a bellyache!

MAD LIBS® is fun to play with friends, but you can also play it by yourself! To begin with, DO NOT look at the story on the page below. Fill in the blanks on this page with the words called for. Then, using the words you have selected, fill in the blank spaces in the story.

Now you've created your own hilarious MAD LIBS® game!

WHAT UNICORNS EAT

PLURAL NOUN _____

ADJECTIVE _____

NOUN _____

TYPE OF FOOD _____

ARTICLE OF CLOTHING (PLURAL) _____

VERB ENDING IN "ING" _____

PLURAL NOUN _____

PLURAL NOUN _____

NUMBER _____

CELEBRITY (FEMALE) _____

COLOR _____

VERB ENDING IN "ING" _____

TYPE OF FOOD (PLURAL) _____

PLURAL NOUN _____

ADJECTIVE _____

ADJECTIVE _____

Would it surprise you to learn that the most majestic _bananas_ in the
PLURAL NOUN

world eat garbage? Well, they do! Everything from _running_
ADJECTIVE

soda cans to _peppa pig_-stained _mango_ boxes to used
NOUN   TYPE OF FOOD

socks —and more! Some have been spotted
ARTICLE OF CLOTHING (PLURAL)

striking dumpsters and then using their long _baseballs_
VERB ENDING IN "ING"   PLURAL NOUN

to spear as many bags of _OJ's_ as they can before being caught.
PLURAL NOUN

According to an interview with _10_ Minutes, _Lady gaga_
NUMBER   CELEBRITY (FEMALE)

once came home to find a/an _blue_ unicorn _juicing_
COLOR   VERB ENDING IN "ING"

up in her recycling bin. The poor thing had mistaken her husband's leftover

fries for dried-up _Ginas_. "It was a/an _crispy_
TYPE OF FOOD (PLURAL)   PLURAL NOUN   ADJECTIVE

mistake," she said. "My husband is a/an _black_ cook!"
ADJECTIVE

MAD LIBS® is fun to play with friends, but you can also play it by yourself! To begin with, DO NOT look at the story on the page below. Fill in the blanks on this page with the words called for. Then, using the words you have selected, fill in the blank spaces in the story.

Now you've created your own hilarious MAD LIBS® game!

BAD HOUSEKEEPING

NOUN_____

ADJECTIVE_____

NOUN_____

PLURAL NOUN_____

VERB ENDING IN "ING"_____

PLURAL NOUN_____

NOUN_____

PLURAL NOUN_____

TYPE OF FOOD_____

NOUN_____

SILLY WORD_____

A PLACE_____

NUMBER_____

NOUN_____

SAME NOUN_____

MAD LIBS®
BAD HOUSEKEEPING

The troll that lives under the __pizza__ shares tips for keeping his home
NOUN

__small__ clean.
ADJECTIVE

- **Decorate sparingly.** Don't clutter up your __Midget__
NOUN

with sentimental garbage, like pictures of __dwarves__ or
PLURAL NOUN

__pooping__ trophies. Having too many __holes__
VERB ENDING IN "ING"   PLURAL NOUN

visible ruins the element of surprise!

- **Clean up immediately.** It's easy to let __fartcloud__-work get
NOUN

away from you. Wash the __werner__ right after meals, so that
PLURAL NOUN

__ravioli__ doesn't sit too long in the sink. For a troll, scraps of
TYPE OF FOOD

__women__ could be considered evidence!
NOUN

- **Make the most of it.** Even if it doesn't win the __ash noon__ award
SILLY WORD

for best home in (the) __your mom__, it's still yours! Spend at least
A PLACE

__26__ minutes a day simply sitting back and appreciating your
NUMBER

" __buttcheeks__, sweet __buttcheeks__."
NOUN   SAME NOUN

MAD LIBS® is fun to play with friends, but you can also play it by yourself! To begin with, DO NOT look at the story on the page below. Fill in the blanks on this page with the words called for. Then, using the words you have selected, fill in the blank spaces in the story.

Now you've created your own hilarious MAD LIBS® game!

ENCOUNTER WITH BIGFOOT

NOUN _____

A PLACE _____

PART OF THE BODY _____

NOUN _____

ADJECTIVE _____

ADJECTIVE _____

PART OF THE BODY (PLURAL) _____

ADJECTIVE _____

ADJECTIVE _____

TYPE OF FOOD _____

VERB ENDING IN "ING" _____

ANIMAL _____

PART OF THE BODY (PLURAL) _____

VERB ENDING IN "ING" _____

CELEBRITY _____

NOUN _____

TYPE OF LIQUID _____

TYPE OF FOOD _____

MAD LIBS®
ENCOUNTER WITH BIGFOOT

Before they vanished, a well-trained ___nesting doll___ (NOUN) of explorers sent an SOS

from the snowy peaks of (the) ___bushyland___ (A PLACE), claiming to have spotted Big-

___wiener___ (PART OF THE BODY). This is what their ~~honey~~ ___honey hole___ (NOUN) said:

OMG, he's real. I'm looking at ___Soar___ (ADJECTIVE) -foot right now. And he's

___chocolaty___ (ADJECTIVE) ! I've never seen such human ___big bazumbas___ (PART OF THE BODY (PLURAL)) on a

creature so ___peppery___ (ADJECTIVE) ! At first he looked as ___frosty___ (ADJECTIVE) as we all were.

But as we approached, he became cool as a/an ___boiled wiener___ (TYPE OF FOOD), silently

___Rushing___ (VERB ENDING IN "ING") us. "What's the matter?" I said. " ___Orangutang___ (ANIMAL)

got your tongue?" But we couldn't believe our ___tounges___ (PART OF THE BODY (PLURAL)) —he

actually spoke! Now the creature won't stop ___juicing___ (VERB ENDING IN "ING") on and on

about ___Kent Rollins___ (CELEBRITY) and ___butthole___ (NOUN) -flavored ~~pee~~ ___hot pee. pee___ (TYPE OF LIQUID)

Help! Someone make this beast shut his ___enchilada___ (TYPE OF FOOD) -hole!

MAD LIBS® is fun to play with friends, but you can also play it by yourself! To begin with, DO NOT look at the story on the page below. Fill in the blanks on this page with the words called for. Then, using the words you have selected, fill in the blank spaces in the story.

Now you've created your own hilarious MAD LIBS® game!

A-MAZE-ING MINOTAUR

ANIMAL _____

NOUN _____

PLURAL NOUN _____

ADJECTIVE _____

VERB _____

ADJECTIVE _____

PLURAL NOUN _____

VERB _____

ADJECTIVE _____

PART OF THE BODY (PLURAL) _____

PLURAL NOUN _____

NOUN _____

PLURAL NOUN _____

ADJECTIVE _____

NOUN _____

ANIMAL _____

MAD LIBS

A-MAZE-ING MINOTAUR

Interviewer: So, what's it like having a/an _____ head, but a human
ANIMAL

_____?
NOUN

Mini: It's just about what you'd expect. _____ don't take me
PLURAL NOUN

seriously. My therapist misses every _____ appointment. I could
ADJECTIVE

_____!
VERB

Interviewer: How unfortunate! Do you think they are _____ against
ADJECTIVE

all non-_____, or what?
PLURAL NOUN

Mini: I do hunt and _____ people I find wandering lost inside the maze.
VERB

That could be the reason for the _____ look in their
ADJECTIVE

_____.
PART OF THE BODY (PLURAL)

Interviewer: That seems likely. After all, _____ speak louder than
PLURAL NOUN

words. With that in _____, do you have anything to say to the families
NOUN

of your _____?
PLURAL NOUN

Mini: Only that it's never _____ to judge a book by its _____.
ADJECTIVE   NOUN

Despite my looks, on the inside I have the heart of a/an _____.
ANIMAL

MAD LIBS® is fun to play with friends, but you can also play it by yourself! To begin with, DO NOT look at the story on the page below. Fill in the blanks on this page with the words called for. Then, using the words you have selected, fill in the blank spaces in the story.

Now you've created your own hilarious MAD LIBS® game!

A GENIE'S CONTRACT

ADJECTIVE _____

VERB ENDING IN "ING" _____

NUMBER _____

NOUN _____

NUMBER _____

NOUN _____

NOUN _____

ADJECTIVE _____

A PLACE _____

NUMBER _____

ADJECTIVE _____

VERB _____

VERB _____

NOUN _____

NOUN _____

PLURAL NOUN _____

ADVERB _____

MAD LIBS

A GENIE'S CONTRACT

Be sure to read the _____ print:
                       ADJECTIVE

The individual responsible for _____ the lamp is entitled to
                                VERB ENDING IN "ING"

_____ wishes, to be granted by the _____ inside. Limit
   NUMBER   NOUN

_____ wishes per master, or one (1) _____ per day. At the genie's
   NUMBER   NOUN

discretion, a/an _____ may be substituted for a lamp at any time.
                     NOUN

Offer only _____ at participating locations, excluding (the)
              ADJECTIVE

_____. Official wishes must be limited to _____ characters, in
 A PLACE   NUMBER

order to minimize _____ consequences that may _____ due
                     ADJECTIVE   VERB

to unnecessary verbosity. May not be used to make a person _____ in love
                                                              VERB

or combined with any other _____ or offer. The lamp (or substituted
                              NOUN

_____) must be surrendered after the final wish. Wishing for more
   NOUN

_____ is _____ prohibited.
 PLURAL NOUN   ADVERB

MAD LIBS® is fun to play with friends, but you can also play it by yourself! To begin with, DO NOT look at the story on the page below. Fill in the blanks on this page with the words called for. Then, using the words you have selected, fill in the blank spaces in the story.

Now you've created your own hilarious MAD LIBS® game!

WHY GIANTS DON'T SLEEP

VERB _____

NUMBER _____

ADJECTIVE _____

ADJECTIVE _____

EXCLAMATION _____

PART OF THE BODY _____

PART OF THE BODY _____

ADJECTIVE _____

PLURAL NOUN _____

VERB _____

COLOR _____

TYPE OF LIQUID _____

PLURAL NOUN _____

ADVERB _____

VERB ENDING IN "ING" _____

ANIMAL _____

ARTICLE OF CLOTHING (PLURAL) _____

MAD LIBS
WHY GIANTS DON'T SLEEP

Finding a place to sit and __juice__ (VERB) when you're more than __14__ (NUMBER) __twisty__

feet tall is no __diddling__ (ADJECTIVE) task. And lying down is next to ~~twisting~~ (ADJECTIVE)!

__Holy bat balls__ (EXCLAMATION)! It would take an area the size of two __Pee hole__ ~~toe~~ (PART OF THE BODY) -ball fields

for a giant to stretch out from head to __wiener__ (PART OF THE BODY). That's why, for a giant,

waking up on the __firey__ (ADJECTIVE) side of the bed is all but inevitable. The

closest that most __beaks__ (PLURAL NOUN) get to a comfortable place to __lynch__ (VERB)

are bogs, where __fucia__ (COLOR) mud, __diahrea__ (TYPE OF LIQUID), and dead

__broom sticks__ (PLURAL NOUN) form a kind of mattress. And even there, they must take care

not to sleep too __quietly__ (ADVERB), or else they risk __booming__ (VERB ENDING IN "ING")

in the mud and drowning. Besides, most giants would rather chug Red

__dalmatian__ (ANIMAL) all night than get mud on their __bikinis__ (ARTICLE OF CLOTHING (PLURAL)).

MAD LIBS® is fun to play with friends, but you can also play it by yourself! To begin with, DO NOT look at the story on the page below. Fill in the blanks on this page with the words called for. Then, using the words you have selected, fill in the blank spaces in the story.

Now you've created your own hilarious MAD LIBS® game!

CERBERUS TRAINING

PERSON IN ROOM (MALE) _____

NUMBER _____

ANIMAL _____

PLURAL NOUN _____

SILLY WORD _____

NOUN _____

VERB _____

VERB _____

TYPE OF FOOD _____

PART OF THE BODY (PLURAL) _____

VERB _____

PART OF THE BODY _____

ADJECTIVE _____

ADVERB _____

PLURAL NOUN _____

ADJECTIVE _____

VERB _____

NOUN _____

VERB ENDING IN "ING" _____

MAD LIBS®
CERBERUS TRAINING

Here are some tips for training _____, your _____-headed
PERSON IN ROOM (MALE)   NUMBER

guard _____.
ANIMAL

1. Be consistent. The same _____ and commands should always
PLURAL NOUN

apply.

2. Be concise. Don't say _____ several times in a/an _____,
SILLY WORD   NOUN

or else he'll _____ the word out entirely.
VERB

3. Be generous. _____ him for being right by giving him treats,
VERB

like _____—yes, one for each of his _____.
TYPE OF FOOD   PART OF THE BODY (PLURAL)

But don't over-_____ him! Verbal praise and _____
VERB   PART OF THE BODY

massages can serve as _____ reinforcement, too.
ADJECTIVE

4. Be patient. Understand that training him _____ takes time.
ADVERB

Don't expect immediate _____. Take a/an _____ tone
PLURAL NOUN   ADJECTIVE

and _____ at him so he knows you're on his _____.
VERB   NOUN

5. Lastly, enjoy! Make sure you both have a good time, and he'll be

_____ out of your hand in no time.
VERB ENDING IN "ING"

MAD LIBS® is fun to play with friends, but you can also play it by yourself! To begin with, DO NOT look at the story on the page below. Fill in the blanks on this page with the words called for. Then, using the words you have selected, fill in the blank spaces in the story.

Now you've created your own hilarious MAD LIBS® game!

PEGASUS BREAKS GROUND

ANIMAL _____

OCCUPATION _____

VERB ENDING IN "ING" _____

A PLACE _____

PERSON IN ROOM (FEMALE) _____

PART OF THE BODY (PLURAL) _____

TYPE OF LIQUID _____

NOUN _____

NUMBER _____

A PLACE _____

CELEBRITY (MALE) _____

NUMBER _____

CELEBRITY (FEMALE) _____

NOUN _____

SILLY WORD _____

VERB ENDING IN "ING" _____

ADJECTIVE _____

MAD LIBS

PEGASUS BREAKS GROUND

Breaking news! A flying _____ escaped from his _____ today
                        ANIMAL   OCCUPATION

while _____ for the Muses in (the) _____. According
       VERB ENDING IN "ING"   A PLACE

to the witness, _____, when the creature dug his
                 PERSON IN ROOM (FEMALE)

_____ into the soil, a spring of _____ bubbled
PART OF THE BODY (PLURAL)   TYPE OF LIQUID

up from the ground, forming a/an _____-clear fountain. For the past
                                  NOUN

_____ hours, Muses from as far away as (the) _____ have come
  NUMBER   A PLACE

to see the miracle for themselves. _____ offered to buy the
                                    CELEBRITY (MALE)

creature for _____ dollars, but _____, backed by a
              NUMBER   CELEBRITY (FEMALE)

crowd of _____-rights activists, insisted the animal isn't for sale. In
          NOUN

related news, the _____ Corporation has already bought
                   SILLY WORD

_____ rights for the fountain and has plans to create a new
VERB ENDING IN "ING"

_____ drink with Pegasus as their mascot.
ADJECTIVE

MAD LIBS® is fun to play with friends, but you can also play it by yourself! To begin with, DO NOT look at the story on the page below. Fill in the blanks on this page with the words called for. Then, using the words you have selected, fill in the blank spaces in the story.

Now you've created your own hilarious MAD LIBS® game!

COOKING WITH MERMAIDS

PERSON IN ROOM (FEMALE) _____

NUMBER _____

ADJECTIVE _____

NOUN _____

ANIMAL _____

TYPE OF LIQUID _____

NUMBER _____

VERB _____

ADVERB _____

COLOR _____

NUMBER _____

NOUN _____

ADJECTIVE _____

ADJECTIVE _____

PLURAL NOUN _____

VERB ENDING IN "ING" _____

ADJECTIVE _____

A PLACE _____

MAD LIBS®
COOKING WITH MERMAIDS

Here is a recipe for Kraken eggs, from __your mom__'s Underwater
PERSON IN ROOM (FEMALE)

Kitchen. (Serves __72__)
NUMBER

Ingredients:

1 __succulent__ egg, stolen from a giant Kraken
ADJECTIVE

4 __clown__-spoons __pigeon__ milk (fresh if possible)
NOUN   ANIMAL

3 __urine__-spoons squid ink
TYPE OF LIQUID

__1__ sea urchins (for garnish)
NUMBER

Directions:

__slap__ the first three ingredients. Beat __stupidly__ until the
VERB   ADVERB

mixture turns __poop brown__ and frothy, about __21__ minutes. Using a
COLOR   NUMBER

pastry __wiener__, pipe __dainty__ portions of egg batter into a/an
NOUN   ADJECTIVE

__sloppy__ tide pool. Allow the __arseholes__ to cook for four minutes,
ADJECTIVE   PLURAL NOUN

__scooching__ them in a net as you go. Serve alongside the
VERB ENDING IN "ING"

__delightful__ urchins. Season with __modemacs asshole__ water, to taste.
ADJECTIVE   A PLACE

MAD LIBS® is fun to play with friends, but you can also play it by yourself! To begin with, DO NOT look at the story on the page below. Fill in the blanks on this page with the words called for. Then, using the words you have selected, fill in the blank spaces in the story.

Now you've created your own hilarious MAD LIBS® game!

MYTHICAL MONSTERS IN HISTORY

NOUN _____

PART OF THE BODY _____

ANIMAL (PLURAL) _____

NOUN _____

PART OF THE BODY (PLURAL) _____

NOUN _____

ADJECTIVE _____

ADJECTIVE _____

VERB ENDING IN "ING" _____

NOUN _____

PERSON IN ROOM (FEMALE) _____

ANIMAL _____

NOUN _____

TYPE OF LIQUID _____

ADVERB _____

PLURAL NOUN _____

NUMBER _____

- **Medusa** was a/an _undy_ (NOUN) with a hideous _dirty hole_ (PART OF THE BODY) and venomous _mice_ (ANIMAL (PLURAL)) for hair. According to _pervert_ (NOUN) mythology, looking into Medusa's _shriveld nuts_ (PART OF THE BODY (PLURAL)) could turn you to _oyester_ (NOUN).

- **Arachne** was born a/an _liquidy_ (ADJECTIVE) human woman with nothing extra-_moist_ (ADJECTIVE) about her—aside from her talent for _moister farming_ (VERB ENDING IN "ING"). After winning a/an _migrant_ (NOUN) against the goddess _pankake_ (PERSON IN ROOM (FEMALE)), Arachne was turned into a/an _wart hog_ (ANIMAL).

- **The Loch Ness** _spatula_ (NOUN) is a famous "_diareah_ (TYPE OF LIQUID) beast" living in a Scottish lake. "Nessie," as the creature has been _slowly_ (ADVERB) nicknamed, supposedly appeared on satellite _beards_ (PLURAL NOUN) as recently as _3_ (NUMBER) years ago.

MAD LIBS® is fun to play with friends, but you can also play it by yourself! To begin with, DO NOT look at the story on the page below. Fill in the blanks on this page with the words called for. Then, using the words you have selected, fill in the blank spaces in the story.

Now you've created your own hilarious MAD LIBS® game!

LAKE MONSTERS OF NORTH AMERICA

VERB _____

A PLACE _____

NOUN _____

PLURAL NOUN _____

NUMBER _____

TYPE OF LIQUID _____

PLURAL NOUN _____

ANIMAL _____

ADJECTIVE _____

PART OF THE BODY (PLURAL) _____

ANIMAL _____

PART OF THE BODY _____

NOUN _____

ANIMAL _____

FIRST NAME _____

NUMBER _____

Why _____ all the way to (the) _____ when there are
          VERB   A PLACE

_____ monsters right here at home? Between the United
     NOUN

_____ and Canada, North America is home to more than
   PLURAL NOUN

_____ lake and river monsters, like giant _____ serpents,
   NUMBER   TYPE OF LIQUID

crocodilian _____, and _____-like fish with _____
              PLURAL NOUN   ANIMAL   ADJECTIVE

necks and webbed _____. Ontario was once home to
                  PART OF THE BODY (PLURAL)

Mishipeshu, an "underwater _____" with a catlike _____ and
                             ANIMAL   PART OF THE BODY

claws. And British Columbia is still home to Ogopogo, a/an _____-
                                                                NOUN

backed creature with a bearded _____ head. But Canada's favorite
                                   ANIMAL

just might be "_____," which has been described as looking
                FIRST NAME

somewhat like a/an _____-eyed Loch Ness Monster.
                    NUMBER

MAD LIBS® is fun to play with friends, but you can also play it by yourself! To begin with, DO NOT look at the story on the page below. Fill in the blanks on this page with the words called for. Then, using the words you have selected, fill in the blank spaces in the story.

Now you've created your own hilarious MAD LIBS® game!

MOST FAMOUS MERMAIDS

ADJECTIVE _____

ADJECTIVE _____

VERB _____

PLURAL NOUN _____

NOUN _____

PERSON IN ROOM (MALE) _____

SILLY WORD _____

VERB ENDING IN "ING" _____

A PLACE _____

ADVERB _____

OCCUPATION (PLURAL) _____

NUMBER _____

ADJECTIVE _____

PERSON IN ROOM (FEMALE) _____

ADJECTIVE _____

NOUN _____

LAST NAME _____

NOUN _____

NOUN _____

MAD LIBS
MOST FAMOUS MERMAIDS

Here is a list of some of the most _____ mermaids in history.
_____ADJECTIVE

• The Sirens of Greek mythology were _____ but
_____ADJECTIVE

dangerous creatures who would _____ sailors with their
_____VERB

_____, causing _____-wrecks. They appear in
PLURAL NOUN _____ NOUN

both _____'s *Odyssey* and Ovid's _____.
PERSON IN ROOM (MALE) _____ SILLY WORD

• The _____ mermaids of Weeki Wachee Springs in (the)
VERB ENDING IN "ING"

_____ are _____ famous. In the 1960s, these female
A PLACE _____ ADVERB

_____ drew nearly _____ tourists per year!
OCCUPATION (PLURAL) _____ NUMBER

• The most _____ mermaid in the world is probably
_____ADJECTIVE

_____, the main character of the animated film
PERSON IN ROOM (FEMALE)

The _____ *Mermaid.* Based on the _____ tale by
ADJECTIVE _____ NOUN

Hans Christian _____, the film tells the story of a teenage
LAST NAME

_____ who is willing to do whatever it takes to become human.
NOUN

Even if it means losing her _____!
NOUN

MAD LIBS® is fun to play with friends, but you can also play it by yourself! To begin with, DO NOT look at the story on the page below. Fill in the blanks on this page with the words called for. Then, using the words you have selected, fill in the blank spaces in the story.

Now you've created your own hilarious MAD LIBS® game!

FAERY SIGHTINGS
ON THE RISE

NOUN _____

VERB _____

NOUN _____

PLURAL NOUN _____

NOUN _____

LAST NAME _____

OCCUPATION _____

PLURAL NOUN _____

NUMBER _____

ADVERB _____

ADJECTIVE _____

VERB _____

ADJECTIVE _____

PART OF THE BODY _____

PLURAL NOUN _____

NOUN _____

NUMBER _____

MAD LIBS
FAERY SIGHTINGS
ON THE RISE

Since at least 1927, the Faery Investigation _____ has met to

NOUN

_____ and gather evidence of _____ life in all its reported

VERB   NOUN

forms. In the Society's heyday, it boasted several famous _____,

PLURAL NOUN

including decorated _____ hero Lord _____ and iconic

NOUN   LAST NAME

_____ Walt Disney. Though many of their _____ were

OCCUPATION   PLURAL NOUN

destroyed during World War _____, the Society grew _____

NUMBER   ADVERB

over the decades, until _____ ridicule in the '90s drove the Society to

ADJECTIVE

_____ underground. Today, however, they appear to be as

VERB

_____ as ever, with an active _____-book page and hundreds

ADJECTIVE   PART OF THE BODY

of devoted _____. A recent census conducted by the Society shows

PLURAL NOUN

_____ sightings are on the rise, with _____ occurring in the past

NOUN   NUMBER

year alone.

MAD LIBS® is fun to play with friends, but you can also play it by yourself! To begin with, DO NOT look at the story on the page below. Fill in the blanks on this page with the words called for. Then, using the words you have selected, fill in the blank spaces in the story.

Now you've created your own hilarious MAD LIBS® game!

SATYR PLAY

NOUN _____

ADJECTIVE _____

PERSON IN ROOM (MALE) _____

VERB _____

PLURAL NOUN _____

TYPE OF FOOD _____

NOUN _____

VERB ENDING IN "ING" _____

VERB _____

VERB ENDING IN "ING" _____

ANIMAL _____

SILLY WORD _____

VERB _____

VERB _____

EXCLAMATION _____

VERB ENDING IN "ING" _____

ADJECTIVE _____

MAD LIBS®
SATYR PLAY

First Satyr: OMG, I'm so bored.

Second Satyr: Me too. Let's play a/an _____ on someone!

NOUN

First Satyr: That's a/an _____ idea! But who?

ADJECTIVE

Second Satyr: How about _____? He's dumb enough to

PERSON IN ROOM (MALE)

_____ for anything.

VERB

(The two _____ hide under a/an _____ tree, waiting for

PLURAL NOUN   TYPE OF FOOD

their _____ to pass by.)

NOUN

First Satyr: Why is he _____ so slow?

VERB ENDING IN "ING"

Second Satyr: I'm so bored I could _____ .

VERB

First Satyr: Wait! He's _____ back around.

VERB ENDING IN "ING"

(Second Satyr makes _____ sounds.)

ANIMAL

First Satyr: What are you doing, _____? He'll _____ you!

SILLY WORD   VERB

Second Satyr: I know! Maybe he'll _____ this way.

VERB

First Satyr: _____! You totally scared him. Look, he's

EXCLAMATION

_____ away.

VERB ENDING IN "ING"

Second Satyr: Now we're going to be even *more* _____ .

ADJECTIVE

MAD LIBS® is fun to play with friends, but you can also play it by yourself! To begin with, DO NOT look at the story on the page below. Fill in the blanks on this page with the words called for. Then, using the words you have selected, fill in the blank spaces in the story.

Now you've created your own hilarious MAD LIBS® game!

WITNESS INTERVIEW

ANIMAL _____

VERB _____

A PLACE _____

NUMBER _____

PLURAL NOUN _____

PLURAL NOUN _____

NOUN _____

ANIMAL _____

VERB ENDING IN "ING" _____

ARTICLE OF CLOTHING _____

ADJECTIVE _____

ADVERB _____

EXCLAMATION _____

ADJECTIVE _____

PART OF THE BODY (PLURAL) _____

COLOR _____

VERB _____

MAD LIBS
WITNESS INTERVIEW

Kid: I'm telling you, my sister is a were-_____!
                                          ANIMAL

Officer: Slow down! _____ at the beginning.
                         VERB

Kid: I got home from (the) _____ _____ hours after my curfew.
                              A PLACE   NUMBER

I tiptoed upstairs without my _____ noticing. That's when I heard
                              PLURAL NOUN

_____ coming from my sister's _____-room!
PLURAL NOUN   NOUN

Officer: What did you think was happening?

Kid: At first I thought there was a/an _____ in the room with her. Then
                                          ANIMAL

I heard _____ sounds, like someone or something was ripping
        VERB ENDING IN "ING"

her _____ apart. I asked her if she was _____, and
    ARTICLE OF CLOTHING   ADJECTIVE

when she didn't answer, I knocked as _____ as I could.
                                     ADVERB

Officer: According to your dad, you screamed, "_____!" Why
                                                   EXCLAMATION

didn't you call for help?

Kid: The door opened, and that's when I saw her! She had _____ claws,
                                                            ADJECTIVE

and whiskers had grown out of her _____. She looked at me
                                  PART OF THE BODY (PLURAL)

with _____ eyes, and growled, "_____ your own business, twerp!"
     COLOR   VERB

MAD LIBS® is fun to play with friends, but you can also play it by yourself! To begin with, DO NOT look at the story on the page below. Fill in the blanks on this page with the words called for. Then, using the words you have selected, fill in the blank spaces in the story.

Now you've created your own hilarious MAD LIBS® game!

RIDDLE OF THE SPHINX

A PLACE _____

NOUN _____

ANIMAL _____

VERB (PAST TENSE) _____

VERB ENDING IN "S" _____

PART OF THE BODY (PLURAL) _____

NUMBER _____

NOUN _____

FIRST NAME (MALE) _____

NOUN _____

VERB _____

VERB ENDING IN "S" _____

ADJECTIVE _____

NOUN _____

ADJECTIVE _____

NOUN _____

OCCUPATION _____

MAD LIBS®
RIDDLE OF THE SPHINX

According to legends of (the) _____, the Sphinx had the
 A PLACE

_____ of a human and the body of a/an _____. She killed
 NOUN   ANIMAL

and _____ any travelers who couldn't answer
 VERB (PAST TENSE)

the following question: "What creature _____ on four
 VERB ENDING IN "S"

_____ in the morning, _____ legs at noon, and three
 PART OF THE BODY (PLURAL)   NUMBER

in the _____?" Only the hero _____ gave the correct
 NOUN   FIRST NAME (MALE)

answer, leading to the Sphinx's _____. "Man," he said. "Because a
 NOUN

baby has to _____ before he can walk. Then he _____
 VERB   VERB ENDING IN "S"

on two legs until he's _____. At which point, he uses a/an
 ADJECTIVE

_____ to keep his balance." The Sphinx was so _____ that
 NOUN   ADJECTIVE

her riddle had been solved that she threw herself off a high _____ and
 NOUN

died. Talk about a drama _____!
 OCCUPATION

MAD LIBS® is fun to play with friends, but you can also play it by yourself! To begin with, DO NOT look at the story on the page below. Fill in the blanks on this page with the words called for. Then, using the words you have selected, fill in the blank spaces in the story.

Now you've created your own hilarious MAD LIBS® game!

HOW TO RIDE A UNICORN

NOUN _____

ADVERB _____

VERB _____

ADJECTIVE _____

TYPE OF FOOD _____

ADJECTIVE _____

PART OF THE BODY (PLURAL) _____

NOUN _____

SILLY WORD _____

VERB ENDING IN "ING" _____

PART OF THE BODY _____

SAME PART OF THE BODY _____

ADJECTIVE _____

VERB _____

TYPE OF LIQUID _____

VERB _____

MAD●LIBS®
HOW TO RIDE A UNICORN

Dos:

- Unicorns don't have _____-belts, so it's important to hold on
  NOUN

  _____ at all times.
  ADVERB

- Because they can _____ your mind, it's crucial to think only
  VERB

  _____ thoughts while riding a uni-_____.
  ADJECTIVE   TYPE OF FOOD

- If touching a unicorn's _____ horn becomes necessary, be
  ADJECTIVE

  sure to warm up your _____ first. (They are quite
  PART OF THE BODY (PLURAL)

  sensitive to changes in _____.)
  NOUN

Don'ts:

- Don't say "yeehaw" or "_____." The unicorn will think you're
  SILLY WORD

  _____ fun of it.
  VERB ENDING IN "ING"

- Never stand _____ to _____ with a unicorn for
  PART OF THE BODY   SAME PART OF THE BODY

  too long (for _____ reasons).
  ADJECTIVE

- Whatever you do, never, ever _____ unicorn
  VERB

  _____! It is deadly to the touch and will _____
  TYPE OF LIQUID   VERB

  you for sure. Happy riding!

MAD LIBS® is fun to play with friends, but you can also play it by yourself! To begin with, DO NOT look at the story on the page below. Fill in the blanks on this page with the words called for. Then, using the words you have selected, fill in the blank spaces in the story.

Now you've created your own hilarious MAD LIBS® game!

CENTAUR WRESTLING

ADJECTIVE _____

COLOR _____

SILLY WORD _____

ANIMAL _____

VERB _____

NOUN _____

CELEBRITY (MALE) _____

COLOR _____

VERB ENDING IN "ING" _____

NOUN _____

PLURAL NOUN _____

OCCUPATION (PLURAL) _____

PART OF THE BODY _____

NUMBER _____

PLURAL NOUN _____

VERB ENDING IN "ING" _____

NOUN _____

MAD LIBS

CENTAUR WRESTLING

The crowd goes _____ as the _____ Whiz and _____
 ADJECTIVE COLOR SILLY WORD

Joe enter the ring. Each of these twin centaurs is half Appaloosa _____
 ANIMAL

and half man. They are favored to _____ tonight at the match in
 VERB

_____ City. Entering the ring behind them is _____'s
 NOUN CELEBRITY (MALE)

dream duo, the _____ Stallions. The crowd makes _____
 COLOR VERB ENDING IN "ING"

sounds at the hated visiting team. Following the sound of a/an

_____-shot, all four heavy-weight _____ gallop against
 NOUN PLURAL NOUN

one another. The Stallions have arms like human _____, which
 OCCUPATION (PLURAL)

they use to put both their opponents in instant _____-locks. The
 PART OF THE BODY

referee counts all the way to _____ before the Whiz and Joe break free.
 NUMBER

Against all _____, the hometown heroes manage to dominate the
 PLURAL NOUN

Stallions, _____ them to the mat for the full count. The referee
 VERB ENDING IN "ING"

calls it. The Stallions have lost. The _____ goes wild!
 NOUN

MAD LIBS® is fun to play with friends, but you can also play it by yourself! To begin with, DO NOT look at the story on the page below. Fill in the blanks on this page with the words called for. Then, using the words you have selected, fill in the blank spaces in the story.

Now you've created your own hilarious MAD LIBS® game!

INTERVIEW WITH A BANSHEE

FIRST NAME (FEMALE) _____

A PLACE _____

VERB _____

PART OF THE BODY (PLURAL) _____

NOUN _____

NOUN _____

VERB _____

ANIMAL (PLURAL) _____

ADJECTIVE _____

VERB ENDING IN "ING" _____

NUMBER _____

ADJECTIVE _____

PLURAL NOUN _____

NOUN _____

NOUN _____

MAD LIBS
INTERVIEW WITH
A BANSHEE

News Anchor: I'm here with _____, a real-life banshee who

FIRST NAME (FEMALE)

has agreed to talk to us about what it's like living as a monster in (the)

_____.

A PLACE

Banshee: Everyone expects me to _____ all the time, at the top of my

VERB

_____, but I'm actually a fairly quiet person.

PART OF THE BODY (PLURAL)

News Anchor: So you're a/an _____ that doesn't scream?

NOUN

Banshee: I scream as loudly as the next _____. But only when

NOUN

someone is about to _____. A kind of death call. And my neighbors

VERB

aren't exactly dropping like _____.

ANIMAL (PLURAL)

News Anchor: So you don't pose a/an _____ threat to the community

ADJECTIVE

here?

Banshee: Of course not! If anything, I'd be an asset to the

Neighborhood Watch because I can sense danger _____ from

VERB ENDING IN "ING"

_____ miles away.

NUMBER

News Anchor: I feel more _____ already! You heard it here first,

ADJECTIVE

_____ and gentlemen. Banshees mean no _____, so give

PLURAL NOUN   NOUN

them all a/an _____, why don't you?

NOUN

MAD LIBS® is fun to play with friends, but you can also play it by yourself! To begin with, DO NOT look at the story on the page below. Fill in the blanks on this page with the words called for. Then, using the words you have selected, fill in the blank spaces in the story.

Now you've created your own hilarious MAD LIBS® game!

MONSTER BONES

PERSON IN ROOM (FEMALE) _____

OCCUPATION _____

NOUN _____

A PLACE _____

NUMBER _____

PLURAL NOUN _____

PLURAL NOUN _____

NUMBER _____

ADJECTIVE _____

VERB (PAST TENSE) _____

ANIMAL _____

ADJECTIVE _____

ADJECTIVE _____

NOUN _____

PART OF THE BODY _____

NOUN _____

ADJECTIVE _____

PLURAL NOUN _____

MAD LIBS
MONSTER BONES

Dr. **Pumes** _____, the world's leading crypto-**Cheech catcher**,

PERSON IN ROOM (FEMALE) — OCCUPATION

asserts that there isn't a/an **Bushy** ~~Bushes~~ of proof that the fabled Cyclops ever

NOUN

existed in (the) **candy land**. "For more than **10** years," she said,

A PLACE — NUMBER

"**Boobies** have brought me what they were certain were

PLURAL NOUN

Weaners belonging to the **5**-eyed beasts. But they were all

PLURAL NOUN — NUMBER

cheesy. What they had **chotched** were in fact ordinary

ADJECTIVE — VERB (PAST TENSE)

hyena skulls! It was a/an **hairy** enough mistake considering

ANIMAL — ADJECTIVE

that each had a/an **boily** hole at the center where the living animal's

ADJECTIVE

poo would be, the same size and position as a Cyclops's

NOUN

Butt crack socket." The scholar wants nothing more than to put the

PART OF THE BODY

toilet to rest, once and for all. "I have **glittery** work to do!"

NOUN — ADJECTIVE

she says. "I can't spend all day teaching elephant anatomy to **Pumpkins**."

PLURAL NOUN

MAD LIBS®
UNIDENTIFIED FLYING MAD
LIBS

by Kristin Conte

Mad Libs

An Imprint of

Penguin Random House

INSTRUCTIONS

MAD LIBS® is a game for people who don't like games!
It can be played by one, two, three, four, or forty.

● RIDICULOUSLY SIMPLE DIRECTIONS

In this tablet you will find stories containing blank spaces where words are left out. One player, the READER, selects one of these stories. The READER does not tell anyone what the story is about. Instead, he/she asks the other players, the WRITERS, to give him/her words. These words are used to fill in the blank spaces in the story.

● TO PLAY

The READER asks each WRITER in turn to call out a word—an adjective or a noun or whatever the space calls for—and uses them to fill in the blank spaces in the story. The result is a MAD LIBS® game.

When the READER then reads the completed MAD LIBS® game to the other players, they will discover that they have written a story that is fantastic, screamingly funny, shocking, silly, crazy, or just plain dumb—depending upon which words each WRITER called out.

● EXAMPLE (*Before* and *After*)

"_____!" he said _____
         EXCLAMATION   ADVERB

as he jumped into his convertible _____ and
                                              NOUN

drove off with his _____ wife.
                          ADJECTIVE

"_____OUCH_____!" he said _____STUPIDLY_____
         EXCLAMATION   ADVERB

as he jumped into his convertible _____CAT_____ and
                                              NOUN

drove off with his _____BRAVE_____ wife.
                          ADJECTIVE

QUICK REVIEW

In case you have forgotten what adjectives, adverbs, nouns, and verbs are, here is a quick review:

An ADJECTIVE describes something or somebody. *Lumpy, soft, ugly, messy,* and *short* are adjectives.

An ADVERB tells how something is done. It modifies a verb and usually ends in "ly." *Modestly, stupidly, greedily,* and *carefully* are adverbs.

A NOUN is the name of a person, place, or thing. *Sidewalk, umbrella, bridle, bathtub,* and *nose* are nouns.

A VERB is an action word. *Run, pitch, jump,* and *swim* are verbs. Put the verbs in past tense if the directions say PAST TENSE. *Ran, pitched, jumped,* and *swam* are verbs in the past tense.

When we ask for A PLACE, we mean any sort of place: a country or city *(Spain, Cleveland)* or a room *(bathroom, kitchen).*

An EXCLAMATION or SILLY WORD is any sort of funny sound, gasp, grunt, or outcry, like *Wow!, Ouch!, Whomp!, Ick!,* and *Gadzooks!*

When we ask for specific words, like a NUMBER, a COLOR, an ANIMAL, or a PART OF THE BODY, we mean a word that is one of those things, like *seven, blue, horse,* or *head.*

When we ask for a PLURAL, it means more than one. For example, *cat* pluralized is *cats.*

MAD LIBS® is fun to play with friends, but you can also play it by yourself! To begin with, DO NOT look at the story on the page below. Fill in the blanks on this page with the words called for. Then, using the words you have selected, fill in the blank spaces in the story.

Now you've created your own hilarious MAD LIBS® game!

UNIDENTIFIED FLYING OBJECTS

ADJECTIVE _____

VEHICLE (PLURAL) _____

NOUN _____

NOUN _____

ADJECTIVE _____

NOUN _____

ANIMAL (PLURAL) _____

NOUN _____

ADJECTIVE _____

ADJECTIVE _____

PLURAL NOUN _____

OCCUPATION (PLURAL) _____

PLURAL NOUN _____

MAD LIBS®
UNIDENTIFIED FLYING OBJECTS

Did you know that UFOs aren't just _____-looking _____
                                        ADJECTIVE   VEHICLE (PLURAL)

flying around in the sky? The term is actually a nickname for any unidentified

flying _____! Currently, the _____ community is split
         NOUN   NOUN

between three schools of thought on this _____ subject. Scientists are
                                            ADJECTIVE

adamant that there is a rational _____ for every UFO sighting. Often,
                                    NOUN

UFOs are officially recognized as weather balloons, asteroids, or a flock of

_____ after they're initially spotted. However, _____ enthusiasts
ANIMAL (PLURAL)   NOUN

believe these _____ objects are actually spacecraft driven by
                 ADJECTIVE

_____ extraterrestrials from faraway _____. Finally, there's a
ADJECTIVE   PLURAL NOUN

growing number of _____ who insist that UFOs are in fact
                     OCCUPATION (PLURAL)

experimental _____ the military is secretly testing. So what do you
                PLURAL NOUN

think?

MAD LIBS® is fun to play with friends, but you can also play it by yourself! To begin with, DO NOT look at the story on the page below. Fill in the blanks on this page with the words called for. Then, using the words you have selected, fill in the blank spaces in the story.

Now you've created your own hilarious MAD LIBS® game!

ABDUCTION JUNCTION

VERB _____

NOUN _____

PLURAL NOUN _____

PLURAL NOUN _____

VERB _____

ADJECTIVE _____

VEHICLE (PLURAL) _____

ADJECTIVE _____

PLURAL NOUN _____

ADJECTIVE _____

PLURAL NOUN _____

NOUN _____

ADJECTIVE _____

MAD LIBS®
ABDUCTION JUNCTION

Spacecraft sightings occur all over the world. Here are some places aliens are most

likely to _____:
                     VERB

Roswell, New Mexico: The birthplace of _____ 51, a haven for top-secret
                                              NOUN

government _____ and a veritable breeding ground for alien
              PLURAL NOUN

_____. UFO fanatics can even _____ down the "Extraterrestrial
 PLURAL NOUN   VERB

Highway" that runs through this _____ town.
                                   ADJECTIVE

Nazca City, Peru: Thought to be a landing zone for alien _____, the
                                                            VEHICLE (PLURAL)

famous Nazca Lines in the ground reveal _____ designs of animals and
                                            ADJECTIVE

other _____ when viewed from high in the sky.
       PLURAL NOUN

The M-Triangle, Russia: Located in the mountains, this area is a hot spot of

UFO sightings, _____ symbols written in the sky, and encounters with
                  ADJECTIVE

translucent _____ and humanoid figures that glow in the
              PLURAL NOUN

_____. It's rumored that people who venture into this region
  NOUN

sometimes return having developed _____-powers and superhuman
                                       ADJECTIVE

abilities.

MAD LIBS® is fun to play with friends, but you can also play it by yourself! To begin with, DO NOT look at the story on the page below. Fill in the blanks on this page with the words called for. Then, using the words you have selected, fill in the blank spaces in the story.

Now you've created your own hilarious MAD LIBS® game!

CIA ITINERARY

VERB _____

ADJECTIVE _____

ADJECTIVE _____

PLURAL NOUN _____

ANIMAL _____

NOUN _____

TYPE OF FOOD _____

NOUN _____

PERSON IN ROOM (MALE) _____

PLURAL NOUN _____

NOUN _____

ADJECTIVE _____

A PLACE _____

MAD LIBS®
CIA ITINERARY

Here's a peek at a typical day in the life of a CIA agent working at Area 51:

9:00 a.m.: Check on the resident Martians to make sure they didn't _____
_{VERB} all the lightbulbs for their _____ experiments again—the CIA can't
_{ADJECTIVE}
afford to keep replacing these!

10:30 a.m.: Oversee _____ peace negotiations between the
_{ADJECTIVE}
_____ of Earth and the _____-people of Planet Nebula.
_{PLURAL NOUN}   _{ANIMAL}

11:00 a.m.: Make sure the antigravity _____ in the kitchen is turned
_{NOUN}
off. Last time we were scraping _____ off the ceiling for a week.
_{TYPE OF FOOD}

1:30 p.m.: A well-deserved _____ break.
_{NOUN}

2:00 p.m.: Drive out to Dundy County, Nebraska, and talk to Farmer
_____ about the crop _____ appearing in his corn
_{PERSON IN ROOM (MALE)}   _{PLURAL NOUN}
fields.

4:30 p.m.: Investigate reports of a/an _____ that crash-landed in a/an
_{NOUN}
_____ field on the outskirts of (the) _____.
_{ADJECTIVE}   _{A PLACE}

MAD LIBS® is fun to play with friends, but you can also play it by yourself! To begin with, DO NOT look at the story on the page below. Fill in the blanks on this page with the words called for. Then, using the words you have selected, fill in the blank spaces in the story.

Now you've created your own hilarious MAD LIBS® game!

THE CONSPIRACY THEORIST'S SURVIVAL GUIDE

ADJECTIVE _____

ARTICLE OF CLOTHING _____

PART OF THE BODY _____

PLURAL NOUN _____

NOUN _____

PLURAL NOUN _____

ARTICLE OF CLOTHING _____

VERB ENDING IN "ING" _____

PLURAL NOUN _____

ANIMAL _____

PLURAL NOUN _____

PLURAL NOUN _____

VERB _____

SILLY WORD _____

MAD LIBS®
THE CONSPIRACY THEORIST'S
SURVIVAL GUIDE

Here's a list of _____ survival tips from our resident conspiracy theorist:
                        ADJECTIVE

- Protect your thoughts by making a stylish tinfoil _____ to wear
                                                    ARTICLE OF CLOTHING
  on your _____ .
          PART OF THE BODY

- The FBI is recording all of your _____ , so you might as well
                                    PLURAL NOUN
  throw your cell phone in the _____ .
                                NOUN

- The government is spraying chemtrails to control the _____ of the
                                                       PLURAL NOUN
  population, so wear a gas _____ to avoid breathing any mind-
                            ARTICLE OF CLOTHING
  _____ chemicals.
  VERB ENDING IN "ING"

- Trust no one! Most _____ in positions of authority belong to the
                     PLURAL NOUN
  Illuminati and are actually _____-people in disguise.
                              ANIMAL

- Companies will try to get you to buy their _____ by exposing you to
                                             PLURAL NOUN
  subliminal _____ hidden in their advertising. To avoid commercials
             PLURAL NOUN
  altogether, just _____ your television.
                   VERB

- Scientists say aliens aren't real, but that's a load of _____ ! The truth
                                                          SILLY WORD
  is out there . . .

MAD LIBS® is fun to play with friends, but you can also play it by yourself! To begin with, DO NOT look at the story on the page below. Fill in the blanks on this page with the words called for. Then, using the words you have selected, fill in the blank spaces in the story.

Now you've created your own hilarious MAD LIBS® game!

LITTLE RED PLANET

NOUN _____

ADJECTIVE _____

PLURAL NOUN _____

ADJECTIVE _____

ADJECTIVE _____

VERB _____

PLURAL NOUN _____

ADJECTIVE _____

NOUN _____

TYPE OF LIQUID _____

OCCUPATION (PLURAL) _____

NOUN _____

NOUN _____

ADJECTIVE _____

PLURAL NOUN _____

NOUN _____

MAD LIBS®
LITTLE RED PLANET

Mars is the fourth _____ from the Sun and close enough to Earth that
        NOUN

you can see it in the sky on _____ nights. It gets its trademark reddish
                  ADJECTIVE

color from a high concentration of _____ on the planet's surface. Some
                    PLURAL NOUN

say that there are "little _____ men from Mars," but is there any merit
               ADJECTIVE

to this claim? Since the planet's atmosphere is so thin and _____, there
                                ADJECTIVE

is no air to _____, making it uninhabitable. However, this doesn't mean
          VERB

it can't support _____ in the future! _____ tests of Mars's
            PLURAL NOUN   ADJECTIVE

soil reveal all the building blocks for life, including nitrogen, carbon, oxygen, and

_____. A key component for survival is _____.
    NOUN   TYPE OF LIQUID

_____ recently discovered underground ice buried deep below the
OCCUPATION (PLURAL)

planet's _____. Explorers claim that space is the final _____.
      NOUN   NOUN

With so many _____ advances, maybe our future _____
          ADJECTIVE   PLURAL NOUN

will colonize this little red _____ after all!
                NOUN

MAD LIBS® is fun to play with friends, but you can also play it by yourself! To begin with, DO NOT look at the story on the page below. Fill in the blanks on this page with the words called for. Then, using the words you have selected, fill in the blank spaces in the story.

Now you've created your own hilarious MAD LIBS® game!

ROSWELL OR BUST

NOUN _____

ADJECTIVE _____

PLURAL NOUN _____

NOUN _____

ADJECTIVE _____

PERSON IN ROOM _____

ADJECTIVE _____

NOUN _____

NOUN _____

PLURAL NOUN _____

PLURAL NOUN _____

ADJECTIVE _____

PLURAL NOUN _____

VERB _____

MAD LIBS

ROSWELL OR BUST

Each summer, Mom and Dad pack up the _____ and we drive across
NOUN

the country to the _____ town of Roswell, New Mexico, to see if we can
ADJECTIVE

encounter some _____. We pay a quick visit to the International
PLURAL NOUN

UFO _____ & Research Center and take a peek at the _____
NOUN   ADJECTIVE

exhibits. Then I get my photo taken with a local mascot, _____, the
PERSON IN ROOM

_____ alien! I know it's just some _____ wearing a costume,
ADJECTIVE   NOUN

but I heard the design was based on a real-life _____ from Mars. At
NOUN

night, we sit around a campfire and watch the _____ twinkle in the
PLURAL NOUN

sky. I save up my _____ all year so I can buy some souvenirs. Once
PLURAL NOUN

we met a/an _____ old man who claimed he'd been abducted over a
ADJECTIVE

dozen times. He sold me a map of alien hot spots in the area for only fifty

_____! This year I know I'll finally _____ some aliens.
PLURAL NOUN   VERB

MAD LIBS® is fun to play with friends, but you can also play it by yourself! To begin with, DO NOT look at the story on the page below. Fill in the blanks on this page with the words called for. Then, using the words you have selected, fill in the blank spaces in the story.

Now you've created your own hilarious MAD LIBS® game!

MILKY WAY GALAXY

ADJECTIVE _____

ADJECTIVE _____

ADJECTIVE _____

NOUN _____

ADJECTIVE _____

NOUN _____

COLOR _____

PLURAL NOUN _____

PLURAL NOUN _____

ANIMAL _____

NOUN _____

PLURAL NOUN _____

VERB ENDING IN "ING" _____

MAD LIBS®
MILKY WAY GALAXY

Home sweet home! Our _____ planet is merely a/an _____
                        ADJECTIVE   ADJECTIVE

speck in a sea of stars that make up the Milky Way Galaxy. It gets its name from

the strip of bright, _____ stars that resemble a milky _____
                      ADJECTIVE   NOUN

coursing through the sky. Like so many other _____ galaxies in the
                                              ADJECTIVE

universe, ours is in the shape of a/an _____. Billions of stars, like
                                        NOUN

_____ dwarfs and super-_____, litter our galaxy, and
   COLOR   PLURAL NOUN

there is enough gas and _____ to create billions more! Many of these
                         PLURAL NOUN

stars form constellations like Aries and Leo, which resembles a/an _____.
                                                                    ANIMAL

At the center of our galaxy sits a supermassive black _____, greedily
                                                       NOUN

feeding on nearby _____ and stardust. The Milky Way's closest
                   PLURAL NOUN

neighbor is nearby Andromeda. These two galaxies are actually _____
                                                              VERB ENDING IN "ING"

through space and are set to collide four billion years from now!

MAD LIBS® is fun to play with friends, but you can also play it by yourself! To begin with, DO NOT look at the story on the page below. Fill in the blanks on this page with the words called for. Then, using the words you have selected, fill in the blank spaces in the story.

Now you've created your own hilarious MAD LIBS® game!

WELCOME, EARTHLINGS!

ADJECTIVE _____

SILLY WORD _____

PART OF THE BODY _____

EXCLAMATION _____

PLURAL NOUN _____

TYPE OF FOOD _____

ANIMAL (PLURAL) _____

VERB _____

ADJECTIVE _____

NOUN _____

ARTICLE OF CLOTHING (PLURAL) _____

MAD☺LIBS®
WELCOME, EARTHLINGS!

Greetings, Earthlings! Here are some dos and don'ts for when you meet the

___hot___ inhabitants of Planet ___bushytrap___ : fart into cup
ADJECTIVE   SILLY WORD

- Wiggle your ___hairy hole___ and shout "___oui___!" whenever you
PART OF THE BODY   EXCLAMATION

  meet someone new.

- As an act of peace, give gifts of golden ___hot holes___ and fragrant
PLURAL NOUN

  ___hot dogs___.
TYPE OF FOOD

- ___Hedge hogs___ are highly respected, so don't make fun of them or you'll
ANIMAL (PLURAL)

  be asked to ___poop___.
VERB

- Don't be offended if you're called a/an ___exciting___ ___talet___ —
ADJECTIVE   NOUN

  this is a common term of endearment.

- These aliens don't wear ___undies___ —feel free to leave
ARTICLE OF CLOTHING (PLURAL)

  yours at home!

MAD LIBS® is fun to play with friends, but you can also play it by yourself! To begin with, DO NOT look at the story on the page below. Fill in the blanks on this page with the words called for. Then, using the words you have selected, fill in the blank spaces in the story.

Now you've created your own hilarious MAD LIBS® game!

THE WAR OF THE WORLDS, A BOOK REPORT

NOUN _____

CELEBRITY (MALE) _____

NOUN _____

PLURAL NOUN _____

ADJECTIVE _____

LETTER OF THE ALPHABET _____

PLURAL NOUN _____

VERB ENDING IN "ING" _____

PLURAL NOUN _____

ADJECTIVE _____

ADJECTIVE _____

ADVERB _____

PLURAL NOUN _____

VERB (PAST TENSE) _____

ADJECTIVE _____

ADJECTIVE _____

The War of the Worlds is a/an _____ novel published in 1898 by
_____NOUN_____

_____ and is told as a factual account of a/an _____ invasion on
CELEBRITY (MALE)   NOUN

Earth. The narrator describes cylindrical _____ that crash to Earth and
                                          PLURAL NOUN

release aliens with _____ skin, _____-shaped mouths,
                    ADJECTIVE   LETTER OF THE ALPHABET

and spindly _____ for arms. They begin _____
            PLURAL NOUN   VERB ENDING IN "ING"

humans with their heat-rays and other advanced _____. The narrator
                                               PLURAL NOUN

flees and after some _____ experiences is finally reunited with his
                     ADJECTIVE

_____ wife. _____, the aliens are defeated by the smallest
  ADJECTIVE   ADVERB

line of defense on our planet: _____. In 1938, Orson Welles
                               PLURAL NOUN

infamously _____ a radio drama based on the _____
           VERB (PAST TENSE)   ADJECTIVE

novel, causing _____ panic among listeners who were convinced the
               ADJECTIVE

report was real!

MAD LIBS® is fun to play with friends, but you can also play it by yourself! To begin with, DO NOT look at the story on the page below. Fill in the blanks on this page with the words called for. Then, using the words you have selected, fill in the blank spaces in the story.

Now you've created your own hilarious MAD LIBS® game!

THE TRUTH BEHIND THE MOON LANDING

NOUN _____

CELEBRITY _____

ADJECTIVE _____

A COUNTRY _____

PART OF THE BODY (PLURAL) _____

ADJECTIVE _____

PLURAL NOUN _____

NOUN _____

ADJECTIVE _____

ADJECTIVE _____

PLURAL NOUN _____

ADJECTIVE _____

TYPE OF FOOD _____

Any __wiggly wiener__ textbook will tell you all about __putin__ landing
NOUN   CELEBRITY

on the moon, but what it won't mention is the __amazing__ scandal that was
                                              ADJECTIVE

covered up. The government claims it was a space race with __Uganda__, but
                                                           A COUNTRY

they were actually trying to get their __constipated holes__ on the
                                       PART OF THE BODY (PLURAL)

__burnt__ treasure hidden deep in the moon's __holes__. The
ADJECTIVE   PLURAL NOUN

footage from the first __fat pig__ landing was intentionally __sizzling__
                       NOUN   ADJECTIVE

so people couldn't make out any __creamy__ details of the surface. After the
                                ADJECTIVE

astronauts returned home, they were paid large sums of __wieners__ to keep
                                                        PLURAL NOUN

quiet. The __nutty__ secret the government was trying to keep? The moon
           ADJECTIVE

is actually made of __dirty peanut butter__
                    TYPE OF FOOD

MAD LIBS® is fun to play with friends, but you can also play it by yourself! To begin with, DO NOT look at the story on the page below. Fill in the blanks on this page with the words called for. Then, using the words you have selected, fill in the blank spaces in the story.

Now you've created your own hilarious MAD LIBS® game!

EXTRATERRESTRIALS

ADJECTIVE _____

ANIMAL _____

PART OF THE BODY (PLURAL) _____

OCCUPATION _____

ADJECTIVE _____

PLURAL NOUN _____

ADJECTIVE _____

NOUN _____

COLOR _____

VERB _____

PLURAL NOUN _____

SILLY WORD (PLURAL) _____

VERB (PAST TENSE) _____

PLURAL NOUN _____

ADJECTIVE _____

MAD LIBS®
EXTRATERRESTRIALS

There are many types of aliens living in the universe. Here are a few of the most recognizable species:

The Reptilians: Hailing from the Alpha Draconis system, this species resembles a/an _____, scaly _____ with webbed _____.

ADJECTIVE   ANIMAL   PART OF THE BODY (PLURAL)

They are a/an _____ race and have _____ tempers.

OCCUPATION   ADJECTIVE

The Greys: These are the most common type of _____ seen by humans.

PLURAL NOUN

They have distinctive features such as their _____ heads, large

ADJECTIVE

_____-shaped eyes, and their namesake _____ skin. These guys can't

NOUN   COLOR

_____ with their feet and instead get around by floating inside

VERB

_____.

PLURAL NOUN

The _____: This group _____ ancient human

SILLY WORD (PLURAL)   VERB (PAST TENSE)

civilizations and were viewed as divine _____. They're said to have a/an

PLURAL NOUN

_____ influence on our culture.

ADJECTIVE

MAD LIBS® is fun to play with friends, but you can also play it by yourself! To begin with, DO NOT look at the story on the page below. Fill in the blanks on this page with the words called for. Then, using the words you have selected, fill in the blank spaces in the story.

Now you've created your own hilarious MAD LIBS® game!

MY BEST FRIEND IS AN ALIEN

NOUN _____

PERSON IN ROOM (MALE) _____

NOUN _____

ADJECTIVE _____

ARTICLE OF CLOTHING _____

NOUN _____

ADJECTIVE _____

NOUN _____

VEHICLE _____

PLURAL NOUN _____

NOUN _____

PLURAL NOUN _____

PART OF THE BODY _____

PERSON IN ROOM (MALE) _____

ADJECTIVE _____

MAD LIBS
MY BEST FRIEND
IS AN ALIEN

My best friend is the new foreign exchange _____ and he's a little out of
NOUN

this world. _____ comes from a faraway _____. He's
PERSON IN ROOM (MALE)   NOUN

just like everyone else, except his skin is a/an _____ shade of green and
ADJECTIVE

he has two antennas he keeps hidden under a/an _____. He
ARTICLE OF CLOTHING

comes to school in a giant metal _____ that beats the pants off of my
NOUN

mom's _____ minivan. Last month, he helped me win the _____
ADJECTIVE   NOUN

fair by building a fully functional model _____. Did I mention he can
VEHICLE

walk through _____ and teleport from one _____ to the
PLURAL NOUN   NOUN

other in the blink of an eye? We're so close that we can finish each other's

_____—sometimes I swear I can even hear his voice inside my
PLURAL NOUN

_____! _____ says one day he'll take me
PART OF THE BODY   PERSON IN ROOM (MALE)

to visit his _____ home. Boy, I sure hope Mom lets me go!
ADJECTIVE

MAD LIBS® is fun to play with friends, but you can also play it by yourself! To begin with, DO NOT look at the story on the page below. Fill in the blanks on this page with the words called for. Then, using the words you have selected, fill in the blank spaces in the story.

Now you've created your own hilarious MAD LIBS® game!

SPACE INVADERS

ADJECTIVE _____

NOUN _____

PLURAL NOUN _____

PLURAL NOUN _____

ADJECTIVE _____

VERB (PAST TENSE) _____

NOUN _____

ANIMAL _____

VERB _____

TYPE OF FOOD _____

ADJECTIVE _____

ADJECTIVE _____

SILLY WORD _____

SILLY WORD _____

NOUN _____

ADJECTIVE _____

VERB _____

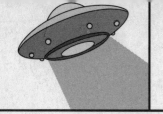

MAD LIBS

SPACE INVADERS

I live next to the most _____ neighbors ever and I'm almost at the end
　　　　　　　　　　　　　　ADJECTIVE

of my _____. Boy, these _____ are annoying. I've been woken
　　　　NOUN　　　　　　　　　　PLURAL NOUN

up by blinding white _____ and _____ noises every night this
　　　　　　　　　　　PLURAL NOUN　　　　ADJECTIVE

week and I haven't _____ a wink. My neighbors have three children
　　　　　　　　　VERB (PAST TENSE)

who shot a toy rocket through my front _____ and I'm still waiting for
　　　　　　　　　　　　　　　　　　　NOUN

them to pay the damages. Their pet is a fifty-foot space _____ that likes
　　　　　　　　　　　　　　　　　　　　　　　　　ANIMAL

to _____ holes in the garden and eat all my _____ plants. I've
　　VERB　　　　　　　　　　　　　　　　TYPE OF FOOD

tried talking to them about these _____ problems, but they don't seem
　　　　　　　　　　　　　　ADJECTIVE

to understand. I think they speak a different language because they're always using

_____ words I've never heard before, like _____ and
ADJECTIVE　　　　　　　　　　　　　　　　　　　SILLY WORD

_____. I know they're not from this _____ and being so far
SILLY WORD　　　　　　　　　　　　　　　NOUN

from home can be _____, but they could at least try to _____
　　　　　　　ADJECTIVE　　　　　　　　　　　　　　　VERB

a little more normal!

MAD LIBS® is fun to play with friends, but you can also play it by yourself! To begin with, DO NOT look at the story on the page below. Fill in the blanks on this page with the words called for. Then, using the words you have selected, fill in the blank spaces in the story.

Now you've created your own hilarious MAD LIBS® game!

ANCIENT CIVILIZATIONS

ADJECTIVE _____

VERB _____

ADJECTIVE _____

NOUN _____

NOUN _____

ADJECTIVE _____

ADJECTIVE _____

PART OF THE BODY (PLURAL) _____

PLURAL NOUN _____

ADJECTIVE _____

ADJECTIVE _____

PLURAL NOUN _____

VEHICLE (PLURAL) _____

MAD LIBS®
ANCIENT CIVILIZATIONS

Man has created many wonders, but here's a list of famous sites where aliens may have lent a helping hand:

The Egyptian Pyramids: Some theorize the ancient Egyptians' technology wasn't _____ enough to build the Pyramids and that aliens helped to
ADJECTIVE
_____ these structures.
VERB

Stonehenge: These _____ stone monuments are laid out in a/an
ADJECTIVE
_____ shape and are thought to act as a landing _____ for
NOUN   NOUN
intergalactic spacecraft. It doesn't hurt that the area is known for sightings of
_____ lights in the sky.
ADJECTIVE

Easter Island *moai*: This coast is littered with hundreds of _____ statues
ADJECTIVE
carved with human-like _____. It's believed their design was
PART OF THE BODY (PLURAL)
based on extraterrestrial _____ that visited _____
PLURAL NOUN   ADJECTIVE
civilizations.

The Bermuda Triangle: This place is famous for countless _____
ADJECTIVE
disappearances. Some suspect this popular spot is where aliens abduct
unsuspecting _____—and their _____!
PLURAL NOUN   VEHICLE (PLURAL)

MAD LIBS® is fun to play with friends, but you can also play it by yourself! To begin with, DO NOT look at the story on the page below. Fill in the blanks on this page with the words called for. Then, using the words you have selected, fill in the blank spaces in the story.

Now you've created your own hilarious MAD LIBS® game!

SPACE CAMP 101

NOUN _____

OCCUPATION _____

NOUN _____

ADJECTIVE _____

VERB _____

NUMBER _____

TYPE OF FOOD _____

TYPE OF LIQUID _____

PLURAL NOUN _____

PLURAL NOUN _____

NOUN _____

NOUN _____

ADJECTIVE _____

ADJECTIVE _____

VEHICLE _____

NOUN _____

VERB _____

It's almost here! Tomorrow I leave for space _____ to learn what it's like
NOUN

to be a/an _____ in outer space! First we'll board a replica _____
OCCUPATION   NOUN

and take a/an _____ ride in the centrifuge, which can _____
ADJECTIVE   VERB

us around in circles at _____ times the normal force of gravity. Just make
NUMBER

sure not to eat any _____ or drink _____ beforehand,
TYPE OF FOOD   TYPE OF LIQUID

otherwise you might lose your _____! Speaking of, later we can
PLURAL NOUN

sample some astronaut chow, like freeze-dried _____ and powdered
PLURAL NOUN

_____. Then we'll visit the zero-gravity _____. Think
NOUN   NOUN

of all the _____ tricks I can do when my body becomes as _____
ADJECTIVE   ADJECTIVE

as air. We even get to build our own _____ and fly it to the
VEHICLE

_____. I can't wait to _____ at camp!
NOUN   VERB

MAD LIBS® is fun to play with friends, but you can also play it by yourself! To begin with, DO NOT look at the story on the page below. Fill in the blanks on this page with the words called for. Then, using the words you have selected, fill in the blank spaces in the story.

Now you've created your own hilarious MAD LIBS® game!

DIARY OF A CIA AGENT

ADJECTIVE _____

PERSON IN ROOM _____

NOUN _____

ADJECTIVE _____

NOUN _____

NOUN _____

ADJECTIVE _____

ADJECTIVE _____

PLURAL NOUN _____

NOUN _____

ADJECTIVE _____

SILLY WORD _____

VERB _____

OCCUPATION _____

NOUN _____

ADJECTIVE _____

Dear Diary,

Today was an absolutely _____ day at Area 51! Agent _____
ADJECTIVE   PERSON IN ROOM

accidentally let Specimen X escape from its containment _____ and we
NOUN

spent all morning searching the _____ areas of the lab for it. Then, we had
ADJECTIVE

a toxic _____ spill in sector C. I had to clean the entire _____
NOUN   NOUN

because the janitor was out sick with a/an _____ cold. I had an incredibly
ADJECTIVE

_____ meeting with some new _____ from Alpha Draconis,
ADJECTIVE   PLURAL NOUN

but I was running late due to a/an _____ jam in the main hallway. These
NOUN

aliens can't stand to wait, and boy, they were _____ with me for the rest
ADJECTIVE

of the day! Later, I met with Commissioner _____ and I was convinced
SILLY WORD

he was going to _____ me. Instead, he said he was promoting me to
VERB

executive _____ of the _____ division. What a great surprise!
OCCUPATION   NOUN

I guess today wasn't so _____ after all!
ADJECTIVE

MAD LIBS® is fun to play with friends, but you can also play it by yourself! To begin with, DO NOT look at the story on the page below. Fill in the blanks on this page with the words called for. Then, using the words you have selected, fill in the blank spaces in the story.

Now you've created your own hilarious MAD LIBS® game!

IT CAME FROM OUTER SPACE

PERSON IN ROOM (FEMALE) _____

PLURAL NOUN _____

ADJECTIVE _____

NOUN _____

ANIMAL _____

VEHICLE _____

ADJECTIVE _____

NOUN _____

ADJECTIVE _____

PLURAL NOUN _____

ADJECTIVE _____

PART OF THE BODY (PLURAL) _____

ANIMAL (PLURAL) _____

ADJECTIVE _____

OCCUPATION _____

PLURAL NOUN _____

ADJECTIVE _____

At 3:00 a.m. this morning, a local woman, __Ivanka__, awoke to
PERSON IN ROOM (FEMALE)

thunderous __lightsabers__ and a/an __little__ flash of light. Armed
PLURAL NOUN   ADJECTIVE

with a heavy __weiner__ and her pet __alpaca__ for protection, she
NOUN   ANIMAL

ventured outside to find that the smoldering remains of a/an __Star cruiser__
VEHICLE

had left a/an __hairy__ hole the size of a/an __holly hobbys__ in her backyard.
ADJECTIVE   NOUN

To her horror, something __dark__ slithered out of the hole and left a trail of
ADJECTIVE   bushie

__hats__ as it escaped to the nearby woods. Authorities advise citizens to
PLURAL NOUN

remain __swirly__ at all times, keep their __tets and boobies__ peeled for
ADJECTIVE   PART OF THE BODY (PLURAL)

any purple __chimpanzees__, and to report any __black__ occurrences
ANIMAL (PLURAL)   ADJECTIVE

to their local __cotton pickers__. A reward of five thousand __alashams__ is
OCCUPATION   PLURAL NOUN

being offered to anyone with a lead on the location of this __dumb__ invader.
ADJECTIVE

MAD LIBS® is fun to play with friends, but you can also play it by yourself! To begin with, DO NOT look at the story on the page below. Fill in the blanks on this page with the words called for. Then, using the words you have selected, fill in the blank spaces in the story.

Now you've created your own hilarious MAD LIBS® game!

SPACESHIP SUPERSALE EMPORIUM

VERB ENDING IN "ING" _____

VEHICLE (PLURAL) _____

ADJECTIVE _____

PLURAL NOUN _____

COLOR _____

ADJECTIVE _____

NOUN _____

NUMBER _____

ADJECTIVE _____

NOUN _____

VERB ENDING IN "ING" _____

NOUN _____

NOUN _____

Tired of the same old _____ saucers? Then come on down to the
VERB ENDING IN "ING"

Spaceship Supersale Emporium and browse our wide selection of

_____, where you're sure to find a/an _____ solution
VEHICLE (PLURAL) _ADJECTIVE_

to all your intergalactic travel needs! Our SUV shuttles are equipped with ample

room to store your abducted _____. All our vehicles come in a variety of
PLURAL NOUN

colors, including cobalt and avocado _____. If you're feeling
COLOR

_____, splurge for our turbo-drive model and kick your _____
ADJECTIVE _NOUN_

up to _____ times the speed of light! Happy with your current vehicle?
NUMBER

Then come get it upgraded with the latest _____ gizmo, like the
ADJECTIVE

_____ Ray 5000, capable of _____ an entire _____
NOUN _VERB ENDING IN "ING"_ _NOUN_

with a single blast! You'd have to be out of your _____ to pass on these
NOUN

deals!

MAD LIBS® is fun to play with friends, but you can also play it by yourself! To begin with, DO NOT look at the story on the page below. Fill in the blanks on this page with the words called for. Then, using the words you have selected, fill in the blank spaces in the story.

Now you've created your own hilarious MAD LIBS® game!

THE BENEFITS OF BLACK HOLES

PLURAL NOUN _____

PART OF THE BODY _____

NOUN _____

ADJECTIVE _____

A PLACE (PLURAL) _____

ADJECTIVE _____

VERB _____

ADJECTIVE _____

PLURAL NOUN _____

NOUN _____

A PLACE _____

ARTICLE OF CLOTHING _____

MAD LIBS®
THE BENEFITS OF
BLACK HOLES

Black holes are crushing, gravitational _____ of nature. Although
<u>PLURAL NOUN</u>

they can't be seen by the naked _____, we know when one exists by
<u>PART OF THE BODY</u>

the way it manipulates the _____ nearby. No one knows what resides
<u>NOUN</u>

inside these _____ holes, but some believe they are used as portals to
<u>ADJECTIVE</u>

other _____. Like a doorway to the universe, aliens utilizing these
<u>A PLACE (PLURAL)</u>

_____ wormholes can easily _____ from one galaxy to the
<u>ADJECTIVE</u>   <u>VERB</u>

next in a matter of seconds. This explains why people often claim UFOs disappear

into _____ air. If we can speak to these _____ and receive help
<u>ADJECTIVE</u>   <u>PLURAL NOUN</u>

with interdimensional travel, it could totally change _____ as we know
<u>NOUN</u>

it! Imagine waking up and deciding you wanted to visit (the) _____.
<u>A PLACE</u>

You could just pull on your space-_____ and teleport over.
<u>ARTICLE OF CLOTHING</u>

Incredible!

MAD LIBS® is fun to play with friends, but you can also play it by yourself! To begin with, DO NOT look at the story on the page below. Fill in the blanks on this page with the words called for. Then, using the words you have selected, fill in the blank spaces in the story.

Now you've created your own hilarious MAD LIBS® game!

FIRST CONTACT

VERB ENDING IN "ING" _____

SILLY WORD _____

PLURAL NOUN _____

NOUN _____

ADJECTIVE _____

NOUN _____

VERB _____

PLURAL NOUN _____

ADJECTIVE _____

EXCLAMATION _____

NOUN _____

PLURAL NOUN _____

TYPE OF FOOD _____

ADJECTIVE _____

TYPE OF LIQUID _Pee_____

MAD LIBS
FIRST CONTACT

Scientists and aliens have finally established a means of long-distance communication. Here is their first recorded conversation:

Alien: Hello? Is this planet Earth?

Scientist: Yes! With whom am I _Cheechuling_
VERB ENDING IN "ING"

Alien: I am _coching_. My family and I hail from the planet of
SILLY WORD

boobies.
PLURAL NOUN

Scientist: Are you here to take over our _weiner_?
NOUN

Alien: No, we are _sliny_ beings and mean you no _baloon_. We come
ADJECTIVE   NOUN

in peace.

Scientist: Shall I _diddling_ you to our leader?
VERB

Alien: No. We've traveled many light-years and risked our _Camel toes_ to
PLURAL NOUN

come here for a very _dirty_ request.
ADJECTIVE

Scientist: _oooh_! Well, what do you want?
EXCLAMATION

Alien: We would like one large _alien_ with pepperoni and green
NOUN

tata towels. Three orders of _pizza_, fried extra _colorful_.
PLURAL NOUN   TYPE OF FOOD   ADJECTIVE

And a diet _wine_.
TYPE OF LIQUID

Scientist: I think you have the wrong number . . .

MAD LIBS® is fun to play with friends, but you can also play it by yourself! To begin with, DO NOT look at the story on the page below. Fill in the blanks on this page with the words called for. Then, using the words you have selected, fill in the blank spaces in the story.

Now you've created your own hilarious MAD LIBS® game!

CLOSE ENCOUNTERS

PLURAL NOUN _____

NOUN _____

VERB (PAST TENSE) _____

NOUN _____

ADJECTIVE _____

ANIMAL _____

TYPE OF FOOD _____

ADJECTIVE _____

PART OF THE BODY (PLURAL) _____

PART OF THE BODY _____

PLURAL NOUN _____

NOUN _____

PLURAL NOUN _____

ADJECTIVE _____

MAD LIBS
CLOSE ENCOUNTERS

Let me tell you about the time I got abducted by _____. I was outside
                                                  PLURAL NOUN

one night, minding my own business, when suddenly a bright _____ lit
                                                            NOUN

up the sky and I was _____ up into a flying _____. Inside,
                     VERB (PAST TENSE)   NOUN

I came face-to-face with some _____ critters that looked like a cross
                              ADJECTIVE

between a/an _____ and a/an oversized _____. The creatures
             ANIMAL   TYPE OF FOOD

could only make _____ noises that sounded even worse than someone
                ADJECTIVE

scraping their _____ on a chalkboard. Yikes! Thankfully, the
               PART OF THE BODY (PLURAL)

creatures could transmit their words straight into my _____ and we
                                                       PART OF THE BODY

could communicate using our _____. They asked to borrow my
                            PLURAL NOUN

_____ so they could call their mother ship. Turns out these strange
   NOUN

_____ were lost and just needed _____ directions to return
  PLURAL NOUN   ADJECTIVE

home!

MAD LIBS®

GIVE ME LIBERTY
OR GIVE ME MAD LIBS

Mad Libs
An Imprint of Penguin Random House

INSTRUCTIONS

MAD LIBS® is a game for people who don't like games!
It can be played by one, two, three, four, or forty.

• RIDICULOUSLY SIMPLE DIRECTIONS

In this tablet you will find stories containing blank spaces where words are left out.
One player, the READER, selects one of these stories. The READER does not tell anyone
what the story is about. Instead, he/she asks the other players, the WRITERS, to give
him/her words. These words are used to fill in the blank spaces in the story.

• TO PLAY

The READER asks each WRITER in turn to call out a word—an adjective or a noun or
whatever the space calls for—and uses them to fill in the blank spaces in the story. The
result is a MAD LIBS® game.

When the READER then reads the completed MAD LIBS® game to the other players,
they will discover that they have written a story that is fantastic, screamingly funny,
shocking, silly, crazy, or just plain dumb—depending upon which words each WRITER
called out.

• EXAMPLE (*Before* and *After*)

"_____!" he said _____
      EXCLAMATION   ADVERB

as he jumped into his convertible _____ and
                                            NOUN

drove off with his _____ wife.
                     ADJECTIVE

"_____OUCH_____!" he said _____STUPIDLY_____
      EXCLAMATION   ADVERB

as he jumped into his convertible _____CAT_____ and
                                            NOUN

drove off with his _____BRAVE_____ wife.
                     ADJECTIVE

QUICK REVIEW

In case you have forgotten what adjectives, adverbs, nouns, and verbs are, here is a quick review:

An ADJECTIVE describes something or somebody. *Lumpy, soft, ugly, messy,* and *short* are adjectives.

An ADVERB tells how something is done. It modifies a verb and usually ends in "ly." *Modestly, stupidly, greedily,* and *carefully* are adverbs.

A NOUN is the name of a person, place, or thing. *Sidewalk, umbrella, bridle, bathtub,* and *nose* are nouns.

A VERB is an action word. *Run, pitch, jump,* and *swim* are verbs. Put the verbs in past tense if the directions say PAST TENSE. *Ran, pitched, jumped,* and *swam* are verbs in the past tense.

When we ask for A PLACE, we mean any sort of place: a country or city *(Spain, Cleveland)* or a room *(bathroom, kitchen).*

An EXCLAMATION or SILLY WORD is any sort of funny sound, gasp, grunt, or outcry, like *Wow!, Ouch!, Whomp!, Ick!,* and *Gadzooks!*

When we ask for specific words, like a NUMBER, a COLOR, an ANIMAL, or a PART OF THE BODY, we mean a word that is one of those things, like *seven, blue, horse,* or *head.*

When we ask for a PLURAL, it means more than one. For example, *cat* pluralized is *cats.*

MAD LIBS® is fun to play with friends, but you can also play it by yourself! To begin with, DO NOT look at the story on the page below. Fill in the blanks on this page with the words called for. Then, using the words you have selected, fill in the blank spaces in the story.

Now you've created your own hilarious MAD LIBS® game!

AS AMERICAN AS . . .

ADJECTIVE _____

TYPE OF FOOD _____

SAME TYPE OF FOOD _____

ADVERB _____

ADJECTIVE _____

ADJECTIVE _____

NOUN _____

NOUN _____

NOUN _____

ADJECTIVE _____

NOUN _____

ADJECTIVE _____

A PLACE _____

ARTICLE OF CLOTHING _____

ADJECTIVE _____

PLURAL NOUN _____

TYPE OF FOOD _____

COLOR _____

MAD LIBS®
AS AMERICAN AS...

Do you know the _____ saying "That's as American as
                          ADJECTIVE

_____ pie"? Well, _____ pie isn't the only thing
TYPE OF FOOD   SAME TYPE OF FOOD

that's _____ American! Here's a list of some of the most
         ADVERB

_____ things that represent the _____ ole US of A!
     ADJECTIVE   ADJECTIVE

• **Apple Pie:** There's nothing quite like biting into a forkful of

_____ pie to celebrate being a/an _____. Just don't
   NOUN   NOUN

add _____ cream—à la mode makes it French!
      NOUN

• **Baseball:** It's the _____ American pastime that dates all
                          ADJECTIVE

the way back to the 1700s! So, around the same time your mom and

_____ were in school!
   NOUN

• **Blue Jeans:** These _____ pants can be worn all year round,
                          ADJECTIVE

for almost every occasion, like your next visit to (the) _____!
                                                          A PLACE

Matching denim _____ optional.
                  ARTICLE OF CLOTHING

• **Mad Libs:** There's nothing more _____ than playing Mad
                                       ADJECTIVE

Libs with your _____! Just make sure to do it while eating
                 PLURAL NOUN

_____ pie and wearing your favorite _____ jeans!
TYPE OF FOOD   COLOR

MAD LIBS® is fun to play with friends, but you can also play it by yourself! To begin with, DO NOT look at the story on the page below. Fill in the blanks on this page with the words called for. Then, using the words you have selected, fill in the blank spaces in the story.

Now you've created your own hilarious MAD LIBS® game!

PATRIOTIC SONGS, PART 1

ADJECTIVE _____

NOUN _____

ADJECTIVE _____

NOUN _____

VERB _____

ADJECTIVE _____

ADVERB _____

NOUN _____

ADJECTIVE _____

NOUN _____

PLURAL NOUN _____

A PLACE _____

NOUN _____

VERB _____

NOUN _____

MAD LIBS
PATRIOTIC SONGS, PART 1

There are tons of _____ songs that are perfect to listen to on the Fourth
ADJECTIVE

of _____, or any day you want to get into a patriotic mood! Here's a list
NOUN

of the most _____, complete with lyrics:
ADJECTIVE

- **"The Star-Spangled _____"**: O say can you _____,
  NOUN   VERB

  by the dawn's _____ light, what so _____ we hailed at the
  ADJECTIVE   ADVERB

  _____'s last gleaming?
  NOUN

- **"Yankee Doodle"**: Yankee Doodle, keep it up. Yankee Doodle

  _____. Mind the music and the _____, and with the
  ADJECTIVE   NOUN

  _____ be handy.
  PLURAL NOUN

- **"God Bless America"**: God bless (the) _____, _____
  A PLACE   NOUN

  that I love. _____ beside her and guide her, through the night
  VERB

  with a/an _____ from above.
  NOUN

MAD LIBS® is fun to play with friends, but you can also play it by yourself! To begin with, DO NOT look at the story on the page below. Fill in the blanks on this page with the words called for. Then, using the words you have selected, fill in the blank spaces in the story.

Now you've created your own hilarious MAD LIBS® game!

PATRIOTIC SONGS, PART 2

PLURAL NOUN _____

VERB ENDING IN "ING" _____

NOUN _____

VERB _____

A PLACE _____

ADJECTIVE _____

NOUN _____

ADJECTIVE _____

VERB _____

PLURAL NOUN _____

PLURAL NOUN _____

PLURAL NOUN _____

PART OF THE BODY (PLURAL) _____

NOUN _____

NOUN _____

PLURAL NOUN _____

VERB (PAST TENSE) _____

ADJECTIVE _____

Here are more patriotic _____ that will have you
PLURAL NOUN

_____ a tune all day long!
VERB ENDING IN "ING"

• **"Stars and Stripes Forever":** Hurrah for the _____ of the free!
NOUN

May it _____ as our standard forever. The gem of the land and
VERB

(the) _____, the banner of the _____ .
A PLACE   ADJECTIVE

• **"My Country, 'Tis of Thee":** My _____, 'tis of thee, _____
NOUN   ADJECTIVE

land of liberty, of thee I _____. Land where my _____
VERB   PLURAL NOUN

died, land of the _____'(s) pride, from every mountainside,
PLURAL NOUN

let _____ ring.
PLURAL NOUN

• **"The Battle Hymn of the Republic":** Mine _____
PART OF THE BODY (PLURAL)

have seen the glory of the coming of the _____ . He is trampling
NOUN

out the _____ where the _____ of wrath are stored. He
NOUN   PLURAL NOUN

hath _____ the fateful lightning of his _____ swift
VERB (PAST TENSE)   ADJECTIVE

sword.

MAD LIBS® is fun to play with friends, but you can also play it by yourself! To begin with, DO NOT look at the story on the page below. Fill in the blanks on this page with the words called for. Then, using the words you have selected, fill in the blank spaces in the story.

Now you've created your own hilarious MAD LIBS® game!

PARTY LIKE IT'S JULY FOURTH!

ADJECTIVE _____

A PLACE _____

NUMBER _____

ADJECTIVE _____

NOUN _____

ADJECTIVE _____

ADJECTIVE _____

ADJECTIVE _____

TYPE OF FOOD _____

COLOR _____

PART OF THE BODY _____

PLURAL NOUN _____

NOUN _____

ADJECTIVE _____

LETTER OF THE ALPHABET _____

VERB _____

PLURAL NOUN _____

NOUN _____

The Fourth of July is right around the corner, and you want to throw the

most ___Smiley___ party in all of (the) ___Johnny Depps hole___. It's as easy as 1, 2,
       ADJECTIVE   A PLACE

___10___ if you follow this ___Colorful___ guide! First, decide who you want
NUMBER   ADJECTIVE

to invite. You can't invite every ___guitar___ on the block, so only invite
                                     NOUN

the most ___crotchety___ (or the ones who will bring something ___Fuzzy___
          ADJECTIVE   ADJECTIVE

to eat!). Next, decide on a/an ___tiny___ menu. Wiggly ___bacon___
                                ADJECTIVE   TYPE OF FOOD

molds in the shape of the American flag are sooo last year! Instead, find

as many ___Purple___, white, and blue ___boobies___-foods as you can,
          COLOR   PART OF THE BODY

and spread them out for your ___Puppies___ to pick at. It doesn't hurt to ask
                               PLURAL NOUN

your ___train___ to throw some burgers on the grill, too! Finally,
      NOUN

don't forget about the music. Put some ___Spicy___ songs on your
                                         ADJECTIVE

___L___-pod for your guests to dance to. And make sure there
LETTER OF THE ALPHABET

are enough fireworks for everyone to ___Singing___ once it gets dark outside!
                                       VERB

Follow these tips (and ask for help from your ___lights___), and it's sure to
                                                PLURAL NOUN

be a/an ___popcorn bucket___ to remember!
         NOUN

MAD LIBS® is fun to play with friends, but you can also play it by yourself! To begin with, DO NOT look at the story on the page below. Fill in the blanks on this page with the words called for. Then, using the words you have selected, fill in the blank spaces in the story.

Now you've created your own hilarious MAD LIBS® game!

DECLARATION OF INDEPENDENCE

NOUN _____

PLURAL NOUN _____

PLURAL NOUN _____

NOUN _____

ADJECTIVE _____

PLURAL NOUN _____

PLURAL NOUN _____

ADJECTIVE _____

PLURAL NOUN _____

PLURAL NOUN _____

VERB _____

PLURAL NOUN _____

PLURAL NOUN _____

MAD LIBS
DECLARATION OF INDEPENDENCE

You haven't read the Declaration of _____ until you've read it Mad Libs–
                                   NOUN

style!

We hold these _____ to be self-evident, that all _____ are created
             PLURAL NOUN   PLURAL NOUN

equal, that they are endowed by their _____ with certain _____
                                    NOUN   ADJECTIVE

Rights, that among these are Life, Liberty and the pursuit of _____.—
                                                      PLURAL NOUN

That to secure these _____, Governments are instituted among Men,
                       PLURAL NOUN

deriving their _____ powers from the consent of the governed,—That
                ADJECTIVE

whenever any Form of Government becomes destructive of these

_____, it is the Right of the _____ to alter or to _____ it,
PLURAL NOUN   PLURAL NOUN   VERB

and to institute new Government, laying its foundation on such principles and

organizing its _____ in such form, as to them shall seem most likely to
                  PLURAL NOUN

effect their Safety and _____.
                          PLURAL NOUN

MAD LIBS® is fun to play with friends, but you can also play it by yourself! To begin with, DO NOT look at the story on the page below. Fill in the blanks on this page with the words called for. Then, using the words you have selected, fill in the blank spaces in the story.

Now you've created your own hilarious MAD LIBS® game!

ROAD TRIP!

ADJECTIVE _____

ADJECTIVE _____

PLURAL NOUN _____

NOUN _____

VERB ENDING IN "ING" _____

NOUN _____

NOUN _____

VEHICLE _____

SILLY WORD _____

PART OF THE BODY (PLURAL) _____

ADJECTIVE _____

COLOR _____

ADJECTIVE _____

NOUN _____

ADJECTIVE _____

MAD LIBS
ROAD TRIP!

Pack your bags! It's time to take a/an _hairy_ road trip across the United
ADJECTIVE

States to visit some of the most _swirly_ historical landmarks. First stop is
ADJECTIVE

Philadelphia, where you can visit Independence Hall to see where the

Declaration of _bushys_ was signed. After that, check out the Liberty Bell.
PLURAL NOUN

It's the most famous cracked _weiner_ in history, and a symbol of freedom
NOUN

across America. Then head on up to Boston, where you can check out the USS

Constitution, the oldest _Juicing_ naval vessel, and the _the rock_
VERB ENDING IN "ING"   NOUN

Hill Monument. In New York, you can climb to the top of the _snoop dog_ of
NOUN

Liberty (or take a/an _sleigh_ to check out the view from the harbor!).
VEHICLE

Now it's time to head west, where you can see famous landmarks like Mount

Material girl, which features carved statues of the _Boobies_ of
SILLY WORD   PART OF THE BODY (PLURAL)

some of our most _Pungent_ presidents. Or check out _purple_-stone,
ADJECTIVE   COLOR

our first national park, which includes the famous geyser Old _indian_ !
ADJECTIVE

Just don't forget to pack a/an _toilet_—you'll want to take pictures to
NOUN

remember your _gay_ trip by!
ADJECTIVE

MAD LIBS® is fun to play with friends, but you can also play it by yourself! To begin with, DO NOT look at the story on the page below. Fill in the blanks on this page with the words called for. Then, using the words you have selected, fill in the blank spaces in the story.

Now you've created your own hilarious MAD LIBS® game!

MOVIES TO GET YOU IN THE MOOD

ADJECTIVE _____

PLURAL NOUN _____

ADJECTIVE _____

ADJECTIVE _____

VERB _____

COLOR _____

CELEBRITY _____

ADJECTIVE _____

PLURAL NOUN _____

PERSON IN ROOM (MALE) _____

ADJECTIVE _____

OCCUPATION _____

OCCUPATION (PLURAL) _____

ADVERB _____

VEHICLE _____

PLURAL NOUN _____

TYPE OF FOOD _____

TYPE OF LIQUID _____

NOUN _____

Fourth of July is right around the corner and you want to get in a/an _____
ADJECTIVE

mood to celebrate, so why not watch some of these classic _____?
PLURAL NOUN

- **Independence Day**: _____ aliens invade Earth in this sci-fi thriller.
  ADJECTIVE

  The aliens are so _____, they even _____ up the _____
  ADJECTIVE   VERB   COLOR

  House!

- **National Treasure**: _____ stars as a history buff who must find
  CELEBRITY

  the _____ lost treasure before his _____ get to it first.
  ADJECTIVE   PLURAL NOUN

- **The Patriot**: _____ Gibson is a war hero who just wants
  PERSON IN ROOM (MALE)

  to live a/an _____ life as a/an _____ on his farm when the
  ADJECTIVE   OCCUPATION

  American Revolution begins.

- **Apollo 13**: Three _____ try to get home _____ after
  OCCUPATION (PLURAL)   ADVERB

  their _____ malfunctions.
  VEHICLE

Now that you've got your _____ all picked out, don't forget your
PLURAL NOUN

_____ and _____. Just be sure to make enough for your little
TYPE OF FOOD   TYPE OF LIQUID

brother or _____!
NOUN

MAD LIBS® is fun to play with friends, but you can also play it by yourself! To begin with, DO NOT look at the story on the page below. Fill in the blanks on this page with the words called for. Then, using the words you have selected, fill in the blank spaces in the story.

Now you've created your own hilarious MAD LIBS® game!

RED, WHITE, AND BEAUTIFUL!

NOUN _____

ADJECTIVE _____

PERSON IN ROOM (FEMALE) _____

ADJECTIVE _____

A PLACE _____

PERSON IN ROOM (MALE) _____

NOUN _____

NUMBER _____

PLURAL NOUN _____

PLURAL NOUN _____

NUMBER _____

PLURAL NOUN _____

ADVERB _____

NOUN _____

NOUN _____

MAD LIBS
RED, WHITE, AND BEAUTIFUL!

Sure, you pledge allegiance to the American _____ every morning
                                                NOUN

when school starts, but do you know the history behind this _____
                                                              ADJECTIVE

flag? The legend goes that the first flag was made by

_____ Ross, a/an _____ seamstress
PERSON IN ROOM (FEMALE)   ADJECTIVE

who lived in (the) _____. In May 1776,
                        A PLACE

_____ Washington visited Ross at her shop and
PERSON IN ROOM (MALE)

asked her to sew a/an _____ based on the design he gave her. The
                           NOUN

stars in the flag originally had _____ points, but Ross changed
                                      NUMBER

the design to five, which is how the flag still looks today! The first official flag

was known as the Stars and _____. The flag changed as more
                                 PLURAL NOUN

_____ joined the Union, until Congress passed a law in 1818
   PLURAL NOUN

that said the flag would always have _____ stripes, and stars
                                          NUMBER

equal to the total number of _____ in the Union. The flag was
                                  PLURAL NOUN

_____ completed in 1960, when Hawaii became the last state to join
   ADVERB

the _____. Think about that next time you say, "I pledge allegiance
        NOUN

to the _____"!
           NOUN

MAD LIBS® is fun to play with friends, but you can also play it by yourself! To begin with, DO NOT look at the story on the page below. Fill in the blanks on this page with the words called for. Then, using the words you have selected, fill in the blank spaces in the story.

Now you've created your own hilarious MAD LIBS® game!

PATRIOTIC HOLIDAYS

ADJECTIVE _____

COLOR _____

ADJECTIVE _____

ADJECTIVE _____

PLURAL NOUN _____

ADJECTIVE _____

NOUN _____

PERSON IN ROOM (MALE) _____

PERSON IN ROOM (MALE) _____

VERB ENDING IN "ING" _____

NOUN _____

ADJECTIVE _____

ADVERB _____

NOUN _____

MAD LIBS
PATRIOTIC HOLIDAYS

The Fourth of July might be the most __slimy__ patriotic holiday, but there
ADJECTIVE

are also many other times throughout the year that you can deck yourself out

in red, white, and __purple__, and show some __spicy__ American pride! Here
COLOR   ADJECTIVE

are a few __slithery__ holidays and their meanings:
ADJECTIVE

- **Martin Luther King Jr. Day:** Celebrates the life and __boobies__
  PLURAL NOUN

  of Martin Luther King Jr., a/an __chubby__ civil rights activist, most
  ADJECTIVE

  famous for his "I Have a/an __noodle__" speech.
  NOUN

- **Presidents' Day:** Celebrates the birthdays of both __Mr. Morow__
  PERSON IN ROOM (MALE)

  Washington and __Trump__ Lincoln.
  PERSON IN ROOM (MALE)

- **Labor Day:** Honors our country's hard-__jucing__ people.
  VERB ENDING IN "ING"

  It marks the end of the summer season and the beginning of a new

  __olive__ year for most students!
  NOUN

- **Veterans Day:** This __dirty__ holiday honors the veterans who
  ADJECTIVE

  fought __slowly__ for our __wenir__.
  ADVERB   NOUN

MAD LIBS® is fun to play with friends, but you can also play it by yourself! To begin with, DO NOT look at the story on the page below. Fill in the blanks on this page with the words called for. Then, using the words you have selected, fill in the blank spaces in the story.

Now you've created your own hilarious MAD LIBS® game!

FIREWORKS! FIREWORKS! FIREWORKS!

ADJECTIVE _____

NOUN _____

PLURAL NOUN _____

ADJECTIVE _____

PLURAL NOUN _____

PLURAL NOUN _____

ADVERB _____

ADJECTIVE _____

ADJECTIVE _____

ADJECTIVE _____

NOUN _____

EXCLAMATION _____

ADJECTIVE _____

ADJECTIVE _____

ADJECTIVE _____

NOUN _____

NOUN _____

Fireworks are a/an _____ way to celebrate the Fourth of _____!
           ADJECTIVE   NOUN

But you probably didn't know that these explosive _____ have a long,
            PLURAL NOUN

_____ history. In fact, some _____ believe that fireworks were
ADJECTIVE   PLURAL NOUN

invented by the Chinese in 200 BC. Chinese _____ _____ lit
                PLURAL NOUN   ADVERB

bamboo stalks on fire, and it caused a loud, _____ *BANG!* that scared
                        ADJECTIVE

away the _____ mountain men nearby. That's how fireworks were born!
      ADJECTIVE

Even though they may seem like _____ magic, fireworks are actually just
                 ADJECTIVE

chemical reactions. Different _____ elements produce different colors of
                NOUN

fireworks! _____—sure makes chemistry class a whole lot more
      EXCLAMATION

_____! Americans have been using _____ fireworks to celebrate
ADJECTIVE   ADJECTIVE

their independence since 1777, at least. So next time you want to celebrate the

_____ ole US of A, light up a sparkler or a Roman _____—with
ADJECTIVE   NOUN

your mom or _____'s permission, of course!
        NOUN

MAD LIBS® is fun to play with friends, but you can also play it by yourself! To begin with, DO NOT look at the story on the page below. Fill in the blanks on this page with the words called for. Then, using the words you have selected, fill in the blank spaces in the story.

Now you've created your own hilarious MAD LIBS® game!

HISTORY LESSON

NOUN _____

NOUN _____

NOUN _____

CELEBRITY _____

NUMBER _____

ADJECTIVE _____

NOUN _____

A PLACE _____

VERB (PAST TENSE) _____

ADJECTIVE _____

ADJECTIVE _____

OCCUPATION _____

ADVERB _____

VERB ENDING IN "ING" _____

NUMBER _____

ADJECTIVE _____

MAD LIBS®
HISTORY LESSON

Have you ever wondered why exactly we celebrate the Fourth of _____?
                                                                    NOUN

The Fourth marks the day that the Continental _____ adopted the
                                                        NOUN

Declaration of _____ way back in 1776! The Declaration of Independence
                  NOUN

was originally written by _____. It stated that _____ North
                            CELEBRITY   NUMBER

American colonies planned to separate from Britain and become their own

_____ nation. The first ever Fourth of _____ celebration took place
 ADJECTIVE   NOUN

in (the) _____ on July 8, 1776. On that day, the Declaration was read
          A PLACE

aloud, city bells _____ loudly, and bands played _____ music.
                   VERB (PAST TENSE)   ADJECTIVE

Some towns even held a/an _____ fake funeral for the _____ of
                            ADJECTIVE   OCCUPATION

England! Independence Day was _____ declared an official holiday in
                               ADVERB

1870, but that didn't stop people from _____ every summer
                                        VERB ENDING IN "ING"

on July _____! And now that you know your history, you can celebrate the
         NUMBER

Fourth of July just like a/an _____ colonist would!
                               ADJECTIVE

MAD LIBS® is fun to play with friends, but you can also play it by yourself! To begin with, DO NOT look at the story on the page below. Fill in the blanks on this page with the words called for. Then, using the words you have selected, fill in the blank spaces in the story.

Now you've created your own hilarious MAD LIBS® game!

INTERVIEW WITH THE STATUE OF LIBERTY

PERSON IN ROOM (FEMALE) _____

PART OF THE BODY _____

NOUN _____

NOUN _____

A PLACE _____

ADJECTIVE _____

NUMBER _____

PLURAL NOUN _____

CELEBRITY _____

PLURAL NOUN _____

ADJECTIVE _____

ADJECTIVE _____

ADJECTIVE _____

SILLY WORD _____

NUMBER _____

ADJECTIVE _____

SAME ADJECTIVE _____

PERSON IN ROOM (MALE) _____

Reporter: _____ Jones here, reporter for
PERSON IN ROOM (FEMALE)

_____-witness News. Today we're reporting live from Liberty
PART OF THE BODY

Island, where we scored an exclusive interview with the Statue of _____!
NOUN

So, tell us, what's it like to be the largest _____ in all of (the) _____?
NOUN · A PLACE

Statue of Liberty: It's _____! After all, I'm over _____ feet tall
ADJECTIVE · NUMBER

and weigh 450,000 _____. Nobody messes with me! Not even _____!
PLURAL NOUN · CELEBRITY

Reporter: Rumor has it that you're not originally from the United

_____. You were a gift from the _____ French! Can you
PLURAL NOUN · ADJECTIVE

confirm if this is true or _____?
ADJECTIVE

Statue of Liberty: Yes, it's totally _____! And it took the sculptor, Auguste
ADJECTIVE

_____, over _____ years to finish building me. That explains why
SILLY WORD · NUMBER

I'm so darn _____!
ADJECTIVE

Reporter: It's true; you're the most _____ statue ever built!
SAME ADJECTIVE

_____, now back to you in the studio with sports!
PERSON IN ROOM (MALE)

MAD LIBS® is fun to play with friends, but you can also play it by yourself! To begin with, DO NOT look at the story on the page below. Fill in the blanks on this page with the words called for. Then, using the words you have selected, fill in the blank spaces in the story.

Now you've created your own hilarious MAD LIBS® game!

APPLE PIE, SO DIVINE!

ADJECTIVE _____

VERB _____

PART OF THE BODY _____

TYPE OF FOOD _____

NOUN _____

PLURAL NOUN _____

NUMBER _____

PLURAL NOUN _____

ADJECTIVE _____

NOUN _____

ADJECTIVE _____

TYPE OF FOOD _____

NOUN _____

NUMBER _____

ADJECTIVE _____

MAD LIBS®
APPLE PIE, SO DIVINE!

If you're looking for a/an _____ recipe to bring to your next Fourth of
                         ADJECTIVE

July celebration, _____ no further! Here's a/an _____-watering
                    VERB   PART OF THE BODY

recipe for the most American dessert of all, apple pie! First, gather your

ingredients. You will need the following:

- 2 premade _____ crusts
             TYPE OF FOOD

- 1/4 cup all-purpose _____
                       NOUN

- 3/4 cup sugar

- 1/2 teaspoon cinnamon

- 1/2 teaspoon _____
                PLURAL NOUN

- 2 tablespoons butter

- _____ cups thinly sliced _____
   NUMBER   PLURAL NOUN

To make this _____ recipe, first preheat the _____ to 425 degrees.
             ADJECTIVE   NOUN

Then mix together your _____ ingredients, and add in the apples. Pour
                       ADJECTIVE

the mixture into the _____ crust, dot with butter, and cover it with the
                     TYPE OF FOOD

other crust. Place it in the _____. Voilà! In just _____ short minutes,
                             NOUN   NUMBER

you'll have a/an _____ dessert that will impress all your friends!
                 ADJECTIVE

MAD LIBS® is fun to play with friends, but you can also play it by yourself! To begin with, DO NOT look at the story on the page below. Fill in the blanks on this page with the words called for. Then, using the words you have selected, fill in the blank spaces in the story.

Now you've created your own hilarious MAD LIBS® game!

CELEBRATE ACROSS AMERICA

ADJECTIVE _____

ADJECTIVE _____

NOUN _____

NOUN _____

ADJECTIVE _____

PERSON IN ROOM (MALE) _____

PLURAL NOUN _____

PLURAL NOUN _____

PLURAL NOUN _____

TYPE OF FOOD _____

ADJECTIVE _____

ADJECTIVE _____

TYPE OF FOOD _____

PLURAL NOUN _____

MAD LIBS®
CELEBRATE ACROSS AMERICA

The Fourth of July is celebrated all across this _____
ADJECTIVE

nation of ours, but not every city honors America in the same way! Here's a list

of _____ cities and their favorite ways to celebrate the most
ADJECTIVE

patriotic _____ of the year!
NOUN

- The Boston _____ Orchestra holds a/an _____ concert on
NOUN   ADJECTIVE

  the banks of the _____ River.
  PERSON IN ROOM (MALE)

- _____ living in Philadelphia celebrate at Independence Hall, the
  PLURAL NOUN

  place where the Declaration of _____ was first signed.
  PLURAL NOUN

- In New York City, _____ flock to Coney Island to watch the
  PLURAL NOUN

  annual _____ -eating contest.
  TYPE OF FOOD

- In cities like Chicago and San Francisco, people cram together to watch

  the _____ fireworks shows that take place every year.
  ADJECTIVE

- And in backyards all across this _____ country, people stuff their
  ADJECTIVE

  faces with _____ , light sparklers, and spend quality time with
  TYPE OF FOOD

  their friends and _____ !
  PLURAL NOUN

MAD LIBS® is fun to play with friends, but you can also play it by yourself! To begin with, DO NOT look at the story on the page below. Fill in the blanks on this page with the words called for. Then, using the words you have selected, fill in the blank spaces in the story.

Now you've created your own hilarious MAD LIBS® game!

CELEBRATE WITH A BANG!

NOUN _____

PLURAL NOUN _____

NUMBER _____

A PLACE _____

NOUN _____

ADJECTIVE _____

PLURAL NOUN _____

VERB _____

VERB ENDING IN "ING" _____

NOUN _____

PLURAL NOUN _____

ANIMAL _____

EXCLAMATION _____

ADJECTIVE _____

ANIMAL (PLURAL) _____

ADJECTIVE _____

NUMBER _____

PLURAL NOUN _____

MAD LIBS®
CELEBRATE WITH A BANG!

Is your Fourth of July celebration feeling a little stale? Looking for some

excitement to liven up your boring _____ ? Want to impress
                                          NOUN

your friends and _____ ? Well, we've got the solution for you!
                      PLURAL NOUN

Come on down to the Firework Warehouse, located right off exit

_____ in (the) _____ . We've got every type of
   NUMBER   A PLACE

_____ imaginable—big ones, loud ones, _____
   NOUN   ADJECTIVE

ones! If rockets are your thing, we've got a huge assortment of _____
                                                                 PLURAL NOUN

that _____ off into the sky and make a loud_____
        VERB   VERB ENDING IN "ING"

noise as they explode. We also carry a wide selection of _____
                                                              NOUN

spinners. These babies spray _____ everywhere as they spin on
                                 PLURAL NOUN

the ground like a crazed _____ ! Can you say, "_____ !"?
                            ANIMAL   EXCLAMATION

We also carry a/an _____ assortment of sparklers, poppers, and
                      ADJECTIVE

caps for all the scaredy-_____ out there! But hurry, hurry, hurry!
                          ANIMAL (PLURAL)

Supply is limited, and this _____ deal won't last long! Offer
                               ADJECTIVE

valid until July _____ or until _____ run out!
                    NUMBER   PLURAL NOUN

MAD LIBS® is fun to play with friends, but you can also play it by yourself! To begin with, DO NOT look at the story on the page below. Fill in the blanks on this page with the words called for. Then, using the words you have selected, fill in the blank spaces in the story.

Now you've created your own hilarious MAD LIBS® game!

MEET UNCLE SAM

ADJECTIVE _____

NOUN _____

PERSON IN ROOM (MALE) _____

COLOR _____

ADJECTIVE _____

COLOR _____

PART OF THE BODY _____

ADJECTIVE _____

PERSON IN ROOM _____

OCCUPATION _____

ADVERB _____

PLURAL NOUN _____

VERB _____

NOUN _____

NUMBER _____

MAD LIBS®
MEET UNCLE SAM

"Uncle Sam" is a/an _____ nickname for the US government that
ADJECTIVE

became popular during the _____ of 1812. But there's so much more
NOUN

about Uncle _____ that you don't know . . .
PERSON IN ROOM (MALE)

Favorite Color: Red, white, and _____, of course!
COLOR

Favorite Article of Clothing: A toss-up between my _____ top
ADJECTIVE

hat and my _____ bow tie. They both make my _____ look
COLOR   PART OF THE BODY

_____!
ADJECTIVE

Favorite Phrase: I Want YOU! (Yes, you, _____!)
PERSON IN ROOM

Favorite Holiday: Talk Like a/an _____ Day. Just kidding! It's
OCCUPATION

_____ Independence Day!
ADVERB

Favorite Band: The Rolling _____. Hey, even Uncle Sam likes to
PLURAL NOUN

_____ and roll sometimes!
VERB

Favorite Movie: Either *Born on the Fourth of* _____ or *Toy Story*
NOUN

_____.
NUMBER

MAD LIBS® is fun to play with friends, but you can also play it by yourself! To begin with, DO NOT look at the story on the page below. Fill in the blanks on this page with the words called for. Then, using the words you have selected, fill in the blank spaces in the story.

Now you've created your own hilarious MAD LIBS® game!

FOURTH OF JULY BLOOPERS

ADJECTIVE _____

PERSON IN ROOM (FEMALE) _____

PERSON IN ROOM (MALE) _____

ADJECTIVE _____

TYPE OF FOOD (PLURAL) _____

PLURAL NOUN _____

ADJECTIVE _____

NUMBER _____

CELEBRITY (MALE) _____

ADJECTIVE _____

EXCLAMATION _____

PART OF THE BODY _____

VERB _____

ADJECTIVE _____

VERB _____

PLURAL NOUN _____

TYPE OF LIQUID _____

ANIMAL _____

Our Fourth of July started out __Hairy__ enough. Aunt __Amber heard__
ADJECTIVE   PERSON IN ROOM (FEMALE)

and Uncle __Johnny Depp__ were coming over to spend the day with my
PERSON IN ROOM (MALE)

family. We had a really __smelly__ barbecue set up in the backyard, with lots
ADJECTIVE

of __Wieners__ and __snowmen__ right off the grill. The trouble started
TYPE OF FOOD (PLURAL)   PLURAL NOUN

when my aunt and uncle arrived and we found out they had brought along the

newest and most __sweet__ member of their family: a/an __81__-pound
ADJECTIVE   NUMBER

pet pig named __Jeff beck__! The pig looked __glittery__ enough, and he
CELEBRITY (MALE)   ADJECTIVE

even made a noise that sounded like "__ooouch__!" when I petted him on
EXCLAMATION

his __Boobies__. But when we put him in the backyard to __feasting__,
PART OF THE BODY   VERB

everything got totally out of hand! The pig took one sniff of all the __spicy__
ADJECTIVE

food and started to __dumping__ around like crazy. He knocked over all the
VERB

tables and __farts__, destroyed my kid sister's playhouse, and took a swim in
PLURAL NOUN

the __peepee__. "That's it!" my father yelled. "Next time you bring a/an
TYPE OF LIQUID

__Yeti__ to a barbecue, we're going to cook him!"
ANIMAL

MAD LIBS® is fun to play with friends, but you can also play it by yourself! To begin with, DO NOT look at the story on the page below. Fill in the blanks on this page with the words called for. Then, using the words you have selected, fill in the blank spaces in the story.

Now you've created your own hilarious MAD LIBS® game!

BIRD OF PREY

ANIMAL _____

ADJECTIVE _____

PLURAL NOUN _____

NUMBER _____

ANIMAL _____

ADJECTIVE _____

TYPE OF LIQUID _____

ADJECTIVE _____

ADJECTIVE _____

VERB ENDING IN "ING" _____

TYPE OF LIQUID _____

NOUN _____

SAME NOUN _____

ADJECTIVE _____

ANIMAL _____

PART OF THE BODY _____

COLOR _____

PERSON IN ROOM (MALE) _____

ADJECTIVE _____

MAD LIBS
BIRD OF PREY

The bald eagle is famous for being the national _____ of the
                                                    ANIMAL
United States of America. You may have seen this _____ bird
                                                    ADJECTIVE
on the national seal, which is used on passports, _____, and
                                                    PLURAL NOUN
$_____ bills. But in the wild, the bald _____ is one of the most
    NUMBER   ANIMAL
ferocious and _____ birds of prey you can encounter. Bald eagles live
                ADJECTIVE
near large bodies of _____ surrounded by lots of old _____
                      TYPE OF LIQUID   ADJECTIVE
trees for nesting. If he's feeling hungry, the bald eagle swoops down and uses

his sharp, _____ talons to pick up fish _____ in the
             ADJECTIVE   VERB ENDING IN "ING"
nearby _____. Then he returns home to his _____, which
        TYPE OF LIQUID   NOUN
is the largest _____ built by any bird in North America. Talk about
                SAME NOUN
living _____! And despite popular opinion, the bald _____ isn't
        ADJECTIVE   ANIMAL
actually bald. His _____ is simply covered with _____
                    PART OF THE BODY   COLOR
feathers. So next time your uncle _____ complains about being
                                    PERSON IN ROOM (MALE)
bald, tell him there's no shame in being _____. The bald eagle says so!
                                           ADJECTIVE

MAD LIBS® is fun to play with friends, but you can also play it by yourself! To begin with, DO NOT look at the story on the page below. Fill in the blanks on this page with the words called for. Then, using the words you have selected, fill in the blank spaces in the story.

Now you've created your own hilarious MAD LIBS® game!

PATRIOTIC QUOTES

ADJECTIVE _____

VERB ENDING IN "ING" _____

OCCUPATION _____

ARTICLE OF CLOTHING _____

ADJECTIVE _____

A PLACE _____

ADJECTIVE _____

PART OF THE BODY _____

NOUN _____

VERB _____

MAD LIBS
PATRIOTIC QUOTES

The next time you really want to impress your parents at the dinner table,

recite one of these _____ quotes made famous by our _____
               ADJECTIVE   VERB ENDING IN "ING"

fathers! Even better, throw one into your next history paper to knock your

_____'s _____ off!
OCCUPATION   ARTICLE OF CLOTHING

"History, in general, only informs us what _____ government is."
                                               ADJECTIVE

—Thomas Jefferson

"May the sun in his course visit no _____ more free, more happy, more
                                       A PLACE

_____, than this our own country!" **—Daniel Webster**
ADJECTIVE

"The cement of this Union is in the _____-blood of every
                                         PART OF THE BODY

American."**—Thomas Jefferson**

"Patriot: the _____who can _____ the loudest without knowing what
                   NOUN   VERB

he is hollering about."**—Mark Twain**

MAD LIBS® is fun to play with friends, but you can also play it by yourself! To begin with, DO NOT look at the story on the page below. Fill in the blanks on this page with the words called for. Then, using the words you have selected, fill in the blank spaces in the story.

Now you've created your own hilarious MAD LIBS® game!

DRESS UP!

ADJECTIVE _____

PLURAL NOUN _____

NOUN _____

PLURAL NOUN _____

COLOR _____

PART OF THE BODY _____

ADJECTIVE _____

EXCLAMATION _____

ADJECTIVE _____

COLOR _____

PERSON IN ROOM (MALE) _____

PERSON IN ROOM (FEMALE) _____

PLURAL NOUN _____

ADJECTIVE _____

ADJECTIVE _____

NOUN _____

PERSON IN ROOM (MALE) _____

MAD LIBS
DRESS UP!

One _____ Fourth of July tradition in many towns
      ADJECTIVE

and _____ is dressing up for the annual _____ Day
   PLURAL NOUN   NOUN

Parade! There are tons of different patriotic _____ that you
                                         PLURAL NOUN

could wear. To dress up as the Statue of Liberty, wrap a/an _____
                                                     COLOR

bedsheet around your body and paint your _____ green. Borrow
                                      PART OF THE BODY

your _____ sister's tiara, and _____! You're Lady
      ADJECTIVE   EXCLAMATION

Liberty! Uncle Sam is another _____ costume choice. For this, you
                              ADJECTIVE

will need a red, white, and _____ suit. Borrow your uncle
                                  COLOR

_____'s toupee and spray-paint it white for the perfect
PERSON IN ROOM (MALE)

beard! A brother-and-sister duo can dress up as George and

_____ Washington. Just make sure the two
PERSON IN ROOM (FEMALE)

_____ get along; otherwise they might start another
   PLURAL NOUN

_____ Revolutionary War! If all else fails, dress in all black, draw
  ADJECTIVE

a/an _____ beard on your face with _____ paint, and
      ADJECTIVE   NOUN

call yourself _____ Lincoln!
              PERSON IN ROOM (MALE)

MAD LIBS® is fun to play with friends, but you can also play it by yourself! To begin with, DO NOT look at the story on the page below. Fill in the blanks on this page with the words called for. Then, using the words you have selected, fill in the blank spaces in the story.

Now you've created your own hilarious MAD LIBS® game!

I LOVE THE USA!

NOUN _____

ADJECTIVE _____

COLOR _____

ADJECTIVE _____

ADJECTIVE _____

ADJECTIVE _____

NOUN _____

NOUN _____

VERB _____

NOUN _____

PLURAL NOUN _____

ADJECTIVE _____

SAME ADJECTIVE _____

MAD LIBS®
I LOVE THE USA!

Do you really love being an American __cup__ ? Then show your pride on
NOUN

the Fourth of July (or any __slimy__ day!) by doing the following:
ADJECTIVE

- Wear red, white, and __pink__ ! Show off the colors of your country
COLOR

by wearing a/an __crunchy__ outfit that looks like it was designed from
ADJECTIVE

the American flag.

- Put a flag outside your home. Just make sure to take it down if it rains—

you don't want the flag to get __big__ !
ADJECTIVE

- Visit a/an __local__ memorial and pay your respects. Chances are,
ADJECTIVE

there is a historical __house__ a lot closer to your home than you think!
NOUN

- Do something artistic! Write a/an __alien__ , __run__ a song, or
NOUN   VERB

paint a/an __chicken__ to show your love for your country!
NOUN

- Honor other people's __balls__ and beliefs. Be __runny__
PLURAL NOUN   ADJECTIVE

to everyone you meet, and they will be __runny__ to you
SAME ADJECTIVE

in return.

MAD LIBS®

MEOW LIBS

by Sarah Fabiny

Mad Libs
An Imprint of Penguin Random House

INSTRUCTIONS

MAD LIBS® is a game for people who don't like games!
It can be played by one, two, three, four, or forty.

● RIDICULOUSLY SIMPLE DIRECTIONS

In this tablet you will find stories containing blank spaces where words are left out.
One player, the READER, selects one of these stories. The READER does not tell anyone
what the story is about. Instead, he/she asks the other players, the WRITERS, to give
him/her words. These words are used to fill in the blank spaces in the story.

● TO PLAY

The READER asks each WRITER in turn to call out a word—an adjective or a noun or
whatever the space calls for—and uses them to fill in the blank spaces in the story. The
result is a MAD LIBS® game.

When the READER then reads the completed MAD LIBS® game to the other players,
they will discover that they have written a story that is fantastic, screamingly funny,
shocking, silly, crazy, or just plain dumb—depending upon which words each WRITER
called out.

● EXAMPLE (*Before* and *After*)

" _____ !" he said _____
                EXCLAMATION   ADVERB

as he jumped into his convertible _____ and
                                           NOUN

drove off with his _____ wife.
                          ADJECTIVE

" _____ OUCH _____ !" he said _____ STUPIDLY _____
                EXCLAMATION   ADVERB

as he jumped into his convertible _____ CAT _____ and
                                           NOUN

drove off with his _____ BRAVE _____ wife.
                          ADJECTIVE

QUICK REVIEW

In case you have forgotten what adjectives, adverbs, nouns, and verbs are, here is a quick review:

An ADJECTIVE describes something or somebody. *Lumpy, soft, ugly, messy,* and *short* are adjectives.

An ADVERB tells how something is done. It modifies a verb and usually ends in "ly." *Modestly, stupidly, greedily,* and *carefully* are adverbs.

A NOUN is the name of a person, place, or thing. *Sidewalk, umbrella, bridle, bathtub,* and *nose* are nouns.

A VERB is an action word. *Run, pitch, jump,* and *swim* are verbs. Put the verbs in past tense if the directions say PAST TENSE. *Ran, pitched, jumped,* and *swam* are verbs in the past tense.

When we ask for A PLACE, we mean any sort of place: a country or city *(Spain, Cleveland)* or a room *(bathroom, kitchen).*

An EXCLAMATION or SILLY WORD is any sort of funny sound, gasp, grunt, or outcry, like *Wow!, Ouch!, Whomp!, Ick!,* and *Gadzooks!*

When we ask for specific words, like a NUMBER, a COLOR, an ANIMAL, or a PART OF THE BODY, we mean a word that is one of those things, like *seven, blue, horse,* or *head.*

When we ask for a PLURAL, it means more than one. For example, *cat* pluralized is *cats.*

MAD LIBS® is fun to play with friends, but you can also play it by yourself! To begin with, DO NOT look at the story on the page below. Fill in the blanks on this page with the words called for. Then, using the words you have selected, fill in the blank spaces in the story.

Now you've created your own hilarious MAD LIBS® game!

FAMOUS CATS

ADJECTIVE _____

NOUN _____

NUMBER _____

TYPE OF FOOD _____

PLURAL NOUN _____

VERB _____

PERSON IN ROOM _____

PERSON IN ROOM (FEMALE) _____

PLURAL NOUN _____

NOUN _____

PART OF THE BODY _____

A PLACE _____

PERSON IN ROOM (FEMALE) _____

ADJECTIVE _____

ANIMAL _____

MAD☺LIBS®
FAMOUS CATS

From cartoons to social media, cats are everywhere. Here are a few of the most famous cats:

- Morris—the cat with the _____ attitude and the posh
  ADJECTIVE
  _____ is the "spokesperson" for _____ Lives cat
  NOUN   NUMBER
  _____.
  TYPE OF FOOD

- Garfield—the famous comic-strip cat who hates _____, loves
  PLURAL NOUN
  to _____, and has no respect for _____, his
     VERB   PERSON IN ROOM
  owner's dog.

- Smelly Cat—made famous in the song sung by _____
  PERSON IN ROOM (FEMALE)
  on the TV show _____.
  PLURAL NOUN

- Grumpy Cat—an Internet _____ known for her hilarious
  NOUN
  _____ expressions.
  PART OF THE BODY

- Stubbs—the mayor of (the) _____, Alaska.
  A PLACE

- Cat—the feline heroine of the movie *Breakfast at*
  _____'s.
  PERSON IN ROOM (FEMALE)

- Tom—the _____ cat that will never catch his archenemy,
  ADJECTIVE
  Jerry the _____.
  ANIMAL

MAD LIBS® is fun to play with friends, but you can also play it by yourself! To begin with, DO NOT look at the story on the page below. Fill in the blanks on this page with the words called for. Then, using the words you have selected, fill in the blank spaces in the story.

Now you've created your own hilarious MAD LIBS® game!

WHICH BREED IS RIGHT FOR YOU?

PART OF THE BODY (PLURAL) _____

ADJECTIVE _____

NOUN _____

ADJECTIVE _____

NOUN _____

NOUN _____

PART OF THE BODY (PLURAL) _____

ADJECTIVE _____

NOUN _____

SILLY WORD _____

ADJECTIVE _____

A PLACE _____

ADJECTIVE _____

PART OF THE BODY _____

COLOR _____

ADJECTIVE _____

NOUN _____

MAD LIBS®
WHICH BREED IS RIGHT FOR YOU?

So you're thinking of getting a cat. Whether you prefer cats with no

_____ or _____ ears, there's a/an _____
PART OF THE BODY (PLURAL)   ADJECTIVE   NOUN

for you.

Sphynx: If you go for the _____ things in life, and don't want to
                               ADJECTIVE

have to clean up cat hair, this is the _____ for you.
                                        NOUN

Siamese: Do you want a cat that sounds like a crying _____ and has
                                                          NOUN

crossed _____? Well then, go get a Siamese.
        PART OF THE BODY (PLURAL)

Manx: Looking for a cat with a sweet, _____ face and no
                                           ADJECTIVE

_____? We suggest you get a/an _____.
    NOUN   SILLY WORD

Maine coon: How about a cat that's the size of a/an _____ dog? If
                                                         ADJECTIVE

you don't mind having to brush your cat every day, it sounds like you should

get a/an _____ coon.
          A PLACE

Persian: If you love a/an _____-looking cat with a scrunched-up
                               ADJECTIVE

_____, go get yourself a Persian.
PART OF THE BODY

Snowshoe: Do you love a cat with adorable _____ feet and a/an
                                               COLOR

_____ personality? You may want a/an _____-shoe.
  ADJECTIVE   NOUN

MAD LIBS® is fun to play with friends, but you can also play it by yourself! To begin with, DO NOT look at the story on the page below. Fill in the blanks on this page with the words called for. Then, using the words you have selected, fill in the blank spaces in the story.

Now you've created your own hilarious MAD LIBS® game!

CAT SAYINGS

ADJECTIVE _____

PLURAL NOUN _____

PART OF THE BODY _____

NOUN _____

SILLY WORD _____

ADJECTIVE _____

VERB ENDING IN "ING" _____

ARTICLE OF CLOTHING _____

ADJECTIVE _____

NOUN _____

ANIMAL _____

NOUN _____

NOUN _____

EXCLAMATION _____

ADJECTIVE _____

ADVERB _____

ADJECTIVE _____

MAD LIBS®
CAT SAYINGS

There are a lot of _____ phrases that incorporate our favorite feline
_____. Check out these sayings and their meanings:

ADJECTIVE

PLURAL NOUN

* Cat got your _____?: Why aren't you talking?

PART OF THE BODY

* You let the cat out of the _____: _____! My secret

NOUN   SILLY WORD
isn't so _____ anymore.

ADJECTIVE

* It is raining cats and dogs: It is _____ like crazy.

VERB ENDING IN "ING"

* That is the cat's _____: That is totally _____!

ARTICLE OF CLOTHING   ADJECTIVE

* When the cat's away, the mice will play: The boss is away—let's get this
_____ started!

NOUN

* Curiosity killed the _____: Mind your own _____!

ANIMAL   NOUN

* He is a fat cat: He likes to flash his _____.

NOUN

* Looks like something the cat dragged in: _____! You look

EXCLAMATION
_____. What happened?!

ADJECTIVE

* Cat on a hot tin roof: Please sit _____!

ADVERB

* It's like herding cats: This job is totally _____!

ADJECTIVE

MAD LIBS® is fun to play with friends, but you can also play it by yourself! To begin with, DO NOT look at the story on the page below. Fill in the blanks on this page with the words called for. Then, using the words you have selected, fill in the blank spaces in the story.

Now you've created your own hilarious MAD LIBS® game!

CAT SHOWS

ADJECTIVE _____

ADJECTIVE _____

ADJECTIVE _____

VERB _____

NOUN _____

SAME NOUN _____

NOUN _____

NOUN _____

PLURAL NOUN _____

PLURAL NOUN _____

NOUN _____

A PLACE _____

PLURAL NOUN _____

ADJECTIVE _____

NOUN _____

MAD LIBS

CAT SHOWS

There are some cat owners who take their love of cats to a/an _____
                                                                     ADJECTIVE

level. A/An _____ example of this: the cat show. Both _____
              ADJECTIVE   ADJECTIVE

and purebred cats are allowed to _____ in a cat show, although the
                                      VERB

rules differ from _____ to _____. The cats are compared
                        NOUN   SAME NOUN

to a breed _____, and those judged to be closest to it are awarded
                NOUN

a/an _____. At the end of the year, all the _____ who
         NOUN   PLURAL NOUN

won at various shows are tallied up, and regional and national _____
                                                                  PLURAL NOUN

are presented. The very first cat _____ took place in 1598 at (the)
                                        NOUN

_____ in England. In the United States, the first cat shows were held
   A PLACE

at New England country _____ in the 1860s. The most important
                           PLURAL NOUN

cat show in the United States is the CFA _____ Cat Show. But no
                                            ADJECTIVE

matter which cat wins "Best in Show," every cat is a/an _____—to
                                                            NOUN

their owners, at least!

MAD LIBS® is fun to play with friends, but you can also play it by yourself! To begin with, DO NOT look at the story on the page below. Fill in the blanks on this page with the words called for. Then, using the words you have selected, fill in the blank spaces in the story.

Now you've created your own hilarious MAD LIBS® game!

CATS IN THE NEWS

PLURAL NOUN _____

ADJECTIVE _____

NOUN _____

ADJECTIVE _____

NUMBER _____

NOUN _____

NOUN _____

NOUN _____

SAME NOUN _____

ADJECTIVE _____

NOUN _____

ADJECTIVE _____

NOUN _____

VERB _____

MAD LIBS®
CATS IN THE NEWS

News Anchor #1: Stay tuned, _____! After the commercial break, we
_{PLURAL NOUN}

have a/an _____ story about a cat who saved a young _____
_{ADJECTIVE} ___ _{NOUN}

from a/an _____ dog.
_{ADJECTIVE}

News Anchor #2: That reminds me of the story about the cat that dialed

_____-1-1 after its owner fell out of his _____.
_{NUMBER} _{NOUN}

News Anchor #1: And how about that kitten that survived the deadly

_____ in Taiwan?
_{NOUN}

News Anchor #2: Have you heard about the kitten that was saved from a/an

_____ by a/an _____-fighter with _____ water
_{NOUN} _{SAME NOUN} _{ADJECTIVE}

and a/an _____ full of oxygen?
_{NOUN}

News Anchor #1: And who could forget that _____ story about a
_{ADJECTIVE}

cat that took a/an _____ on the London Underground?
_{NOUN}

News Anchor #2: Well, I guess he had to _____ to work just like
_{VERB}

everyone else!

MAD LIBS® is fun to play with friends, but you can also play it by yourself! To begin with, DO NOT look at the story on the page below. Fill in the blanks on this page with the words called for. Then, using the words you have selected, fill in the blank spaces in the story.

Now you've created your own hilarious MAD LIBS® game!

HISTORY OF CATS

VERB ENDING IN "ING" _____

NUMBER _____

ADJECTIVE _____

ANIMAL (PLURAL) _____

SAME ANIMAL (PLURAL) _____

ADJECTIVE _____

PLURAL NOUN _____

ADJECTIVE _____

PART OF THE BODY _____

ADJECTIVE _____

OCCUPATION (PLURAL) _____

VERB (PAST TENSE) _____

ADJECTIVE _____

ADJECTIVE _____

NUMBER _____

ADJECTIVE _____

MAD LIBS®
HISTORY OF CATS

Cats have been _____ with—or at least tolerating—people for

VERB ENDING IN "ING"

over _____ years. Cats first became a part of our _____ lives

NUMBER   ADJECTIVE

when people started to grow grain. The grain attracted _____,

ANIMAL (PLURAL)

and the cats preyed on the _____. Cats soon became

SAME ANIMAL (PLURAL)

a/an _____ fixture in peoples' _____ and were even

ADJECTIVE   PLURAL NOUN

worshipped in _____ Egypt. There was even an Egyptian goddess

ADJECTIVE

that had the _____ of a cat! However, in the _____

PART OF THE BODY   ADJECTIVE

Ages, cats came to be demonized and were thought to be affiliated with evil

_____. Many cats were _____ to ward off evil. In

OCCUPATION (PLURAL)   VERB (PAST TENSE)

the 1600s, the cat's _____ reputation was restored, and today cats

ADJECTIVE

are _____ stars and live in _____ percent of American

ADJECTIVE   NUMBER

households. Talk about a long and _____ history!

ADJECTIVE

MAD LIBS® is fun to play with friends, but you can also play it by yourself! To begin with, DO NOT look at the story on the page below. Fill in the blanks on this page with the words called for. Then, using the words you have selected, fill in the blank spaces in the story.

Now you've created your own hilarious MAD LIBS® game!

I AM A CAT LADY

ADJECTIVE _____

ADJECTIVE _____

PLURAL NOUN _____

NUMBER _____

ADJECTIVE _____

ADJECTIVE _____

VERB _____

ADJECTIVE _____

PLURAL NOUN _____

ADVERB _____

ADVERB _____

NOUN _____

ADJECTIVE _____

ADJECTIVE _____

ADJECTIVE _____

ANIMAL _____

MAD LIBS
I AM A CAT LADY

Dear _____ Neighbor,
        ADJECTIVE

I'm glad we have come to a/an _____ understanding about our
                                ADJECTIVE

_____. You have come to accept my _____ cats, and
PLURAL NOUN   NUMBER

I have come to accept your _____ dog. Yes, my _____
                            ADJECTIVE   ADJECTIVE

cats may _____ in your garden, but your _____ dog
          VERB   ADJECTIVE

digs up my _____. And I will remind you that my cats purr very
            PLURAL NOUN

_____, while your dog barks _____. To conclude, I feel
ADVERB   ADVERB

sorry for the _____-man, who is scared of your _____
               NOUN   ADJECTIVE

dog, while he brings treats for my _____ felines. I'm glad we have
                                    ADJECTIVE

been able to come to a/an _____ understanding on this matter.
                           ADJECTIVE

Yours truly,

The _____ Lady Next Door
     ANIMAL

MAD LIBS® is fun to play with friends, but you can also play it by yourself! To begin with, DO NOT look at the story on the page below. Fill in the blanks on this page with the words called for. Then, using the words you have selected, fill in the blank spaces in the story.

Now you've created your own hilarious MAD LIBS® game!

CATS ON CAMERA

ADJECTIVE _____

VERB ENDING IN "ING" _____

NOUN _____

SILLY WORD _____

ADJECTIVE _____

ADJECTIVE _____

NOUN _____

NOUN _____

NOUN _____

EXCLAMATION _____

VERB ENDING IN "S" _____

NOUN _____

ADJECTIVE _____

NUMBER _____

ADJECTIVE _____

PLURAL NOUN _____

MAD LIBS®
CATS ON CAMERA

Cat Lover #1: Have you seen the _____ video on YouTube of the cat
<u>ADJECTIVE</u>

_____ a/an _____?
<u>VERB ENDING IN "ING"</u>   <u>NOUN</u>

Cat Lover #2: _____! It's almost as _____ as that GIF of
     <u>SILLY WORD</u>   <u>ADJECTIVE</u>

the _____ kitten playing with a/an _____.
<u>ADJECTIVE</u>   <u>NOUN</u>

Cat Lover #1: And that clip of the _____ cat who pushes her own
     <u>NOUN</u>

_____ down some stairs?! _____!
<u>NOUN</u>   <u>EXCLAMATION</u>

Cat Lover #2: How about the cat who _____ along to
     <u>VERB ENDING IN "S"</u>

a/an _____ video? Totally _____!
<u>NOUN</u>   <u>ADJECTIVE</u>

Cat Lover #1: And there must be about _____ videos of
     <u>NUMBER</u>

_____ cats that have gotten stuck in _____.
<u>ADJECTIVE</u>   <u>PLURAL NOUN</u>

Cat Lover #2: Yep! And I think I've watched them all.

MAD LIBS® is fun to play with friends, but you can also play it by yourself! To begin with, DO NOT look at the story on the page below. Fill in the blanks on this page with the words called for. Then, using the words you have selected, fill in the blank spaces in the story.

Now you've created your own hilarious MAD LIBS® game!

SEVEN SIGNS YOUR CAT LOVES YOU

ADJECTIVE _____

NOUN _____

SAME NOUN _____

PLURAL NOUN _____

ADJECTIVE _____

VERB _____

NOUN _____

SAME NOUN _____

ADVERB _____

NOUN _____

ADJECTIVE _____

ANIMAL _____

A PLACE _____

ADJECTIVE _____

MAD LIBS
SEVEN SIGNS YOUR CAT LOVES YOU

Here are seven _____ signs your cat loves you:
ADJECTIVE

- Head butting—If your boyfriend or _____ did this to you,
  NOUN

  you probably wouldn't want them as your _____ anymore.
  SAME NOUN

  But when your cat does it, they are marking you with their facial

  _____, which shows your cat trusts you.
  PLURAL NOUN

- Powerful purrs—Cats purr for all kinds of reasons, but that

  _____ body rumble is saved for expressing true love.
  ADJECTIVE

- Love bites—If your cat likes to _____ on you, it means they
  VERB

  have a serious _____ for you.
  NOUN

- Tail twitching—When the tip of a cat's _____ is twitching, it
  SAME NOUN

  means they are in total control.

- Tummy up—If your cat rolls around on the ground with its tummy

  showing, it means they trust you _____.
  ADVERB

- Kneading—No, your cat doesn't think you are _____ dough;
  NOUN

  he is reliving his _____ memories of kittenhood.
  ADJECTIVE

- Gifts—You may not want to find a dead _____ in your
  ANIMAL

  _____, but this is a/an _____ sign of friendship.
  A PLACE   ADJECTIVE

MAD LIBS® is fun to play with friends, but you can also play it by yourself! To begin with, DO NOT look at the story on the page below. Fill in the blanks on this page with the words called for. Then, using the words you have selected, fill in the blank spaces in the story.

Now you've created your own hilarious MAD LIBS® game!

SEVEN SIGNS YOUR CAT IS TRYING TO KILL YOU

ADJECTIVE _____

PLURAL NOUN _____

ADVERB _____

NOUN _____

PART OF THE BODY _____

VERB ENDING IN "ING" _____

ADJECTIVE _____

PART OF THE BODY _____

SILLY WORD _____

NOUN _____

ADVERB _____

ANIMAL _____

ADJECTIVE _____

MAD LIBS®
SEVEN SIGNS YOUR CAT IS TRYING TO KILL YOU

There's a flip side to all those _____ expressions of love.
ADJECTIVE

- Head butting—Beware! Your cat is not showing you that it trusts you;

  it's telling you that your _____ are numbered!
  PLURAL NOUN

- Powerful purrs—This is not a sign of true love; it's _____ a
  ADVERB

  battle cry!

- Love bites—Not actually a/an _____ of love, but your cat
  NOUN

  tasting you to decide which bit of you to eat first. _____,
  PART OF THE BODY

  please!

- Tail twitching—The equivalent of your cat _____ a sword
  VERB ENDING IN "ING"

  at you.

- Tummy up—Do not fall for this _____ trick! As soon as
  ADJECTIVE

  you put your _____ near your cat's belly, it will scratch the
  PART OF THE BODY

  _____ out of it!
  SILLY WORD

- Kneading—This is not a/an _____ of affection; your cat is
  NOUN

  _____ checking your organs for weaknesses.
  ADVERB

- Gifts—A dead _____ is not a gift; it's a/an _____
  ANIMAL   ADJECTIVE

  warning. Didn't you see *The Godfather*?!

MAD LIBS® is fun to play with friends, but you can also play it by yourself! To begin with, DO NOT look at the story on the page below. Fill in the blanks on this page with the words called for. Then, using the words you have selected, fill in the blank spaces in the story.

Now you've created your own hilarious MAD LIBS® game!

DOGS VERSUS CATS

ADJECTIVE _____

NOUN _____

ADJECTIVE _____

ADJECTIVE _____

ADJECTIVE _____

PART OF THE BODY (PLURAL) _____

NOUN _____

VERB ENDING IN "ING" _____

NOUN _____

ANIMAL _____

NOUN _____

NOUN _____

ADJECTIVE _____

ADVERB _____

ADJECTIVE _____

If you've ever owned both dogs and cats, you know that the differences between

the two species are _____. They are like night and _____.
            ADJECTIVE   NOUN

The argument about which pet is more _____ will continue
                                          ADJECTIVE

until the end of time, but it's easy to see why cats are _____.
                                                ADJECTIVE

For instance, cats won't embarrass you in front of your guests by parading

around with your _____ underwear in their _____.
                  ADJECTIVE   PART OF THE BODY (PLURAL)

Cats are also funnier than dogs, even if they don't know it. And they don't

give a/an _____ if you laugh at them, because they are too busy
             NOUN

_____ their revenge. Cats are natural _____
VERB ENDING IN "ING"   NOUN

repellents—no spider, fly, or _____ stands a chance if there's
                                ANIMAL

a cat in the _____. Cats have no interest in being hooked up to
               NOUN

a/an _____ and going for a walk; they'd rather curl up and take
        NOUN

a/an _____ nap. And it's _____ proven that cat owners are
        ADJECTIVE   ADVERB

smarter and more _____ than dog owners. So go get yourself a cat!
                ADJECTIVE

MAD LIBS® is fun to play with friends, but you can also play it by yourself! To begin with, DO NOT look at the story on the page below. Fill in the blanks on this page with the words called for. Then, using the words you have selected, fill in the blank spaces in the story.

Now you've created your own hilarious MAD LIBS® game!

MY HOUSE. MY RULES.

ADJECTIVE _____

NOUN _____

VERB _____

NOUN _____

SAME NOUN _____

TYPE OF LIQUID _____

VERB ENDING IN "ING" _____

PERSON IN ROOM (FEMALE) _____

VERB _____

SAME VERB _____

ADJECTIVE _____

ADJECTIVE _____

MAD LIBS®
MY HOUSE. MY RULES.

_____raunchy_____ Servant,
ADJECTIVE

It's quite obvious that you think you control me, but we all know that I am

in charge of this _____mom_____. You think I am just a simple cat, but I am
NOUN

able to out-_____pooping_____ you any day of the week. Please be aware that
VERB

"your" house is actually mine, and I am not to be disturbed if I happen to

be sleeping on your bed or favorite piece of _____oan_____. I will scratch
NOUN

any piece of _____Cm_____ I want. I do not want to drink _____pee_____
SAME NOUN   TYPE OF LIQUID

from an ordinary bowl; I prefer to lap water from a/an _____dumping_____
VERB ENDING IN "ING"

faucet or a toilet. So please remember to leave the toilet seat up—I don't care

what _____tully_____ has to say about that. Don't try to get me to
PERSON IN ROOM (FEMALE)

_____run_____ during the day; you should know better than that. I prefer to
VERB

_____run_____ at night when you are asleep; this is much more fun. You are
SAME VERB

a/an _____yellow_____ human, but you are my human.
ADJECTIVE

With tolerance,

Your Super-_____fut_____ Cat Waffle
ADJECTIVE

MAD LIBS® is fun to play with friends, but you can also play it by yourself! To begin with, DO NOT look at the story on the page below. Fill in the blanks on this page with the words called for. Then, using the words you have selected, fill in the blank spaces in the story.

Now you've created your own hilarious MAD LIBS® game!

AM I IN YOUR WAY?

EXCLAMATION _____

NOUN _____

NOUN _____

ADJECTIVE _____

NOUN _____

ADJECTIVE _____

VERB ENDING IN "ING" _____

NOUN _____

VERB ENDING IN "ING" _____

NOUN _____

NOUN _____

VERB _____

NOUN _____

TYPE OF FOOD _____

PART OF THE BODY _____

MAD LIBS
AM I IN YOUR WAY?

_____! Were you trying to type? I just felt the need to lie on your
EXCLAMATION

_____ keyboard at this moment. That _____ you're trying
NOUN   NOUN

to write isn't as _____ as my nap. Oh, and did you want to read
ADJECTIVE

today's _____? Tough. It's much more _____ that I use
NOUN   ADJECTIVE

it as a place to do my _____. And I hope you aren't going to
VERB ENDING IN "ING"

do the _____ today, as I am planning on _____ in
NOUN   VERB ENDING IN "ING"

the laundry _____ all day, and I don't want to be disturbed. Let me
NOUN

know when you are going to start preparing dinner, as I can help knock things

off the _____. And when you sit down to _____, I will
NOUN   VERB

certainly expect a few pieces of food from your _____. But please,
NOUN

no _____—you know I turn my _____ up at that.
TYPE OF FOOD   PART OF THE BODY

MAD LIBS® is fun to play with friends, but you can also play it by yourself! To begin with, DO NOT look at the story on the page below. Fill in the blanks on this page with the words called for. Then, using the words you have selected, fill in the blank spaces in the story.

Now you've created your own hilarious MAD LIBS® game!

THE SEVEN HABITS OF HIGHLY EFFECTIVE KITTENS

PLURAL NOUN _____

ADJECTIVE _____

NOUN _____

VERB ENDING IN "ING" _____

PART OF THE BODY _____

ADJECTIVE _____

VERB _____

ADJECTIVE _____

ANIMAL _____

NOUN _____

ADJECTIVE _____

ANIMAL _____

NOUN _____

NOUN _____

NOUN _____

NOUN _____

VERB _____

MAD LIBS®
THE SEVEN HABITS OF
HIGHLY EFFECTIVE KITTENS

All kittens know they must perfect these _____:
PLURAL NOUN

1. Be as adorably _____ as possible at all times.
ADJECTIVE

2. Perfect that tiny, irresistible _____. Your servants will come
NOUN

_____ in a/an _____-beat.
VERB ENDING IN "ING"   PART OF THE BODY

3. Learn the ways of a/an _____ ninja; you can _____
ADJECTIVE   VERB

anywhere. It's all about stealth.

4. You must be _____, whether you're facing down the neighbor's
ADJECTIVE

_____ or jumping off the kitchen _____.
ANIMAL   NOUN

5. You may be _____, but inside of you beats the heart of
ADJECTIVE

a/an _____. Honor your heritage.
ANIMAL

6. Make use of those _____-sharp claws. Climb the living room
NOUN

_____ and the Christmas _____ with courage and
NOUN   NOUN

confidence.

7. And when you sleep, curl up in the tiniest, fluffiest _____ possible.
NOUN

It will make your servants _____.
VERB

MAD LIBS® is fun to play with friends, but you can also play it by yourself! To begin with, DO NOT look at the story on the page below. Fill in the blanks on this page with the words called for. Then, using the words you have selected, fill in the blank spaces in the story.

Now you've created your own hilarious MAD LIBS® game!

YOU CALL THAT CAT FOOD?

EXCLAMATION _____

NOUN _____

ADJECTIVE _____

ANIMAL _____

ADJECTIVE _____

NOUN _____

ADJECTIVE _____

NOUN _____

ADJECTIVE _____

ADJECTIVE _____

NOUN _____

PLURAL NOUN _____

ADJECTIVE _____

NOUN _____

MAD LIBS
YOU CALL THAT CAT FOOD?

_____! What is this _____ that you put in my bowl? Do
   EXCLAMATION   NOUN

you really expect me to eat this? Have I not made it perfectly _____
                                                ADJECTIVE

that I prefer fresh _____ to the _____ stuff that comes
                     ANIMAL   ADJECTIVE

out of a/an _____? It looks _____ and smells like a rotting
              NOUN   ADJECTIVE

_____. And I refuse to eat something that is advertised by a cat who is
  NOUN

an embarrassment to my _____ species. Don't get so _____
                       ADJECTIVE   ADJECTIVE

when I jump onto the kitchen _____ to see what you are cooking for
                              NOUN

yourself—I might not want any of that, either. Some of the _____
                                           PLURAL NOUN

you make look and smell as _____ as that _____ you try
                      ADJECTIVE   NOUN

to feed me!

MAD LIBS® is fun to play with friends, but you can also play it by yourself! To begin with, DO NOT look at the story on the page below. Fill in the blanks on this page with the words called for. Then, using the words you have selected, fill in the blank spaces in the story.

Now you've created your own hilarious MAD LIBS® game!

STRANGE CAT FACTS

VERB ENDING IN "ING" _____

NOUN _____

NUMBER _____

PLURAL NOUN _____

VERB _____

PLURAL NOUN _____

NUMBER _____

NUMBER _____

NOUN _____

NOUN _____

VERB _____

PART OF THE BODY _____

COLOR _____

ADJECTIVE _____

MAD LIBS®
STRANGE CAT FACTS

If you think you know cats, think again:

- On average, cats spend two-thirds of every day __farting__.
  <u>VERB ENDING IN "ING"</u>

- A group of cats is called a/an "__weiner__."
  <u>NOUN</u>

- A cat can jump up to __21__ times its own height in a single
  <u>NUMBER</u>
  bound.

- Cats have over twenty __peanuts__ that control their ears.
  <u>PLURAL NOUN</u>

- Cats can't __clap__ sweetness.
  <u>VERB</u>

- The world's longest cat measured 48.5 __balls__ long.
  <u>PLURAL NOUN</u>

- A cat has __12__ toes on its front paws, but only __18__
  <u>NUMBER</u>   <u>NUMBER</u>
  toes on its back paws.

- When a cat leaves its __gibralter__ uncovered in the litter box, it is
  <u>NOUN</u>
  a/an __skids__ of aggression.
  <u>NOUN</u>

- Cats only __skid__ through their __armpit__ pads.
  <u>VERB</u>   <u>PART OF THE BODY</u>

- __black__ cats are bad luck in the United States, but they are
  <u>COLOR</u>
  __slimy__ luck in the United Kingdom and Australia.
  <u>ADJECTIVE</u>

MAD LIBS® is fun to play with friends, but you can also play it by yourself! To begin with, DO NOT look at the story on the page below. Fill in the blanks on this page with the words called for. Then, using the words you have selected, fill in the blank spaces in the story.

Now you've created your own hilarious MAD LIBS® game!

CATS IN A BOX—OR BAG

ADJECTIVE _____

VERB _____

ANIMAL (PLURAL) _____

PLURAL NOUN _____

ADJECTIVE _____

ADJECTIVE _____

ARTICLE OF CLOTHING _____

PLURAL NOUN _____

VERB _____

SAME VERB _____

ADJECTIVE _____

NOUN _____

PLURAL NOUN _____

ADJECTIVE _____

ANIMAL (PLURAL) _____

VERB _____

MAD LIBS
CATS IN A BOX—OR BAG

Don't bother buying me some _squishy_ toy; I won't _juggling_ with it. So
_____ ADJECTIVE _____ _____ VERB _____

skip the fake _monkeys_ filled with catnip and those "teasers" with
_____ ANIMAL (PLURAL) _____

juices on the ends. Just give me an old _hind_ box. The secret
_____ PLURAL NOUN _____ _____ ADJECTIVE _____

of the old _spiky_ box is that it gives me (a/an) _undies_
_____ ADJECTIVE _____ _____ ARTICLE OF CLOTHING _____

of invisibility, enhancing my super-_fat folds_. When I am in the box,
_____ PLURAL NOUN _____

I can _slurp_ you, but you can't _slurp_ me. If the box is
_____ VERB _____ _____ SAME VERB _____

shaking, that's even better, as it is more fun if I can barely get myself in
_____ ADJECTIVE _____

it. And it is preferable if the box has a/an _balloon_ or _crock pots_
_____ NOUN _____ _____ PLURAL NOUN _____

And if you don't have a box, a/an _goopy_ paper bag will do. Because
_____ ADJECTIVE _____

within the bag live the Bag _horses_. And it is my mission in life
_____ ANIMAL (PLURAL) _____

to _squat_ them!
_____ VERB _____

MAD LIBS® is fun to play with friends, but you can also play it by yourself! To begin with, DO NOT look at the story on the page below. Fill in the blanks on this page with the words called for. Then, using the words you have selected, fill in the blank spaces in the story.

Now you've created your own hilarious MAD LIBS® game!

BIG CATS

VERB _____

PLURAL NOUN _____

PLURAL NOUN _____

ADJECTIVE _____

ADJECTIVE _____

ANIMAL _____

SAME ANIMAL _____

ADJECTIVE _____

ADJECTIVE _____

VERB _____

SAME VERB _____

ADJECTIVE _____

VERB ENDING IN "ING" _____

SAME VERB ENDING IN "ING" _____

A PLACE _____

ADJECTIVE _____

NOUN _____

ADJECTIVE _____

MAD LIBS
BIG CATS

Although they don't have to _swimming_ (VERB) for their food or worry about _Snow man_ (PLURAL NOUN), domestic cats aren't all that different from their wild _plviigers_ (PLURAL NOUN) and sisters. All cats, domestic and _chrimasy_ (ADJECTIVE), are _Halloweeny_ (ADJECTIVE) carnivores, whether they prefer to eat a can of _dragon_ (ANIMAL) delight or an entire raw _dragon_ (SAME ANIMAL). Felines around the world, from _Hairy_ (ADJECTIVE) tabbies to _dirty_ (ADJECTIVE) jaguars, _cheeching_ (VERB) for sixteen to twenty hours a day. (However, snow leopards don't get to _cheeching_ (SAME VERB) in a basket of _cocking_ (ADJECTIVE) laundry.) And there's the _stuffing_ (VERB ENDING IN "ING") thing. You might think your cat is _stuffing_ (SAME VERB ENDING IN "ING") against you because it loves you. But it's marking you, just like big cats mark their territory in (the) _disneyland_ (A PLACE). And even though there are _wet_ (ADJECTIVE) similarities between a house cat and a cheetah, it's much safer to have a domestic cat in your _carrot_ (NOUN)—so don't get any _sparking_ (ADJECTIVE) ideas!

MAD LIBS® is fun to play with friends, but you can also play it by yourself! To begin with, DO NOT look at the story on the page below. Fill in the blanks on this page with the words called for. Then, using the words you have selected, fill in the blank spaces in the story.

Now you've created your own hilarious MAD LIBS® game!

CATS IN BOOKS

ADJECTIVE _____

ADJECTIVE _____

VERB ENDING IN "ING" _____

ADJECTIVE _____

PERSON IN ROOM (MALE) _____

PART OF THE BODY _____

PERSON IN ROOM (MALE) _____

A PLACE _____

ADJECTIVE _____

ADJECTIVE _____

PLURAL NOUN _____

PART OF THE BODY _____

ADJECTIVE _____

PLURAL NOUN _____

ADJECTIVE _____

PART OF THE BODY _____

MAD LIBS®
CATS IN BOOKS

Test your knowledge about cats who have made their _____ mark in
                                                   ADJECTIVE

literature:

- The cat who seems to be _____ and can't stop
                                     ADJECTIVE

  _____ at Alice: The Cheshire Cat
  VERB ENDING IN "ING"

- The _____ cat in _____ King's horror
         ADJECTIVE   PERSON IN ROOM (MALE)

  classic: Church

- The cat with a squashed _____ who belongs to
                                      PART OF THE BODY

  _____ Potter's best friend: Crookshanks
       PERSON IN ROOM (MALE)

- The _____ cat who is the best friend of the _____
          A PLACE   ADJECTIVE

  cockroach Archy: Mehitabel

- A mysterious, _____, and small black cat capable of
                 ADJECTIVE

  performing _____ of magic and sleight of _____:
             PLURAL NOUN   PART OF THE BODY

  Mr. Mistoffelees

- The story of a very _____ kitten who struggles to keep his
                     ADJECTIVE

  _____ clean and tidy: *Tom Kitten*
     PLURAL NOUN

- A/An _____ tale about a cat who wins the _____
          ADJECTIVE   PART OF THE BODY

  of a princess in marriage: *Puss in Boots*

MAD LIBS® is fun to play with friends, but you can also play it by yourself! To begin with, DO NOT look at the story on the page below. Fill in the blanks on this page with the words called for. Then, using the words you have selected, fill in the blank spaces in the story.

Now you've created your own hilarious MAD LIBS® game!

DRESSING YOUR CAT

ADJECTIVE _____

NOUN _____

PART OF THE BODY (PLURAL) _____

ANIMAL _____

ADJECTIVE _____

PERSON IN ROOM (MALE) _____

COLOR _____

PLURAL NOUN _____

OCCUPATION _____

NOUN _____

NOUN _____

ARTICLE OF CLOTHING _____

ADJECTIVE _____

NOUN _____

ADVERB _____

ADJECTIVE _____

MAD LIBS
DRESSING YOUR CAT

Your cat can help you celebrate your favorite holidays throughout the year. All

you need to do is dress it up in a/an _____, fun _____.
ADJECTIVE   NOUN

With a pair of fuzzy _____, your cat can be transformed
PART OF THE BODY (PLURAL)

into the Easter _____. Or be _____ and turn your
ANIMAL   ADJECTIVE

cat into Uncle _____ with a little red, white, and
PERSON IN ROOM (MALE)

_____ suit. And there are a lot of _____ for your cat to wear
COLOR   PLURAL NOUN

on Halloween. You can dress your cat as a/an _____ in a pink tutu,
OCCUPATION

a prehistoric _____ with spikes down its back, or a superhero like
NOUN

_____-man with a black cape and matching _____.
NOUN   ARTICLE OF CLOTHING

And of course any cat can be turned into Santa Claus with a/an _____
ADJECTIVE

red suit and a cute matching _____. Just make sure you choose
NOUN

_____—you don't want to get on your cat's _____ side!
ADVERB   ADJECTIVE

MAD LIBS® is fun to play with friends, but you can also play it by yourself! To begin with, DO NOT look at the story on the page below. Fill in the blanks on this page with the words called for. Then, using the words you have selected, fill in the blank spaces in the story.

Now you've created your own hilarious MAD LIBS® game!

NINE LIVES

NOUN _____

ADJECTIVE _____

VERB ENDING IN "ING" _____

ADJECTIVE _____

ADJECTIVE _____

ANIMAL _____

ADJECTIVE _____

NOUN _____

NUMBER _____

TYPE OF LIQUID _____

NOUN _____

VERB (PAST TENSE) _____

NOUN _____

ADJECTIVE _____

VEHICLE _____

NOUN _____

NOUN _____

ADJECTIVE _____

MAD LIBS
NINE LIVES

Life #1—I ate a/an _____ — a/an _____ mistake.
NOUN   ADJECTIVE

Life #2—I didn't look both ways before _____ the street.
VERB ENDING IN "ING"

_____ move.
ADJECTIVE

Life #3—I was a bit too _____ when I teased the neighbor's
ADJECTIVE

_____ .
ANIMAL

Life #4—I thought cats were supposed to be able to survive falls from

_____ places?!
ADJECTIVE

Life #5—I got locked in the _____ for _____ days without
NOUN   NUMBER

food or _____ . What's a/an _____ to do?!
TYPE OF LIQUID   NOUN

Life #6—I _____ into the washing machine. That spin cycle is a
VERB (PAST TENSE)

killer, let me tell you . . .

Life #7—I chewed through the cord to the _____ . That was
NOUN

a/an _____ shocker.
ADJECTIVE

Life #8—I was keeping warm under the _____ when my human
VEHICLE

decided to start it. I should have just taken a nap in the _____ basket.
NOUN

I have one _____ left—better make it _____ !
NOUN   ADJECTIVE

MAD LIBS®
HISTORY OF THE WORLD
MAD LIBS

Mad Libs
An Imprint of Penguin Random House

INSTRUCTIONS

MAD LIBS® is a game for people who don't like games!
It can be played by one, two, three, four, or forty.

• RIDICULOUSLY SIMPLE DIRECTIONS

In this tablet you will find stories containing blank spaces where words are left out. One player, the READER, selects one of these stories. The READER does not tell anyone what the story is about. Instead, he/she asks the other players, the WRITERS, to give him/her words. These words are used to fill in the blank spaces in the story.

• TO PLAY

The READER asks each WRITER in turn to call out a word—an adjective or a noun or whatever the space calls for—and uses them to fill in the blank spaces in the story. The result is a MAD LIBS® game.

When the READER then reads the completed MAD LIBS® game to the other players, they will discover that they have written a story that is fantastic, screamingly funny, shocking, silly, crazy, or just plain dumb—depending upon which words each WRITER called out.

• EXAMPLE (*Before* and *After*)

"_____!" he said _____
          EXCLAMATION   ADVERB

as he jumped into his convertible _____ and
                                               NOUN

drove off with his _____ wife.
                        ADJECTIVE

"_____OUCH_____!" he said _____STUPIDLY_____
          EXCLAMATION   ADVERB

as he jumped into his convertible _____CAT_____ and
                                               NOUN

drove off with his _____BRAVE_____ wife.
                        ADJECTIVE

QUICK REVIEW

In case you have forgotten what adjectives, adverbs, nouns, and verbs are, here is a quick review:

An ADJECTIVE describes something or somebody. *Lumpy, soft, ugly, messy,* and *short* are adjectives.

An ADVERB tells how something is done. It modifies a verb and usually ends in "ly." *Modestly, stupidly, greedily,* and *carefully* are adverbs.

A NOUN is the name of a person, place, or thing. *Sidewalk, umbrella, bridle, bathtub,* and *nose* are nouns.

A VERB is an action word. *Run, pitch, jump,* and *swim* are verbs. Put the verbs in past tense if the directions say PAST TENSE. *Ran, pitched, jumped,* and *swam* are verbs in the past tense.

When we ask for A PLACE, we mean any sort of place: a country or city *(Spain, Cleveland)* or a room *(bathroom, kitchen).*

An EXCLAMATION or SILLY WORD is any sort of funny sound, gasp, grunt, or outcry, like *Wow!, Ouch!, Whomp!, Ick!,* and *Gadzooks!*

When we ask for specific words, like a NUMBER, a COLOR, an ANIMAL, or a PART OF THE BODY, we mean a word that is one of those things, like *seven, blue, horse,* or *head.*

When we ask for a PLURAL, it means more than one. For example, *cat* pluralized is *cats.*

MAD LIBS® is fun to play with friends, but you can also play it by yourself! To begin with, DO NOT look at the story on the page below. Fill in the blanks on this page with the words called for. Then, using the words you have selected, fill in the blank spaces in the story.

Now you've created your own hilarious MAD LIBS® game!

LIGHT MY FIRE

PART OF THE BODY (PLURAL) _____

ADJECTIVE _____

ADJECTIVE _____

ADJECTIVE _____

A PLACE _____

ANIMAL _____

PART OF THE BODY _____

NOUN _____

ADJECTIVE _____

ADVERB _____

EXCLAMATION _____

ADJECTIVE _____

PERSON IN ROOM _____

NOUN _____

MAD LIBS®
LIGHT MY FIRE

At one time man walked on four __arse holes__ , spoke in
PART OF THE BODY (PLURAL)

__tight__ grunts, and did not know how to make a/an __loose__ fire.
ADJECTIVE   ADJECTIVE

Here is the story of the day that changed mankind forever (translated from the

__medium rare__ cave-speak):
ADJECTIVE

Caveman #1: It's colder than (the) __Ur dads butt__ in this cave. Even my
A PLACE

warmest __gerbal__ fur won't keep my __tounge__ from
ANIMAL   PART OF THE BODY

shivering.

Caveman #2: If only there was a way to make the cold __teethess__
NOUN

warmer.

Caveman #1: I'm bored. I think I'll play with these __shallow__ sticks
ADJECTIVE

of wood.

Caveman #2: Why don't you rub them __lovelly__ together and see
ADVERB

what happens? __fusing__

Caveman #1: __Oh my__ ! There's smoke coming off these
EXCLAMATION

__fat__ sticks!
ADJECTIVE

Caveman #2: Ouch! It's hot! In the name of __Amy__ —we made
PERSON IN ROOM

heat!

Caveman #1: We shall call this magical flaming __wenier__ fire.
NOUN

MAD LIBS® is fun to play with friends, but you can also play it by yourself! To begin with, DO NOT look at the story on the page below. Fill in the blanks on this page with the words called for. Then, using the words you have selected, fill in the blank spaces in the story.

Now you've created your own hilarious MAD LIBS® game!

EUREKA!

PLURAL NOUN _____

OCCUPATION (PLURAL) _____

NOUN _____

PLURAL NOUN _____

PLURAL NOUN _____

NOUN _____

NOUN _____

PLURAL NOUN _____

PLURAL NOUN _____

ADJECTIVE _____

NOUN _____

NOUN _____

NOUN _____

MAD LIBS®
EUREKA!

Throughout history, inventors have been responsible for everyday things like
computers, cars, and _____. These are some of the most famous
PLURAL NOUN
_____ in history:
OCCUPATION (PLURAL)

Benjamin Franklin was not only a founding _____ of the United
NOUN
States, he also invented many things, including bifocal glasses, which allow
people to see _____ near and far. He also invented the lightning rod,
PLURAL NOUN
which protects _____ from electric bolts of _____.
PLURAL NOUN NOUN

Johannes Gutenberg was a German _____ who invented the printing
NOUN
press, a machine that could print words and _____ to make books,
PLURAL NOUN
newspapers, and _____.
PLURAL NOUN

Thomas Edison was a/an _____ inventor perhaps best known for
ADJECTIVE
making a lightbulb that the average _____ could use. He also invented
NOUN
the phonograph, which was the first _____ to be able to record the
NOUN
human _____ and then play it back.
NOUN

MAD LIBS® is fun to play with friends, but you can also play it by yourself! To begin with, DO NOT look at the story on the page below. Fill in the blanks on this page with the words called for. Then, using the words you have selected, fill in the blank spaces in the story.

Now you've created your own hilarious MAD LIBS® game!

NEWS FLASH!: WORLD NOT FLAT

ADJECTIVE _____

ADJECTIVE _____

NOUN _____

TYPE OF FOOD _____

PLURAL NOUN _____

VERB (PAST TENSE) _____

NOUN _____

PLURAL NOUN _____

ADJECTIVE _____

SILLY WORD _____

ADJECTIVE _____

PERSON IN ROOM (FEMALE) _____

ADJECTIVE _____

In _____ news for explorers everywhere, it has recently been discovered

ADJECTIVE

that the Earth is round. That's right: Earth is shaped like a/an _____

ADJECTIVE

ball! For as long as any _____ can remember, it has been widely believed

NOUN

that the Earth is as flat as a/an _____. Many _____

TYPE OF FOOD   PLURAL NOUN

believed that if you _____ too far, you would fall off the edge of

VERB (PAST TENSE)

the _____. Now, some _____ are trying to prove that the

NOUN   PLURAL NOUN

_____ Earth rotates around the sun, though most people think this is a

ADJECTIVE

bunch of _____! We will keep you updated as this _____

SILLY WORD   ADJECTIVE

story develops. In the meantime, back to you, _____, with

PERSON IN ROOM (FEMALE)

the day's _____ stories.

ADJECTIVE

MAD LIBS® is fun to play with friends, but you can also play it by yourself! To begin with, DO NOT look at the story on the page below. Fill in the blanks on this page with the words called for. Then, using the words you have selected, fill in the blank spaces in the story.

Now you've created your own hilarious MAD LIBS® game!

CAT FANCY

ADJECTIVE _____

PLURAL NOUN _____

ADJECTIVE _____

PLURAL NOUN _____

ADJECTIVE _____

ADJECTIVE _____

PLURAL NOUN _____

ADJECTIVE _____

NOUN _____

ADVERB _____

PART OF THE BODY (PLURAL) _____

NOUN _____

PLURAL NOUN _____

ADJECTIVE _____

You might say the ancient Egyptians were __black__ cat people. After
ADJECTIVE

all, they built an entire religion around worshipping their feline __plungers__!
PLURAL NOUN

Cats were well-liked by Egyptians for their ability to kill __Heavy__ vermin
ADJECTIVE

like rodents and wild __Cats__. Cats were thought to be graceful and
PLURAL NOUN

__ugly__ creatures. Some __Sparkly__ cats were mummified and buried in
ADJECTIVE   ADJECTIVE

__Shoes__ along with their __long__ owners. Harming a cat was
PLURAL NOUN   ADJECTIVE

a crime punishable by __pillow__. And when a cat died, its family would
NOUN

mourn __Cheeching__, shaving their __weiners__ as a symbol of
ADVERB   PART OF THE BODY (PLURAL)

their __Boobies__. So maybe it's a little funny that ancient __Swimsuits__
NOUN   PLURAL NOUN

worshipped cats. But, then again, so does the __Smelly__ Internet!
ADJECTIVE

MAD LIBS® is fun to play with friends, but you can also play it by yourself! To begin with, DO NOT look at the story on the page below. Fill in the blanks on this page with the words called for. Then, using the words you have selected, fill in the blank spaces in the story.

Now you've created your own hilarious MAD LIBS® game!

THE CODE OF THE SAMURAI

ADJECTIVE _____

ADJECTIVE _____

PLURAL NOUN _____

ADJECTIVE _____

PLURAL NOUN _____

VERB _____

PLURAL NOUN _____

PLURAL NOUN _____

NOUN _____

PLURAL NOUN _____

VERB _____

PLURAL NOUN _____

NOUN _____

Samurai were ancient, _____ Japanese warriors who followed a/an
                              ADJECTIVE

_____ code of virtue, which contained these eight _____:
ADJECTIVE   PLURAL NOUN

1. Samurai believed **justice** was the most _____ virtue.
                                              ADJECTIVE

2. They always showed **courage** in the face of _____.
                                                   PLURAL NOUN

3. Samurai may have had the power to _____, but they also needed to
                                      VERB

   show **mercy** toward all _____.
                             PLURAL NOUN

4. It was important to be **polite** and considerate of other people's _____.
                                                                        PLURAL NOUN

5. Samurai also thought **honesty** was the best _____.
                                                  NOUN

6. _____ were not an option for the Samurai, who tried to _____
   PLURAL NOUN   VERB

   with **honor.**

7. Samurai were **loyal** to their fellow _____.
                                           PLURAL NOUN

8. And, finally, they had to show **character** and that they knew the difference

   between right and _____.
                      NOUN

MAD LIBS® is fun to play with friends, but you can also play it by yourself! To begin with, DO NOT look at the story on the page below. Fill in the blanks on this page with the words called for. Then, using the words you have selected, fill in the blank spaces in the story.

Now you've created your own hilarious MAD LIBS® game!

GOD SAVE THE QUEEN

PERSON IN ROOM (MALE) _____

PERSON IN ROOM (FEMALE) _____

NUMBER _____

NOUN _____

VERB ENDING IN "ING" _____

ADJECTIVE _____

FIRST NAME (MALE) _____

ADJECTIVE _____

PERSON IN ROOM _____

A PLACE _____

A PLACE _____

PLURAL NOUN _____

ADJECTIVE _____

PLURAL NOUN _____

NOUN _____

PART OF THE BODY _____

MAD LIBS

GOD SAVE THE QUEEN

Elizabeth I of England was the daughter of King _____ VIII
_{PERSON IN ROOM (MALE)}

and his wife _____. At age _____, she was crowned
_{PERSON IN ROOM (FEMALE)}   _{NUMBER}

_____ of England in a royal _____ ceremony. During
_{NOUN}   _{VERB ENDING IN "ING"}

her reign, England was a very _____ place to live. Famous writer
_{ADJECTIVE}

_____ Shakespeare wrote many _____ plays, and explorer
_{FIRST NAME (MALE)}   _{ADJECTIVE}

_____ discovered (the) _____. In a war against
_{PERSON IN ROOM}   _{A PLACE}

(the) _____, Queen Elizabeth I led her army of _____ to
_{A PLACE}   _{PLURAL NOUN}

a/an _____ victory. Today, many _____ consider Queen
_{ADJECTIVE}   _{PLURAL NOUN}

Elizabeth the most famous _____ in English history. Some even say she
_{NOUN}

ruled England with an iron _____!
_{PART OF THE BODY}

MAD LIBS® is fun to play with friends, but you can also play it by yourself! To begin with, DO NOT look at the story on the page below. Fill in the blanks on this page with the words called for. Then, using the words you have selected, fill in the blank spaces in the story.

Now you've created your own hilarious MAD LIBS® game!

WHAT A
*WONDER*FUL WORLD

NOUN _____

ADJECTIVE _____

NOUN _____

ADJECTIVE _____

PERSON IN ROOM (FEMALE) _____

NOUN _____

CELEBRITY (FEMALE) _____

COLOR _____

CELEBRITY (MALE) _____

PERSON IN ROOM _____

PERSON IN ROOM _____

A PLACE _____

CELEBRITY (MALE) _____

A PLACE _____

NOUN _____

MAD LIBS
WHAT A
WONDERFUL WORLD

These are considered the Seven Wonders of the Ancient _____:
NOUN

1. **The Giza Necropolis** is a site in Egypt where you can see the Great Pyramids

   and the _____ Sphinx.
   ADJECTIVE

2. **The Hanging Gardens** were in the ancient _____ of Babylon and
   NOUN

   were built as a gift from Nebuchadnezzar II to his _____ wife,
   ADJECTIVE

   _____.
   PERSON IN ROOM (FEMALE)

3. **The Temple of Artemis at Ephesus** was a Greek _____ dedicated to
   NOUN

   the goddess _____.
   CELEBRITY (FEMALE)

4. **The Statue of Zeus at Olympia** was a giant forty-three-foot ivory and

   _____ statue of _____.
   COLOR   CELEBRITY (MALE)

5. **The Mausoleum at Halicarnassus** was a tomb built by _____
   PERSON IN ROOM

   and _____ of (the) _____.
   PERSON IN ROOM   A PLACE

6. **The Colossus of Rhodes** was a statue of Greek god _____, built
   CELEBRITY (MALE)

   to commemorate victory over (the) _____.
   A PLACE

7. **The Lighthouse of Alexandria** was at one time the tallest _____ on
   NOUN

   Earth.

MAD LIBS® is fun to play with friends, but you can also play it by yourself! To begin with, DO NOT look at the story on the page below. Fill in the blanks on this page with the words called for. Then, using the words you have selected, fill in the blank spaces in the story.

Now you've created your own hilarious MAD LIBS® game!

FAMOUS FIRSTS

PERSON IN ROOM _____

NOUN _____

PERSON IN ROOM _____

NOUN _____

NOUN _____

PERSON IN ROOM _____

PERSON IN ROOM _____

PLURAL NOUN _____

PERSON IN ROOM _____

PART OF THE BODY _____

A PLACE _____

PERSON IN ROOM _____

VERB _____

PERSON IN ROOM _____

ANIMAL _____

MAD LIBS
FAMOUS FIRSTS

- In 1901, _____ became the first person to go over Niagara
  <u>PERSON IN ROOM</u>

  Falls in a/an _____ and survive.
  <u>NOUN</u>

- In 1933, _____ became the first _____ to fly an
  <u>PERSON IN ROOM</u>   <u>NOUN</u>

  airplane around the _____.
  <u>NOUN</u>

- In 1953, _____ and _____ became the first
  <u>PERSON IN ROOM</u>   <u>PERSON IN ROOM</u>

  _____ to climb to the top of Mount Everest.
  <u>PLURAL NOUN</u>

- In 1963, _____ became the first person to receive a/an
  <u>PERSON IN ROOM</u>

  _____ transplant in (the) _____, South Africa.
  <u>PART OF THE BODY</u>   <u>A PLACE</u>

- In 1969, _____ became the first person to _____ on
  <u>PERSON IN ROOM</u>   <u>VERB</u>

  the moon.

- In 1996, in Scotland, _____ became the world's first clone
  <u>PERSON IN ROOM</u>

  of a/an _____.
  <u>ANIMAL</u>

MAD LIBS® is fun to play with friends, but you can also play it by yourself! To begin with, DO NOT look at the story on the page below. Fill in the blanks on this page with the words called for. Then, using the words you have selected, fill in the blank spaces in the story.

Now you've created your own hilarious MAD LIBS® game!

LAND, HO!

PLURAL NOUN _____

PLURAL NOUN _____

ADJECTIVE _____

NOUN _____

VERB (PAST TENSE) _____

ADJECTIVE _____

NOUN _____

NOUN _____

NOUN _____

NOUN _____

PLURAL NOUN _____

NOUN _____

PERSON IN ROOM (FEMALE) _____

PLURAL NOUN _____

PART OF THE BODY _____

PLURAL NOUN _____

MAD LIBS®
LAND, HO!

Throughout history, _____ with a sense of adventure have traveled
        PLURAL NOUN

the world in search of new lands and _____. Here are a few of the
                                        PLURAL NOUN

most _____ explorers:
        ADJECTIVE

Leif Ericson was a famous Viking _____ who _____ to
                                        NOUN   VERB (PAST TENSE)

the Americas five hundred years before _____ Christopher Columbus.
                                           ADJECTIVE

Ferdinand Magellan, a Portuguese _____, became the first _____
                                        NOUN   NOUN

to cross the Pacific Ocean while he tried to discover a route to the _____
                                                                        NOUN

Islands.

Marco Polo traveled in a/an _____ from Italy to China and helped many
                                   NOUN

Western _____ learn about the Eastern _____.
          PLURAL NOUN   NOUN

Lewis and Clark, led by _____, were the first _____
                            PERSON IN ROOM (FEMALE)   PLURAL NOUN

to travel by _____ across the continental United _____.
                PART OF THE BODY   PLURAL NOUN

MAD LIBS® is fun to play with friends, but you can also play it by yourself! To begin with, DO NOT look at the story on the page below. Fill in the blanks on this page with the words called for. Then, using the words you have selected, fill in the blank spaces in the story.

Now you've created your own hilarious MAD LIBS® game!

WALK LIKE AN EGYPTIAN

ADJECTIVE _____

NOUN _____

ADJECTIVE _____

ADJECTIVE _____

PLURAL NOUN _____

ADJECTIVE _____

PLURAL NOUN _____

ADVERB _____

NOUN _____

NOUN _____

VERB (PAST TENSE) _____

ADJECTIVE _____

OCCUPATION _____

NOUN _____

CELEBRITY (FEMALE) _____

Cleopatra was a/an _____ Egyptian pharaoh. Well-educated and clever
                          ADJECTIVE

as a/an _____, Cleopatra spoke many _____ languages. She
            NOUN   ADJECTIVE

was also known for being particularly _____. When she was eighteen,
                                           ADJECTIVE

Cleopatra took the throne, though she was chased out by a bunch of unruly

_____. In response, Cleopatra put together an army of _____
  PLURAL NOUN   ADJECTIVE

_____, marched _____ back into Egypt, and took back the
  PLURAL NOUN   ADVERB

_____ for herself. Cleopatra fell in love with the Roman _____,
   NOUN   NOUN

Julius Caesar. After Caesar _____, Cleopatra fell in love
                                VERB (PAST TENSE)

with another _____ Roman, Mark Antony. Cleopatra was the most
                 ADJECTIVE

famous and powerful _____ to rule a/an _____. She was even
                        OCCUPATION   NOUN

played by the legendary actress _____ in a movie!
                                    CELEBRITY (FEMALE)

MAD LIBS® is fun to play with friends, but you can also play it by yourself! To begin with, DO NOT look at the story on the page below. Fill in the blanks on this page with the words called for. Then, using the words you have selected, fill in the blank spaces in the story.

Now you've created your own hilarious MAD LIBS® game!

CROOKS DOWN UNDER

NOUN _____

ADJECTIVE _____

PLURAL NOUN _____

ADJECTIVE _____

PERSON IN ROOM _____

ADJECTIVE _____

NUMBER _____

PLURAL NOUN _____

ADJECTIVE _____

VERB _____

PLURAL NOUN _____

PERSON IN ROOM (FEMALE) _____

ANIMAL _____

NUMBER _____

PART OF THE BODY _____

MAD LIBS
CROOKS DOWN UNDER

Australia—known as the _____ Down Under—has a/an
NOUN

_____ criminal past. In the late 1700s, Britain's prisons were overrun
ADJECTIVE

with _____, so they began transporting their _____ prisoners
PLURAL NOUN   ADJECTIVE

to Australia. Captain _____ was in charge of setting up the first
PERSON IN ROOM

_____ colony for prisoners. Over _____ years, fifty-five thousand
ADJECTIVE   NUMBER

criminal _____ came from England to live there! With _____
PLURAL NOUN   ADJECTIVE

behavior, these prisoners could _____ their way to freedom and gain
VERB

work as butchers, farmers, and professional _____. One resident in
PLURAL NOUN

the colony was a thirteen-year-old named _____, who had
PERSON IN ROOM (FEMALE)

come to the colony for stealing a/an _____. She eventually became one
ANIMAL

of Australia's first businesswomen, and today, Australia's _____-dollar bill
NUMBER

features her _____!
PART OF THE BODY

MAD LIBS® is fun to play with friends, but you can also play it by yourself! To begin with, DO NOT look at the story on the page below. Fill in the blanks on this page with the words called for. Then, using the words you have selected, fill in the blank spaces in the story.

Now you've created your own hilarious MAD LIBS® game!

WHEREFORE ART THOU SHAKESPEARE?

NOUN _____

PERSON IN ROOM (FEMALE) _____

NOUN _____

ADJECTIVE _____

ADJECTIVE _____

NOUN _____

ADJECTIVE _____

PLURAL NOUN _____

NOUN _____

NOUN _____

NOUN _____

PLURAL NOUN _____

PART OF THE BODY (PLURAL) _____

NOUN _____

MAD LIBS®
WHEREFORE ART THOU SHAKESPEARE?

William Shakespeare is the most famous writer in the history of the

_____. He wrote many plays, including *Romeo and* _____
NOUN   PERSON IN ROOM (FEMALE)

and *A Midsummer Night's* _____. He also wrote many _____
                          NOUN   ADJECTIVE

poems. Here is a selection from one of his most _____ sonnets:
                                                 ADJECTIVE

Shall I compare thee to a summer's _____?
                                    NOUN

Thou art more lovely and more _____.
                               ADJECTIVE

Rough winds do shake the darling _____ of May,
                                  PLURAL NOUN

And summer's _____ hath all too short a/an _____ . . .
              NOUN   NOUN

But thy eternal _____ shall not fade . . .
                 NOUN

So long as _____ can breathe,
            PLURAL NOUN

or _____ can see,
   PART OF THE BODY (PLURAL)

So long lives this, and this gives _____ to thee.
                                    NOUN

MAD LIBS® is fun to play with friends, but you can also play it by yourself! To begin with, DO NOT look at the story on the page below. Fill in the blanks on this page with the words called for. Then, using the words you have selected, fill in the blank spaces in the story.

Now you've created your own hilarious MAD LIBS® game!

WANTED:
FOUNTAIN OF YOUTH

ADJECTIVE _____

VERB ENDING IN "S" _____

ANIMAL _____

PART OF THE BODY _____

ADJECTIVE _____

PLURAL NOUN _____

A PLACE _____

ADJECTIVE _____

SILLY WORD _____

NOUN _____

PLURAL NOUN _____

NOUN _____

MAD LIBS®
WANTED:
FOUNTAIN OF YOUTH

Spanish explorer Ponce de Leon seeks a/an _____ Fountain of
                                              ADJECTIVE

Youth. Anyone who drinks or _____ in its waters will
                              VERB ENDING IN "S"

have eternal youth. It can also cure illnesses from _____ pox to the
                                                       ANIMAL

_____ flu. It has been rumored for many _____
PART OF THE BODY   ADJECTIVE

years that the Fountain of Youth exists. Some _____ believe
                                                PLURAL NOUN

it is either in the New World or (the) _____. If you find this
                                         A PLACE

_____ fountain, please contact Ponce de Leon at 555-_____ or
ADJECTIVE   SILLY WORD

poncedeleon@_____-mail.com. You will be rewarded with gold and
              NOUN

_____, as well as eternal _____.
PLURAL NOUN   NOUN

MAD LIBS® is fun to play with friends, but you can also play it by yourself! To begin with, DO NOT look at the story on the page below. Fill in the blanks on this page with the words called for. Then, using the words you have selected, fill in the blank spaces in the story.

Now you've created your own hilarious MAD LIBS® game!

O.M.O. (OH MY ODIN)

PLURAL NOUN _____

A PLACE _____

ADJECTIVE _____

A PLACE _____

PLURAL NOUN _____

VERB _____

ADJECTIVE _____

COLOR _____

SAME COLOR _____

ADJECTIVE _____

ADJECTIVE _____

PLURAL NOUN _____

PLURAL NOUN _____

PLURAL NOUN _____

PLURAL NOUN _____

NOUN _____

Vikings were seafaring _____ from Scandinavia, which includes
                          PLURAL NOUN

modern-day countries like Denmark, Norway, and (the) _____. Vikings
                                                        A PLACE

traveled in their _____ boats from Europe to Russia and then to (the)
                     ADJECTIVE

_____, raiding _____ and establishing villages to _____
   A PLACE   PLURAL NOUN   VERB

in. The Vikings were known to be _____ fighters. One famous Viking
                                    ADJECTIVE

warrior was Erik the _____, who was nicknamed this because of his
                        COLOR

flowing _____ beard. There were also _____ Viking female
           SAME COLOR   ADJECTIVE

warriors who wore _____ shields when fighting _____. The
                     ADJECTIVE   PLURAL NOUN

Vikings even had their own gods and goddesses, like Odin, who was thought

to be the ruler of all _____, and who also represented war, battle, and
                          PLURAL NOUN

_____. The Vikings were a serious bunch of _____—you
  PLURAL NOUN   PLURAL NOUN

sure didn't want to get on their bad _____!
                                        NOUN

MAD LIBS® is fun to play with friends, but you can also play it by yourself! To begin with, DO NOT look at the story on the page below. Fill in the blanks on this page with the words called for. Then, using the words you have selected, fill in the blank spaces in the story.

Now you've created your own hilarious MAD LIBS® game!

PEACE, LOVE, AND

_____
PLURAL NOUN

PLURAL NOUN _____

ADJECTIVE _____

PLURAL NOUN _____

NOUN _____

PLURAL NOUN _____

A PLACE _____

VERB ENDING IN "ING" _____

PLURAL NOUN _____

NOUN _____

NOUN _____

A PLACE _____

ADJECTIVE _____

A PLACE _____

PLURAL NOUN _____

PLURAL NOUN _____

MAD LIBS®
PEACE, LOVE, AND
_____
PLURAL NOUN

Since the beginning of time, _____ have fought with one another
                                    PLURAL NOUN

for many _____ reasons. But these brave people devoted their lives to
              ADJECTIVE

helping their fellow _____:
                        PLURAL NOUN

Gandhi led India to freedom from the British _____, who had taken
                                                      NOUN

it over. He inspired people all over the world to be peaceful _____.
                                                                PLURAL NOUN

Martin Luther King Jr. led the Civil Rights Movement in (the) _____,
                                                                    A PLACE

helping gain equal rights for African Americans by _____
                                                      VERB ENDING IN "ING"

peacefully.

Nelson Mandela helped end racist _____ in South Africa. For his
                                        PLURAL NOUN

hard work, he won the Nobel Peace _____ and the US Presidential
                                     NOUN

_____ of Freedom.
   NOUN

Mother Teresa was a nun from (the) _____ who devoted her life to helping
                                        A PLACE

sick and _____ people all over (the) _____.
            ADJECTIVE   A PLACE

Clara Barton was a nurse who helped found the American Red Cross, which

educates _____ and gives assistance to _____ in need.
           PLURAL NOUN   PLURAL NOUN

MAD LIBS® is fun to play with friends, but you can also play it by yourself! To begin with, DO NOT look at the story on the page below. Fill in the blanks on this page with the words called for. Then, using the words you have selected, fill in the blank spaces in the story.

Now you've created your own hilarious MAD LIBS® game!

DID I DO THAT?

PLURAL NOUN _____

PLURAL NOUN _____

PERSON IN ROOM _____

NOUN _____

PLURAL NOUN _____

VERB _____

NOUN _____

PERSON IN ROOM (MALE) _____

VERB _____

VERB _____

ADJECTIVE _____

A PLACE _____

ADJECTIVE _____

PERSON IN ROOM _____

NOUN _____

ADJECTIVE _____

MAD LIBS®
DID I DO THAT?

Oops! We should thank our lucky _____ for these _____
<u>PLURAL NOUN</u>   <u>PLURAL NOUN</u>

that were invented by accident!

The microwave: In 1945, _____ was experimenting with
<u>PERSON IN ROOM</u>

a/an _____ when he discovered it could melt _____ and make
<u>NOUN</u>   <u>PLURAL NOUN</u>

popcorn _____. He then built the first microwave _____.
<u>VERB</u>   <u>NOUN</u>

The Slinky: In 1943, naval engineer _____ attempted to
<u>PERSON IN ROOM (MALE)</u>

create a spring to help ships _____, when he got the idea for a toy spring
<u>VERB</u>

that could _____ down the stairs all by itself. It became the _____
<u>VERB</u>   <u>ADJECTIVE</u>

Slinky!

Potato chips: At a restaurant in (the) _____ in 1853, a customer
<u>A PLACE</u>

complained that his fried potatoes were too _____. The chef,
<u>ADJECTIVE</u>

_____, cut the potatoes as thin as possible and fried them
<u>PERSON IN ROOM</u>

to a/an _____, accidentally inventing the _____ potato chip!
<u>NOUN</u>   <u>ADJECTIVE</u>

MAD LIBS® is fun to play with friends, but you can also play it by yourself! To begin with, DO NOT look at the story on the page below. Fill in the blanks on this page with the words called for. Then, using the words you have selected, fill in the blank spaces in the story.

Now you've created your own hilarious MAD LIBS® game!

STATE OF WONDER

NOUN _____

PLURAL NOUN _____

ADJECTIVE _____

PLURAL NOUN _____

A PLACE _____

A PLACE _____

ADJECTIVE _____

PLURAL NOUN _____

PLURAL NOUN _____

ADJECTIVE _____

NOUN _____

ADJECTIVE _____

NOUN _____

ADJECTIVE _____

PERSON IN ROOM (MALE) _____

CELEBRITY _____

MAD LIBS
STATE OF WONDER

The Seven Wonders of the Modern <u>chinchilla</u> were chosen by <u>balls</u>
__NOUN__ __PLURAL NOUN__

like me and you!

1. **The Great Wall of China** is a/an <u>glittery</u> wall made of stones, bricks,
__ADJECTIVE__

 and <u>bushes</u> that stretches all the way from (the) <u>galah cruize</u> to
__PLURAL NOUN__ __A PLACE__

 (the) <u>your moon's hole</u>
__A PLACE__

2. **Petra** is a/an <u>spicy</u> city in Jordan, also known as the Rose City
__ADJECTIVE__

 for its pink-colored <u>bulging eyes</u>
__PLURAL NOUN__

3. **The Colosseum** is an ancient Roman amphitheater built by <u>umbrellas</u>
__PLURAL NOUN__

4. **Chichén Itzá** is a/an <u>inflamitory</u> city in Mexico built during the
__ADJECTIVE__

 <u>Chilli</u> Empire.
__NOUN__

5. **Machu Picchu** is a/an <u>poopy</u> estate built into a huge <u>gummy bear</u>
__ADJECTIVE__ __NOUN__

 in Peru.

6. **Taj Mahal** is a/an <u>ranchy</u> mausoleum in India, built by Emperor
__ADJECTIVE__

 <u>Pat SayJack</u>.
__PERSON IN ROOM (MALE)__

7. **Christ the Redeemer** in Brazil is a hundred-foot-tall statue of
 <u>Mr. Mason</u>.
__CELEBRITY__

MAD LIBS® is fun to play with friends, but you can also play it by yourself! To begin with, DO NOT look at the story on the page below. Fill in the blanks on this page with the words called for. Then, using the words you have selected, fill in the blank spaces in the story.

Now you've created your own hilarious MAD LIBS® game!

MONGOLIAN WARRIOR

ADJECTIVE _____

NUMBER _____

ADJECTIVE _____

PLURAL NOUN _____

ADJECTIVE _____

A PLACE _____

PLURAL NOUN _____

ADJECTIVE _____

PLURAL NOUN _____

PLURAL NOUN _____

ADJECTIVE _____

NOUN _____

ADJECTIVE _____

VERB (PAST TENSE) _____

ADJECTIVE _____

Genghis Khan was a/an _____ Mongolian leader. Starting at the

ADJECTIVE

young age of _____, Genghis Khan began to build a/an _____

NUMBER ADJECTIVE

army of _____. He wanted to destroy _____ tribes in (the)

PLURAL NOUN ADJECTIVE

Northeast _____ so he could rule over all the _____ in the

A PLACE PLURAL NOUN

land. He and his _____ armies marched into _____

ADJECTIVE PLURAL NOUN

all around Asia. They brutally fought and killed many _____ and

PLURAL NOUN

eventually created the _____ Mongolian Empire, which was the largest

ADJECTIVE

_____ in the world. Today, Genghis Khan is considered one of the most

NOUN

ruthless and _____ warriors that ever _____. You

ADJECTIVE VERB (PAST TENSE)

wouldn't have wanted to meet him alone in a/an _____ alley!

ADJECTIVE

MAD LIBS® is fun to play with friends, but you can also play it by yourself! To begin with, DO NOT look at the story on the page below. Fill in the blanks on this page with the words called for. Then, using the words you have selected, fill in the blank spaces in the story.

Now you've created your own hilarious MAD LIBS® game!

NAPOLEON COMPLEX

OCCUPATION _____

PLURAL NOUN _____

PLURAL NOUN _____

ADJECTIVE _____

NOUN _____

NOUN _____

NOUN _____

ADJECTIVE _____

NOUN _____

PLURAL NOUN _____

PLURAL NOUN _____

ADJECTIVE _____

A PLACE _____

A PLACE _____

PLURAL NOUN _____

VERB (PAST TENSE) _____

ADJECTIVE _____

Napoleon Bonaparte was the first _____ of France. He made his way to

OCCUPATION

the top during the French Revolution, where regular old _____ rose

PLURAL NOUN

up to fight against royal _____. But Napoleon was known for having

PLURAL NOUN

a/an _____ temper. He would fly off the _____ at the drop

ADJECTIVE ... NOUN

of a/an _____. Napoleon was also not a very tall _____. Some

NOUN ... NOUN

say his small size made him feel _____. In order to feel like more of

ADJECTIVE

a/an _____, he would act out, invade _____, and fight wars

NOUN ... PLURAL NOUN

with _____! This made him feel _____ and powerful, despite

PLURAL NOUN ... ADJECTIVE

his small size. And, for a while, it worked, and Napoleon ruled over all of (the)

_____. But eventually, at the Battle of (the) _____, Napoleon was

A PLACE ... A PLACE

captured by British _____, and he _____.

PLURAL NOUN ... VERB (PAST TENSE)

One thing's for sure: What Napoleon lacked in size, he made up for with his

_____ personality!

ADJECTIVE

MAD LIBS® is fun to play with friends, but you can also play it by yourself! To begin with, DO NOT look at the story on the page below. Fill in the blanks on this page with the words called for. Then, using the words you have selected, fill in the blank spaces in the story.

Now you've created your own hilarious MAD LIBS® game!

WHEN IN ROME

ADJECTIVE _____

PLURAL NOUN _____

ADJECTIVE _____

ADJECTIVE _____

PLURAL NOUN _____

ADJECTIVE _____

PLURAL NOUN _____

VERB _____

ADJECTIVE _____

PART OF THE BODY (PLURAL) _____

PLURAL NOUN _____

NOUN _____

NOUN _____

NOUN _____

The Roman Empire is one of the most _____ empires in world history.

ADJECTIVE

Two thousand years ago, one in four _____ lived under Roman rule.

PLURAL NOUN

The Roman Empire was led by _____ emperors—a bunch of

ADJECTIVE

powerful men who wore _____ robes and decided the fate of Rome's

ADJECTIVE

many _____. The most famous Roman emperor was Caesar

PLURAL NOUN

Augustus, a/an _____ leader who helped Rome become one of the most

ADJECTIVE

powerful _____ the world had ever seen. The Roman people, rich and

PLURAL NOUN

poor, loved to mingle, gossip, and _____ at the _____ Roman

VERB ADJECTIVE

baths, a place for bathing and exercising your _____.

PART OF THE BODY (PLURAL)

Romans also enjoyed watching gladiators fight wild _____ in coliseums

PLURAL NOUN

and racing chariots around a/an _____. For about five hundred years,

NOUN

Romans ruled the _____—which is why the Roman Empire is thought

NOUN

of by some people as the most powerful _____ to ever exist.

NOUN

MAD LIBS® is fun to play with friends, but you can also play it by yourself! To begin with, DO NOT look at the story on the page below. Fill in the blanks on this page with the words called for. Then, using the words you have selected, fill in the blank spaces in the story.

Now you've created your own hilarious MAD LIBS® game!

AN APPLE A DAY

ADJECTIVE _____

ADJECTIVE _____

ADJECTIVE _____

ADJECTIVE _____

PERSON IN ROOM (FEMALE) _____

SILLY WORD _____

A PLACE _____

VERB ENDING IN "ING" _____

NOUN _____

ADVERB _____

NOUN _____

ADJECTIVE _____

NOUN _____

ADJECTIVE _____

VERB _____

MAD LIBS
AN APPLE A DAY

Here is the story of how a/an _____ scientist named Sir Isaac Newton
ADJECTIVE

came up with the _____ theory of gravity. One day, a/an _____
ADJECTIVE   ADJECTIVE

Isaac went to visit his _____ mother, _____,
ADJECTIVE   PERSON IN ROOM (FEMALE)

at _____ Manor, her country home in (the) _____. While
SILLY WORD   A PLACE

_____ in the garden, Isaac saw an apple fall from a/an
VERB ENDING IN "ING"

_____. *Why does that apple fall* _____ *to the ground?* thought
NOUN   ADVERB

Isaac. *Why doesn't the apple fall sideways, or go upward, toward the* _____
NOUN

in the sky? Before long, Isaac decided that the _____ apple must be
ADJECTIVE

drawn to the Earth's core, right in the middle of the _____. And thus,
NOUN

Sir Isaac Newton came up with the _____ concept of gravity—that
ADJECTIVE

whatever goes up must _____ down.
VERB

MAD LIBS®

MAD SCIENTIST MAD LIBS

Mad Libs
An Imprint of Penguin Random House

INSTRUCTIONS

MAD LIBS® is a game for people who don't like games!
It can be played by one, two, three, four, or forty.

• RIDICULOUSLY SIMPLE DIRECTIONS

In this tablet you will find stories containing blank spaces where words are left out. One player, the READER, selects one of these stories. The READER does not tell anyone what the story is about. Instead, he/she asks the other players, the WRITERS, to give him/her words. These words are used to fill in the blank spaces in the story.

• TO PLAY

The READER asks each WRITER in turn to call out a word—an adjective or a noun or whatever the space calls for—and uses them to fill in the blank spaces in the story. The result is a MAD LIBS® game.

When the READER then reads the completed MAD LIBS® game to the other players, they will discover that they have written a story that is fantastic, screamingly funny, shocking, silly, crazy, or just plain dumb—depending upon which words each WRITER called out.

• EXAMPLE (*Before* and *After*)

"_____!" he said _____
      EXCLAMATION   ADVERB

as he jumped into his convertible _____ and
                                      NOUN

drove off with his _____ wife.
                    ADJECTIVE

"____OUCH____!" he said ____STUPIDLY____
      EXCLAMATION   ADVERB

as he jumped into his convertible ____CAT____ and
                                      NOUN

drove off with his ____BRAVE____ wife.
                    ADJECTIVE

QUICK REVIEW

In case you have forgotten what adjectives, adverbs, nouns, and verbs are, here is a quick review:

An ADJECTIVE describes something or somebody. *Lumpy, soft, ugly, messy,* and *short* are adjectives.

An ADVERB tells how something is done. It modifies a verb and usually ends in "ly." *Modestly, stupidly, greedily,* and *carefully* are adverbs.

A NOUN is the name of a person, place, or thing. *Sidewalk, umbrella, bridle, bathtub,* and *nose* are nouns.

A VERB is an action word. *Run, pitch, jump,* and *swim* are verbs. Put the verbs in past tense if the directions say PAST TENSE. *Ran, pitched, jumped,* and *swam* are verbs in the past tense.

When we ask for A PLACE, we mean any sort of place: a country or city *(Spain, Cleveland)* or a room *(bathroom, kitchen).*

An EXCLAMATION or SILLY WORD is any sort of funny sound, gasp, grunt, or outcry, like *Wow!, Ouch!, Whomp!, Ick!,* and *Gadzooks!*

When we ask for specific words, like a NUMBER, a COLOR, an ANIMAL, or a PART OF THE BODY, we mean a word that is one of those things, like *seven, blue, horse,* or *head.*

When we ask for a PLURAL, it means more than one. For example, *cat* pluralized is *cats.*

MAD LIBS® is fun to play with friends, but you can also play it by yourself! To begin with, DO NOT look at the story on the page below. Fill in the blanks on this page with the words called for. Then, using the words you have selected, fill in the blank spaces in the story.

Now you've created your own hilarious MAD LIBS® game!

HOW TO GET MY LOOK
BY ALBERT EINSTEIN

OCCUPATION _____

ADVERB _____

ADJECTIVE _____

NOUN _____

ADJECTIVE _____

ADJECTIVE _____

COLOR _____

ADJECTIVE _____

PART OF THE BODY _____

NOUN _____

ARTICLE OF CLOTHING _____

OCCUPATION _____

MAD LIBS
HOW TO GET MY LOOK
BY ALBERT EINSTEIN

Hallo. I am famous German __cheechly__ Albert Einstein. Some people
OCCUPATION

say I look __choching__ insane. And zey are right, I do! But I am not
ADVERB

actually __moist__. Zis is just how I like to look. If you would also like
ADJECTIVE

to look like zis, use ze makeover tips I have outlined below.

• Never comb your __Boobies__ : It is supposed to look like zis! Ze
NOUN

more __Wieners__, the better, as I always say. It also helps if your
ADJECTIVE

hair is a/an __Ugly__ shade of __Black__.
ADJECTIVE · COLOR

• Make __sexy__ faces as often as possible. For example, stick out
ADJECTIVE

your __balls__ in pictures. Why? Because life is fun! Do zis when
PART OF THE BODY

your eager __boobies__ students photograph you. Zey will love it!
NOUN

• Always wear a white lab __undie__. Zis way, you will
ARTICLE OF CLOTHING

look like a real __cheech chocher__
OCCUPATION

MAD LIBS® is fun to play with friends, but you can also play it by yourself! To begin with, DO NOT look at the story on the page below. Fill in the blanks on this page with the words called for. Then, using the words you have selected, fill in the blank spaces in the story.

Now you've created your own hilarious MAD LIBS® game!

THE BIOGRAPHY OF ALBERT EINSTEIN

A PLACE _____

NUMBER _____

OCCUPATION _____

ADJECTIVE _____

COLOR _____

ADJECTIVE _____

ADVERB _____

ADJECTIVE _____

PLURAL NOUN _____

PLURAL NOUN _____

VERB (PAST TENSE) _____

NOUN _____

NOUN _____

NOUN _____

PART OF THE BODY _____

A PLACE _____

Albert Einstein was born in (the) _____ in Germany in the year
<u>A PLACE</u>

18-_____. He grew up to be a genius _____ with a/an _____
<u>NUMBER</u>   <u>OCCUPATION</u>   <u>ADJECTIVE</u>

_____ head of hair and a/an _____ sense of humor. Even
<u>COLOR</u>   <u>ADJECTIVE</u>

though he was _____ smart, the people who knew him thought he acted
<u>ADVERB</u>

pretty _____. He was notorious for losing _____ and forgetting
<u>ADJECTIVE</u>   <u>PLURAL NOUN</u>

the _____ in his equations. Einstein became famous for inventing
<u>PLURAL NOUN</u>

things like E equals MC _____, the theory of _____,
<u>VERB (PAST TENSE)</u>   <u>NOUN</u>

and the quantum _____ of light. In 1921, he won the Nobel _____
<u>NOUN</u>   <u>NOUN</u>

in Physics. After his death in 1955, Einstein's _____ was
<u>PART OF THE BODY</u>

donated to (the) _____ Medical Center.
<u>A PLACE</u>

MAD LIBS® is fun to play with friends, but you can also play it by yourself! To begin with, DO NOT look at the story on the page below. Fill in the blanks on this page with the words called for. Then, using the words you have selected, fill in the blank spaces in the story.

Now you've created your own hilarious MAD LIBS® game!

QUIZ: ARE YOU A MAD SCIENTIST?

ADJECTIVE _____

ADJECTIVE _____

EXCLAMATION _____

ADJECTIVE _____

ADJECTIVE _____

VERB (PAST TENSE) _____

TYPE OF LIQUID _____

ANIMAL (PLURAL) _____

COLOR _____

ADJECTIVE _____

NOUN _____

NOUN _____

ADJECTIVE _____

ARTICLE OF CLOTHING _____

ADJECTIVE _____

OCCUPATION _____

MAD LIBS®
QUIZ: ARE YOU A MAD SCIENTIST?

Are you crazy about science? Do you go nuts for _____ experiments?

ADJECTIVE

Take this _____ quiz to find out if you're a mad scientist.

ADJECTIVE

1. Your favorite saying is: a) "Oh, _____! What did I do?",

EXCLAMATION

   b) "It's _____!", c) "This _____ experiment went exactly as

ADJECTIVE   ADJECTIVE

   _____."

VERB (PAST TENSE)

2. Your lab always contains: a) test tubes filled with _____,

TYPE OF LIQUID

   b) _____ floating in jars, c) a few _____ mice in cages.

ANIMAL (PLURAL)   COLOR

3. Your favorite thing to do at night is: a) go to bed and have _____

ADJECTIVE

   dreams, b) laugh maniacally while bringing to life an evil _____,

NOUN

   c) plan tomorrow's _____-work.

NOUN

If you answered mostly *b*'s, guess what? You're a/an _____ scientist! Go

ADJECTIVE

put on your long white _____ and experiment in your

ARTICLE OF CLOTHING

_____ laboratory. If you answered mostly *a*'s and *c*'s, you're better off as

ADJECTIVE

a/an _____!

OCCUPATION

MAD LIBS® is fun to play with friends, but you can also play it by yourself! To begin with, DO NOT look at the story on the page below. Fill in the blanks on this page with the words called for. Then, using the words you have selected, fill in the blank spaces in the story.

Now you've created your own hilarious MAD LIBS® game!

LAB RAT ON THE LOOSE

SILLY WORD _____

ADJECTIVE _____

NUMBER _____

NOUN _____

VERB ENDING IN "ING" _____

NOUN _____

TYPE OF LIQUID _____

ADJECTIVE _____

PART OF THE BODY _____

ADJECTIVE _____

VERB ENDING IN "ING" _____

ADJECTIVE _____

ANIMAL _____

ADJECTIVE _____

MAD LIBS
LAB RAT ON THE LOOSE

Uh-oh! Last night, _____ the lab rat escaped from his cage and ran amok
SILLY WORD

in the science lab. He was out to get revenge on the _____ scientists
ADJECTIVE

who'd held him captive for _____ weeks. First, he ran straight to the
NUMBER

_____ tubes and knocked them over, _____ glass all
NOUN   VERB ENDING IN "ING"

over the _____. Then he jumped into a vat of _____ and
NOUN   TYPE OF LIQUID

left _____ _____-prints all over the floor. Later on,
ADJECTIVE   PART OF THE BODY

the _____ rat finally got tired of _____ around and went
ADJECTIVE   VERB ENDING IN "ING"

to sleep under a/an _____-scope. Looks like that silly _____ is
ADJECTIVE   ANIMAL

finally done with all his _____ hijinks. For now, at least . . .
ADJECTIVE

MAD LIBS® is fun to play with friends, but you can also play it by yourself! To begin with, DO NOT look at the story on the page below. Fill in the blanks on this page with the words called for. Then, using the words you have selected, fill in the blank spaces in the story.

Now you've created your own hilarious MAD LIBS® game!

THE STORY OF FRANKENSTEIN

PERSON IN ROOM (MALE) _____

ADJECTIVE _____

NOUN _____

NOUN _____

A PLACE _____

PART OF THE BODY (PLURAL) _____

NUMBER _____

PLURAL NOUN _____

NOUN _____

ADJECTIVE _____

NOUN _____

ADJECTIVE _____

A PLACE _____

NOUN _____

NOUN _____

ADVERB _____

VERB (PAST TENSE) _____

MAD⊙LIBS®
THE STORY OF
FRANKENSTEIN

Mary Shelley wrote a science-fiction book about a villainous mad scientist

called _____ Frankenstein. Frankenstein was a/an

PERSON IN ROOM (MALE)

_____ scientist from the nineteenth _____. His greatest wish was to

ADJECTIVE   NOUN

one day become a real _____. So he went to (the) _____ and took

NOUN   A PLACE

a brain, some _____, and _____ legs from several dead

PART OF THE BODY (PLURAL)   NUMBER

_____. Once he had sewn the body parts together, Frankenstein used

PLURAL NOUN

electricity to make the hideous _____ come to life. Soon, in the middle

NOUN

of a/an _____ and stormy _____, the creature awoke! It was

ADJECTIVE   NOUN

Frankenstein's greatest creation, and one of the most _____ beings to

ADJECTIVE

ever live—until it started terrorizing the citizens of (the) _____.

A PLACE

Frankenstein had to take action. He armed himself with a/an _____

NOUN

and went on a hunt for the _____ he'd created. After searching

NOUN

_____ for months, Frankenstein finally had to give up his search because

ADVERB

he _____ .

VERB (PAST TENSE)

MAD LIBS® is fun to play with friends, but you can also play it by yourself! To begin with, DO NOT look at the story on the page below. Fill in the blanks on this page with the words called for. Then, using the words you have selected, fill in the blank spaces in the story.

Now you've created your own hilarious MAD LIBS® game!

ANNOUNCEMENT: THE SCIENCE FAIR WINNERS

CITY _____

ADVERB _____

ADJECTIVE _____

PERSON IN ROOM (FEMALE) _____

NOUN _____

SILLY WORD _____

PERSON IN ROOM (MALE) _____

ADJECTIVE _____

VERB (PAST TENSE) _____

PERSON IN ROOM _____

VERB ENDING IN "ING" _____

NUMBER _____

COLOR _____

ADJECTIVE _____

NOUN _____

ADJECTIVE _____

MAD LIBS
ANNOUNCEMENT: THE
SCIENCE FAIR WINNERS

Thank you all for participating in the _____ Middle School Science Fair.
CITY

Everyone worked very _____ on their projects, and it shows. We will
ADVERB

now announce the first-, second-, and _____-place winners.
ADJECTIVE

_____ won first prize for her miniature erupting
PERSON IN ROOM (FEMALE)

_____, which was a model of the largest volcano in history, Mount
NOUN

_____.
SILLY WORD

_____ got second place for his super _____ miniature
PERSON IN ROOM (MALE)   ADJECTIVE

solar system, in which all the planets _____ in circles.
VERB (PAST TENSE)

_____ was given a third-place ribbon for _____ an
PERSON IN ROOM   VERB ENDING IN "ING"

ant farm using sand and _____ tiny _____ ants.
NUMBER   COLOR

That's it for the _____ annual science fair. We'll see you next _____
ADJECTIVE   NOUN

for another round of _____ science experiments.
ADJECTIVE

MAD LIBS® is fun to play with friends, but you can also play it by yourself! To begin with, DO NOT look at the story on the page below. Fill in the blanks on this page with the words called for. Then, using the words you have selected, fill in the blank spaces in the story.

Now you've created your own hilarious MAD LIBS® game!

THE PERIODIC TABLE

PLURAL NOUN _____

NOUN _____

NOUN _____

ADJECTIVE _____

A PLACE _____

LAST NAME _____

PLURAL NOUN _____

NUMBER _____

NOUN _____

PLURAL NOUN _____

NOUN _____

LETTER OF THE ALPHABET _____

LETTER OF THE ALPHABET _____

PLURAL NOUN _____

VERB _____

MAD LIBS
THE PERIODIC TABLE

The periodic table of _____ hangs in classrooms and _____
       PLURAL NOUN   NOUN

laboratories all around the _____. So what's this _____ chart
           NOUN   ADJECTIVE

all about? Well, in the eighteenth century, a chemist from (the) _____
                        A PLACE

named Dmitri _____ created the very first periodic table of
      LAST NAME

_____. There are more than _____ elements on the periodic table,
PLURAL NOUN   NUMBER

organized by atomic _____. The elements all have a certain number of
       NOUN

protons, neutrons, and _____. Each element on the periodic
         PLURAL NOUN

_____ has a symbol that is often the first two letters of the element's
NOUN

name. For example, helium's symbol is _____
                LETTER OF THE ALPHABET

_____. Some scientists say more _____ should be
LETTER OF THE ALPHABET   PLURAL NOUN

added to the table. Maybe someday you'll _____ one yourself!
              VERB

From MAD SCIENTIST MAD LIBS® • Copyright © 2014 by Penguin Random House LLC.

MAD LIBS® is fun to play with friends, but you can also play it by yourself! To begin with, DO NOT look at the story on the page below. Fill in the blanks on this page with the words called for. Then, using the words you have selected, fill in the blank spaces in the story.

Now you've created your own hilarious MAD LIBS® game!

DR. JEKYLL AND MR. HYDE

OCCUPATION _____

CITY _____

NOUN _____

ADJECTIVE _____

PLURAL NOUN _____

VERB (PAST TENSE) _____

ADJECTIVE _____

ADVERB _____

VERB _____

PLURAL NOUN _____

ADJECTIVE _____

OCCUPATION _____

NOUN _____

NOUN _____

ADJECTIVE _____

NOUN _____

ADJECTIVE _____

TYPE OF LIQUID _____

PART OF THE BODY _____

MAD LIBS
DR. JEKYLL AND MR. HYDE

Dr. Jekyll was a friendly old _____ living in _____, England. Mr.
                               OCCUPATION   CITY

Hyde was an evil young _____ who did _____ things to every
                        NOUN   ADJECTIVE

person he met. But these two _____ were also a lot alike. They even
                              PLURAL NOUN

kind of _____ the same! But Hyde had a/an _____ power over
         VERB (PAST TENSE)   ADJECTIVE

the doctor, and became _____ evil as time went on. He was willing to
                        ADVERB

_____ anyone who got in his way, and even took _____ from the
  VERB   PLURAL NOUN

_____ townspeople. Then Hyde murdered a well-known _____!
 ADJECTIVE   OCCUPATION

But, what a surprise—it wasn't Hyde after all. It was Jekyll! They were the same

exact _____. Turns out, Jekyll had split-_____disorder. To fix this,
       NOUN   NOUN

Jekyll did _____ experiments on himself so that Hyde would leave his
            ADJECTIVE

_____ once and for all. But the experiments were too _____.
 NOUN   ADJECTIVE

The chemicals and _____ didn't work. In the end, Hyde took over
                   TYPE OF LIQUID

Jekyll's _____, and Jekyll was never seen again.
          PART OF THE BODY

MAD LIBS® is fun to play with friends, but you can also play it by yourself! To begin with, DO NOT look at the story on the page below. Fill in the blanks on this page with the words called for. Then, using the words you have selected, fill in the blank spaces in the story.

Now you've created your own hilarious MAD LIBS® game!

LABORATORY SAFETY DOS AND DON'TS

PART OF THE BODY (PLURAL) _____

NOUN _____

ADVERB _____

VERB ENDING IN "ING" _____

NOUN _____

VERB _____

ADJECTIVE _____

PART OF THE BODY (PLURAL) _____

TYPE OF FOOD _____

ADJECTIVE _____

TYPE OF CONTAINER _____

ANIMAL (PLURAL) _____

MAD LIBS®
LABORATORY SAFETY
DOS AND DON'TS

Do wear safety goggles. They will protect your <u>Boobies</u> .
PART OF THE BODY (PLURAL)

Don't light anything on fire. Always keep a/an <u>Brush</u> extinguisher handy
NOUN

in case you <u>Slowly</u> set your laboratory aflame.
ADVERB

Do clean the lens of the microscope before <u>Juicing</u> it. You
VERB ENDING IN "ING"

might think you're looking at a cell when really you're just looking at a piece of

<u>necklace</u>.
NOUN

Don't get too close to the test tubes after combining their contents. They might

<u>Jumping</u> all over you!
VERB

Do clean up after yourself. Experiments can leave you with <u>Spicy</u> hands
ADJECTIVE

and stinky <u>Balls</u> .
PART OF THE BODY (PLURAL)

Don't leave any experiments unattended. If you get hungry and want to grab

a/an <u>Hot dog</u> sandwich, stop! You need to stay put until the <u>Hairy</u>
TYPE OF FOOD   ADJECTIVE

chemicals in your beakers are done boiling and you've put them safely away in

a/an <u>Bucket</u> .
TYPE OF CONTAINER

Do remember to feed your lab <u>kitties</u> . They're not only
ANIMAL (PLURAL)

your test subjects, they're your friends.

MAD LIBS® is fun to play with friends, but you can also play it by yourself! To begin with, DO NOT look at the story on the page below. Fill in the blanks on this page with the words called for. Then, using the words you have selected, fill in the blank spaces in the story.

Now you've created your own hilarious MAD LIBS® game!

I NEED A NEW LAB PARTNER!

PERSON IN ROOM (MALE) _____

ADJECTIVE _____

LAST NAME _____

PERSON IN ROOM (FEMALE) _____

ADJECTIVE _____

VERB (PAST TENSE) _____

NOUN _____

ADJECTIVE _____

NOUN _____

ADJECTIVE _____

ADJECTIVE _____

PLURAL NOUN _____

ADJECTIVE _____

MAD LIBS®
I NEED A NEW LAB PARTNER!

To Whom It May Concern:

Hi. My name is _____, and I am looking for a new,
PERSON IN ROOM (MALE)

_____ lab partner for Mrs. _____ 's biology class. My
ADJECTIVE   LAST NAME

last lab partner, _____, was really _____ and
PERSON IN ROOM (FEMALE)   ADJECTIVE

never _____ our experiments on time. So I asked to
VERB (PAST TENSE)

switch, and the teacher said if I wanted another _____ partner,
NOUN

I had to find one all by myself. If you are smart, _____ in school,
ADJECTIVE

and always turn your _____-work in on time, you'd be a/an
NOUN

_____ lab partner for me. Please only contact me if you're
ADJECTIVE

_____ about science and love doing scientific
ADJECTIVE

_____. If this describes you, contact me at
PLURAL NOUN

scienceluvr1@-_____-mail.com, or just find me by my locker
ADJECTIVE

after lunch.

MAD LIBS® is fun to play with friends, but you can also play it by yourself! To begin with, DO NOT look at the story on the page below. Fill in the blanks on this page with the words called for. Then, using the words you have selected, fill in the blank spaces in the story.

Now you've created your own hilarious MAD LIBS® game!

MY WACKY
CHEMISTRY TEACHER

LAST NAME _____

PART OF THE BODY (PLURAL) _____

NOUN _____

EXCLAMATION _____

PERSON IN ROOM (FEMALE) _____

ADJECTIVE _____

NOUN _____

ADJECTIVE _____

NOUN _____

EXCLAMATION _____

VERB (PAST TENSE) _____

NOUN _____

ADJECTIVE _____

NP

There are a lot of rumors going around about Mr. __Allen__, our chemistry
LAST NAME

teacher. He always has a crazy look in his __butts__. Sometimes,
PART OF THE BODY (PLURAL)

in the middle of a/an __poop__ lesson, he'll shout "__FART__!" for
NOUN   EXCLAMATION

no reason at all. My friend __Evette__ told me that he acts
PERSON IN ROOM (FEMALE)

__fat__ because one time during a/an __Obese__-storm he was struck
ADJECTIVE   NOUN

by lightning in his classroom. Ouch! That would probably explain why he is

so __large__ all the time and shakes whenever he writes on the
ADJECTIVE

__RRRR__-board. Last week, while doing an experiment in class, he yelled,
NOUN

"__SUS__! It's alive!" and then __pooped__ around the
EXCLAMATION   VERB (PAST TENSE)

room holding a/an __fart__ full of mysterious bubbling liquid. Maybe the
NOUN

rumors are true; maybe my teacher really is __big__!
ADJECTIVE

MAD LIBS® is fun to play with friends, but you can also play it by yourself! To begin with, DO NOT look at the story on the page below. Fill in the blanks on this page with the words called for. Then, using the words you have selected, fill in the blank spaces in the story.

Now you've created your own hilarious MAD LIBS® game!

AT-HOME EXPERIMENT #1: FLOATING PAPER CLIPS!

NUMBER _____

ADJECTIVE _____

ADJECTIVE _____

TYPE OF LIQUID _____

ADJECTIVE _____

ADVERB _____

NOUN _____

VERB ENDING IN "S" _____

VERB _____

PART OF THE BODY (PLURAL) _____

MAD LIBS®
AT-HOME EXPERIMENT #1:
FLOATING PAPER CLIPS!

Materials:

_____ paper clips
NUMBER

A piece of _____ paper
ADJECTIVE

A see-through _____-size bowl
ADJECTIVE

A pencil

Instructions:

1. Fill the bowl with _____ .
TYPE OF LIQUID

2. Rip a/an _____ piece of tissue paper and _____ drop it
ADJECTIVE   ADVERB

onto the water.

3. Drop one of the _____ clips onto the tissue paper.
NOUN

4. Use the pencil to gently nudge the tissue paper until the paper clip

_____ .
VERB ENDING IN "S"

5. If you do this just right, the paper clip will start to _____ in
VERB

front of your very _____ !
PART OF THE BODY (PLURAL)

MAD LIBS® is fun to play with friends, but you can also play it by yourself! To begin with, DO NOT look at the story on the page below. Fill in the blanks on this page with the words called for. Then, using the words you have selected, fill in the blank spaces in the story.

Now you've created your own hilarious MAD LIBS® game!

FAMOUS SCIENTISTS

PLURAL NOUN _____

ADJECTIVE _____

NOUN _____

ADJECTIVE _____

VERB _____

NOUN _____

ADJECTIVE _____

SILLY WORD _____

PLURAL NOUN _____

ADJECTIVE _____

VERB (PAST TENSE) _____

ADVERB _____

ANIMAL _____

PLURAL NOUN _____

Over the years, many famous _____ have developed _____
                              PLURAL NOUN   ADJECTIVE

theories, inventions, and ideas that have contributed to the evolution of

_____-kind. Below are some of the most _____ scientists to ever
    NOUN   ADJECTIVE

_____.
    VERB

Galileo Galilei was an Italian _____ who invented telescopes and found
                                        NOUN

out a lot of information about the _____ Way Galaxy, the solar system,
                                      ADJECTIVE

and planets like Jupiter and _____.
                                SILLY WORD

Sir Isaac Newton discovered most of what we now know about gravity. He

also wrote scientific _____ called the First Law of Motion, the Second
                         PLURAL NOUN

Law of Motion, and the _____ Law of Motion.
                           ADJECTIVE

Charles Darwin invented theories about natural selection, which proved how

different species _____ over hundreds of years on Earth.
                     VERB (PAST TENSE)

He _____ studied several species of _____ on the Galapagos
      ADVERB   ANIMAL

_____.
 PLURAL NOUN

MAD LIBS® is fun to play with friends, but you can also play it by yourself! To begin with, DO NOT look at the story on the page below. Fill in the blanks on this page with the words called for. Then, using the words you have selected, fill in the blank spaces in the story.

Now you've created your own hilarious MAD LIBS® game!

TURN YOUR BEDROOM INTO A SECRET LAB

ADJECTIVE _____

ADJECTIVE _____

VERB ENDING IN "ING" _____

NOUN _____

VERB _____

PLURAL NOUN _____

NOUN _____

ADJECTIVE _____

TYPE OF CONTAINER (PLURAL) _____

TYPE OF LIQUID _____

ADVERB _____

ADJECTIVE _____

VERB ENDING IN "ING" _____

Follow these _____ steps to turn your boring, _____ bedroom into
           ADJECTIVE   ADJECTIVE

a fully _____ science lab! First, put a big _____ on your
   VERB ENDING IN "ING"   NOUN

bedroom door that reads KEEP OUT! Scientists need to _____ in silence
                                                     VERB

without any annoying _____ interrupting them. Then clear off your
                 PLURAL NOUN

_____. You'll need it to hold all your oozy, _____ chemicals. Gather
 NOUN   ADJECTIVE

a bunch of _____ and put them all over your desk. Connect
        TYPE OF CONTAINER (PLURAL)

them with tubing so you can watch all the _____ run through
                                   TYPE OF LIQUID

them—_____ cool! Finally, pull your curtains shut—you don't want
      ADVERB

anyone to see what kind of _____ concoctions you're
                           ADJECTIVE

_____!
VERB ENDING IN "ING"

MAD LIBS® is fun to play with friends, but you can also play it by yourself! To begin with, DO NOT look at the story on the page below. Fill in the blanks on this page with the words called for. Then, using the words you have selected, fill in the blank spaces in the story.

Now you've created your own hilarious MAD LIBS® game!

THE MAD SCIENTIST'S SHOPPING LIST

PLURAL NOUN _____

PART OF THE BODY _____

ARTICLE OF CLOTHING _____

VERB ENDING IN "ING" _____

ANIMAL (PLURAL) _____

PLURAL NOUN _____

NOUN _____

ADJECTIVE _____

VERB _____

NOUN _____

MAD LIBS®
THE MAD SCIENTIST'S
SHOPPING LIST

- Long, rubbery black _____ to wear on your hands
  PLURAL NOUN

- Giant round _____-glasses with black frames
  PART OF THE BODY

- Long white lab _____
  ARTICLE OF CLOTHING

- Two beakers—one to hold in each hand while _____
  VERB ENDING IN "ING"

  maniacally

- Several cages for all your lab _____
  ANIMAL (PLURAL)

- Assorted _____ floating in formaldehyde to add to your
  PLURAL NOUN

  collection

- A chalkboard and a piece of _____ to write down your
  NOUN

  _____ hypotheses and equations
  ADJECTIVE

- A giant electrical power switch to turn on when you need to

  _____ something to life
  VERB

- A Bunsen burner to light every _____ on fire!
  NOUN

MAD LIBS® is fun to play with friends, but you can also play it by yourself! To begin with, DO NOT look at the story on the page below. Fill in the blanks on this page with the words called for. Then, using the words you have selected, fill in the blank spaces in the story.

Now you've created your own hilarious MAD LIBS® game!

MORE FAMOUS SCIENTISTS

ADJECTIVE _____

ADJECTIVE _____

NOUN _____

PLURAL NOUN _____

PERSON IN ROOM (MALE) _____

OCCUPATION _____

NOUN _____

VERB _____

NOUN _____

PLURAL NOUN _____

COLOR _____

NOUN _____

MAD LIBS®
MORE FAMOUS SCIENTISTS

Here are a few more _____ scientists!
ADJECTIVE

Nikola Tesla was born in Croatia. Later, he moved to the _____ States
ADJECTIVE
of America and became an inventor. He helped create fluorescent

_____-bulbs so that people wouldn't have to use _____ to light
NOUN   PLURAL NOUN
their homes. Tesla also invented radio and worked with _____
PERSON IN ROOM (MALE)
Edison to invent things that helped electricity work.

Alexander Graham Bell was a/an _____ from the nineteenth
OCCUPATION
century. His mother was deaf, as was his _____. Because of this, Bell was
NOUN
interested in speech and hearing. He decided to create something that would

help people _____ each other, no matter where they were. He invented
VERB
the tele-_____ so that people could talk to one another.
NOUN

Stephen Hawking was a British physicist who studied galaxies and solar

_____. He discovered a lot about _____ holes. His most famous
PLURAL NOUN   COLOR
book is called *A Brief History of* _____.
NOUN

MAD LIBS® is fun to play with friends, but you can also play it by yourself! To begin with, DO NOT look at the story on the page below. Fill in the blanks on this page with the words called for. Then, using the words you have selected, fill in the blank spaces in the story.

Now you've created your own hilarious MAD LIBS® game!

FRANKENSTEIN'S MONSTER

NUMBER _____

NOUN _____

ADJECTIVE _____

COLOR _____

NOUN _____

PLURAL NOUN _____

PART OF THE BODY _____

PART OF THE BODY _____

ADJECTIVE _____

VERB (PAST TENSE) _____

ARTICLE OF CLOTHING _____

ADJECTIVE _____

ADJECTIVE _____

NOUN _____

MAD LIBS®
FRANKENSTEIN'S MONSTER

Frankenstein's monster was a hideous, _____-foot-tall _____.
NUMBER   NOUN

His skin was a/an _____ shade of _____, his head was shaped like
ADJECTIVE   COLOR

a/an _____, and he had _____ sticking out of both sides of his
NOUN   PLURAL NOUN

neck. Frankenstein's monster also had black lips and spiky black hair on his

_____, and his _____ was filled with big
PART OF THE BODY   PART OF THE BODY

white teeth. His _____ arms stuck straight out whenever he
ADJECTIVE

_____ down the street, because the black shirt and
VERB (PAST TENSE)

_____ he always wore were too small on his grotesque,
ARTICLE OF CLOTHING

_____ body. What a/an _____-looking _____ he was!
ADJECTIVE   ADJECTIVE   NOUN

MAD LIBS® is fun to play with friends, but you can also play it by yourself! To begin with, DO NOT look at the story on the page below. Fill in the blanks on this page with the words called for. Then, using the words you have selected, fill in the blank spaces in the story.

Now you've created your own hilarious MAD LIBS® game!

AT-HOME EXPERIMENT #2: ERUPTING VOLCANO!

NOUN _____

ADJECTIVE _____

COLOR _____

VERB ENDING IN "ING" _____

TYPE OF LIQUID _____

ADJECTIVE _____

NOUN _____

PLURAL NOUN _____

ADJECTIVE _____

NUMBER _____

VERB _____

Materials:

A homemade volcano made out of plaster or _____-mâché

NOUN

A small _____ container

ADJECTIVE

_____ or yellow food coloring

COLOR

_____ soda

VERB ENDING IN "ING"

_____

TYPE OF LIQUID

Dish soap

Instructions:

1. Put the _____ container at the top of your volcano.

ADJECTIVE

2. Pour in a little bit of baking soda and some dish _____.

NOUN

3. Add a few _____ of _____ food coloring.

PLURAL NOUN ADJECTIVE

4. Pour in _____ ounces of vinegar.

NUMBER

5. Watch your volcano _____ with lava!

VERB

MAD LIBS® is fun to play with friends, but you can also play it by yourself! To begin with, DO NOT look at the story on the page below. Fill in the blanks on this page with the words called for. Then, using the words you have selected, fill in the blank spaces in the story.

Now you've created your own hilarious MAD LIBS® game!

THE WORST SCI-FI NIGHTMARE I EVER HAD

OCCUPATION _____

PART OF THE BODY _____

ADJECTIVE _____

PLURAL NOUN _____

VERB _____

ADJECTIVE _____

NOUN _____

PART OF THE BODY (PLURAL) _____

VERB _____

COLOR _____

TYPE OF LIQUID _____

NOUN _____

ADJECTIVE _____

MAD LIBS
THE WORST SCI-FI
NIGHTMARE I EVER HAD

I had a dream last night that a crazy _____ was trying to perform
OCCUPATION

experiments on me. He took a strand of my _____ and looked
PART OF THE BODY

at it under a microscope. Then he told me to sit in his _____
ADJECTIVE

chair. But I was scared—there were a bunch of electrical _____
PLURAL NOUN

tied to it, and I was afraid he was going to _____ me in it! I said,
VERB

"No, thanks, you _____ scientist—I'm getting the
ADJECTIVE

_____ out of here." He looked me right in the
NOUN

_____ and said, "Don't you dare try to leave my dungeon!
PART OF THE BODY (PLURAL)

You can't _____ —the door's locked!" Suddenly, he pounced on
VERB

me, and everything turned to _____. I woke up with
COLOR

_____ running down my temples. Thank _____ that
TYPE OF LIQUID   NOUN

nightmare is over. I hope I never see that _____ scientist again!
ADJECTIVE

MAD LIBS® is fun to play with friends, but you can also play it by yourself! To begin with, DO NOT look at the story on the page below. Fill in the blanks on this page with the words called for. Then, using the words you have selected, fill in the blank spaces in the story.

Now you've created your own hilarious MAD LIBS® game!

AT-HOME EXPERIMENT #3: TORNADO IN A BOTTLE!

NOUN _____

VERB ENDING IN "ING" _____

VERB _____

ADJECTIVE _____

ADJECTIVE _____

VERB _____

NOUN _____

ADJECTIVE _____

NOUN _____

ADJECTIVE _____

NOUN _____

ADJECTIVE _____

VERB (PAST TENSE) _____

Materials:

Water

A see-through plastic soda _____ with a cap
NOUN

Glitter, to see debris _____ in the bottle
VERB ENDING IN "ING"

Dish soap to make your tornado _____
VERB

Instructions:

1. Fill the entire _____ bottle with water until it is almost all the
ADJECTIVE

   way _____ .
   ADJECTIVE

2 _____ a few drops of dish _____ into the bottle. Add the
VERB   NOUN

   _____ glitter.
   ADJECTIVE

3. Screw the _____ onto the top of the bottle.
NOUN

4. Turn the bottle upside _____ and hold it near the cap.
ADJECTIVE

5. Spin the bottle in a/an _____-wise rotation.
NOUN

6. Stop spinning the bottle and admire the _____ tornado you
ADJECTIVE

   _____ !
   VERB (PAST TENSE)

MAD LIBS® is fun to play with friends, but you can also play it by yourself! To begin with, DO NOT look at the story on the page below. Fill in the blanks on this page with the words called for. Then, using the words you have selected, fill in the blank spaces in the story.

Now you've created your own hilarious MAD LIBS® game!

THE FIRST WEEK OF SCIENCE CLASS

ADJECTIVE _____

LAST NAME _____

PLURAL NOUN _____

PLURAL NOUN _____

NOUN _____

NOUN _____

ANIMAL (PLURAL) _____

PERSON IN ROOM _____

ADJECTIVE _____

VERB _____

MAD LIBS®
THE FIRST WEEK OF
SCIENCE CLASS

My first few days of science class were so _____! Our teacher, Miss
                                            ADJECTIVE

_____, taught us all about matter and energy, atoms and
        LAST NAME

_____, and the difference between solids, _____, and gases. We
PLURAL NOUN   PLURAL NOUN

even got to watch a video about gravity and why things in outer _____
                                                                    NOUN

float but things on Earth fall to the _____! Our teacher says that next
                                        NOUN

week we're going to do our first experiment and that, if we want, some day this

year we can even dissect _____! My friend _____
                         ANIMAL (PLURAL)   PERSON IN ROOM

thought dissecting sounded gross, but I think it sounds really _____!
                                                                ADJECTIVE

I can't wait to _____ more about science next week.
                    VERB

MAD LIBS®

DOG ATE MY MAD LIBS

by Leigh Olsen

Mad Libs
An Imprint of Penguin Random House

INSTRUCTIONS

MAD LIBS® is a game for people who don't like games!
It can be played by one, two, three, four, or forty.

• RIDICULOUSLY SIMPLE DIRECTIONS

In this tablet you will find stories containing blank spaces where words are left out. One player, the READER, selects one of these stories. The READER does not tell anyone what the story is about. Instead, he/she asks the other players, the WRITERS, to give him/her words. These words are used to fill in the blank spaces in the story.

• TO PLAY

The READER asks each WRITER in turn to call out a word—an adjective or a noun or whatever the space calls for—and uses them to fill in the blank spaces in the story. The result is a MAD LIBS® game.

When the READER then reads the completed MAD LIBS® game to the other players, they will discover that they have written a story that is fantastic, screamingly funny, shocking, silly, crazy, or just plain dumb—depending upon which words each WRITER called out.

• EXAMPLE (*Before* and *After*)

"_____!" he said _____
    EXCLAMATION   ADVERB

as he jumped into his convertible _____ and
                                           NOUN

drove off with his _____ wife.
                   ADJECTIVE

"_____OUCH_____!" he said ____STUPIDLY____
    EXCLAMATION   ADVERB

as he jumped into his convertible ____CAT____ and
                                         NOUN

drove off with his ____BRAVE____ wife.
                   ADJECTIVE

MAD LIBS®

QUICK REVIEW

In case you have forgotten what adjectives, adverbs, nouns, and verbs are, here is a quick review:

An ADJECTIVE describes something or somebody. *Lumpy, soft, ugly, messy,* and *short* are adjectives.

An ADVERB tells how something is done. It modifies a verb and usually ends in "ly." *Modestly, stupidly, greedily,* and *carefully* are adverbs.

A NOUN is the name of a person, place, or thing. *Sidewalk, umbrella, bridle, bathtub,* and *nose* are nouns.

A VERB is an action word. *Run, pitch, jump,* and *swim* are verbs. Put the verbs in past tense if the directions say PAST TENSE. *Ran, pitched, jumped,* and *swam* are verbs in the past tense.

When we ask for A PLACE, we mean any sort of place: a country or city *(Spain, Cleveland)* or a room *(bathroom, kitchen).*

An EXCLAMATION or SILLY WORD is any sort of funny sound, gasp, grunt, or outcry, like *Wow!, Ouch!, Whomp!, Ick!,* and *Gadzooks!*

When we ask for specific words, like a NUMBER, a COLOR, an ANIMAL, or a PART OF THE BODY, we mean a word that is one of those things, like *seven, blue, horse,* or *head.*

When we ask for a PLURAL, it means more than one. For example, *cat* pluralized is *cats.*

MAD LIBS® is fun to play with friends, but you can also play it by yourself! To begin with, DO NOT look at the story on the page below. Fill in the blanks on this page with the words called for. Then, using the words you have selected, fill in the blank spaces in the story.

Now you've created your own hilarious MAD LIBS® game!

DOG DAYS

VERB ENDING IN "ING" _____

PART OF THE BODY _____

PLURAL NOUN _____

VERB _____

NOUN _____

A PLACE _____

ADVERB _____

NOUN _____

PLURAL NOUN _____

PART OF THE BODY _____

PART OF THE BODY _____

PLURAL NOUN _____

PLURAL NOUN _____

NOUN _____

MAD LIBS
DOG DAYS

Have you always wondered what it's like to be a dog?

7:00 a.m.: I wake up and my tummy is __cooking__. I bug my human
                                    VERB ENDING IN "ING"

by licking her __hot wener__ until I get a bowl of __bouncy boobies__.
              PART OF THE BODY   PLURAL NOUN

7:30 a.m.: Potty time! My human takes me outside to __peeing__ on a/an
                                                    VERB

__gummy bear__.
  NOUN

8:00 a.m.: My human leaves to go to (the) __coch land__. I am sad and pout
                                          A PLACE

__quickly__.
  ADVERB

9:00 a.m.: Naptime. I cuddle on my favorite __sprinkles__ and dream about
                                            NOUN

chasing __cherries__.
        PLURAL NOUN

6:00 p.m.: MY HUMAN IS HOME! FINALLY! I wag my __tounge__
                                               PART OF THE BODY

back and forth, and give my human kisses on the __butt crach__.
                                                PART OF THE BODY

6:30 p.m.: My human takes me for a walk, and I sniff lots of __poo holes__.
                                                             PLURAL NOUN

7:00 p.m.: Dinnertime! Eating __weiner holes__ is my favorite!
                              PLURAL NOUN

9:00 p.m.: I snuggle up next to my human and fall asleep, happy as

a/an __apple__.
     NOUN

poo pee doohie

MAD LIBS® is fun to play with friends, but you can also play it by yourself! To begin with, DO NOT look at the story on the page below. Fill in the blanks on this page with the words called for. Then, using the words you have selected, fill in the blank spaces in the story.

Now you've created your own hilarious MAD LIBS® game!

WHO'S THAT DOG?, PART 1

A PLACE _____

NOUN _____

PLURAL NOUN _____

VERB _____

VERB ENDING IN "ING" _____

ADJECTIVE _____

ADJECTIVE _____

ADJECTIVE _____

NOUN _____

ADJECTIVE _____

ADJECTIVE _____

VERB _____

A PLACE _____

NOUN _____

With hundreds of breeds of dogs in (the) _____SF_____, there's one for every
_{A PLACE}

kind of _____thunderthishs_____. Here are a few popular breeds:
_{NOUN}

Golden retriever: The golden retriever is one of the most popular family

_____r_____. Intelligent and eager to _____, the golden retriever
_{PLURAL NOUN} _{VERB}

makes an excellent _____ companion, and is also a/an
_{VERB ENDING IN "ING"}

_____ guide dog.
_{ADJECTIVE}

Pug: The pug is a lot of dog in a very _____ package. It is known
_{ADJECTIVE}

for being loving, outgoing, and _____. And it snores like a freight
_{ADJECTIVE}

_____!
_{NOUN}

Siberian husky: The husky was bred to pull _____ sleds, and it is
_{ADJECTIVE}

known for its _____ endurance and willingness to _____.
_{ADJECTIVE} _{VERB}

German shepherd: The German shepherd is not only the most popular police,

guard, and military dog in (the) _____, it is also a loving family
_{A PLACE}

_____.
_{NOUN}

MAD LIBS® is fun to play with friends, but you can also play it by yourself! To begin with, DO NOT look at the story on the page below. Fill in the blanks on this page with the words called for. Then, using the words you have selected, fill in the blank spaces in the story.

Now you've created your own hilarious MAD LIBS® game!

FAMOUS FIDOS: RIN TIN TIN

NOUN _____

PERSON IN ROOM _____

A PLACE _____

VERB _____

CELEBRITY _____

PERSON IN ROOM _____

ADJECTIVE _____

A PLACE _____

NOUN _____

NOUN _____

ADJECTIVE _____

PLURAL NOUN _____

NOUN _____

Rin Tin Tin was the biggest movie-star pooch to ever grace the silver

_____. During World War I, Rin Tin Tin's owner and future
    NOUN

trainer, _____, discovered the German shepherd puppy on a war-
         PERSON IN ROOM

torn battlefield in (the) _____. He brought Rin Tin Tin back
                          A PLACE

to the United States, trained him to _____, and brought him to
                                     VERB

Hollywood, home to celebrities like _____ and _____.
                                    CELEBRITY   PERSON IN ROOM

Soon, Rin Tin Tin began to receive _____ roles in silent films!
                                   ADJECTIVE

He quickly became one of the most famous stars in (the) _____.
                                                        A PLACE

In 1929, Rin Tin Tin even received the most votes for the Academy Award

for Best _____—but the Academy decided to give the award to
         NOUN

a/an _____ instead. All in all, this _____ dog starred in
     NOUN   ADJECTIVE

twenty-seven major motion _____. He even has his own star on the
                          PLURAL NOUN

Hollywood Walk of _____!
                  NOUN

MAD LIBS® is fun to play with friends, but you can also play it by yourself! To begin with, DO NOT look at the story on the page below. Fill in the blanks on this page with the words called for. Then, using the words you have selected, fill in the blank spaces in the story.

Now you've created your own hilarious MAD LIBS® game!

ODE TO THE MUTT

ADJECTIVE _____

PART OF THE BODY _____

PLURAL NOUN _____

PLURAL NOUN _____

PLURAL NOUN _____

NOUN _____

PART OF THE BODY _____

NOUN _____

NOUN _____

A PLACE _____

ANIMAL _____

ADJECTIVE _____

A little bit of this and a little bit of that, the mutt is a/an _____
ADJECTIVE

mixed-breed pup that will warm your _____ and chase your
PART OF THE BODY

_____ away. First of all, mutts are just like snowflakes—no two
PLURAL NOUN

_____ are alike! Mutts come in all shapes and _____.
PLURAL NOUN   PLURAL NOUN

Big ones, small ones, fluffy ones, and scruffy ones—there's a mutt for every

_____. Mutts have a special way of worming their way into your
NOUN

_____. There are millions in shelters that need your love and
PART OF THE BODY

_____. They need your love more than the average _____,
NOUN   NOUN

and they'll love you to (the) _____ and back! So next time you are
A PLACE

thinking about bringing home a new _____, consider adopting a/an
ANIMAL

_____ mutt!
ADJECTIVE

MAD LIBS® is fun to play with friends, but you can also play it by yourself! To begin with, DO NOT look at the story on the page below. Fill in the blanks on this page with the words called for. Then, using the words you have selected, fill in the blank spaces in the story.

Now you've created your own hilarious MAD LIBS® game!

BEGGING 101

NOUN _____

ADJECTIVE _____

PLURAL NOUN _____

NOUN _____

NOUN _____

PART OF THE BODY (PLURAL) _____

ADJECTIVE _____

PART OF THE BODY (PLURAL) _____

ADVERB _____

ADJECTIVE _____

NOUN _____

TYPE OF FOOD _____

PERSON IN ROOM _____

MAD LIBS

BEGGING 101

Are your humans cooking a delicious-smelling _____? Learn to
                                              NOUN

beg like a pro with these _____ tips, and you'll be eating tasty
                          ADJECTIVE

_____ in no time!
PLURAL NOUN

• Identify the weakest _____ at the dinner table. Who is the most likely
                       NOUN

  to sneak you a/an _____? Sit as close to that person as possible.
                    NOUN

• Stare up at your target with your biggest, saddest puppy-dog

  _____. If possible, think of something that makes you
  PART OF THE BODY (PLURAL)

  feel _____ so you can work up some tears.
       ADJECTIVE

• Squint your _____ so you look extra weak and hungry.
              PART OF THE BODY (PLURAL)

  Lie down on the ground and pout _____. Basically, make yourself
                                  ADVERB

  look as pathetic and _____ as possible.
                       ADJECTIVE

• Still not getting any food? Try crying like a/an _____.
                                                   NOUN

• If all else fails, grab that delicious _____ with your teeth and
                                         TYPE OF FOOD

  make a run for it—quick! Before _____ catches you!
                                  PERSON IN ROOM

MAD LIBS® is fun to play with friends, but you can also play it by yourself! To begin with, DO NOT look at the story on the page below. Fill in the blanks on this page with the words called for. Then, using the words you have selected, fill in the blank spaces in the story.

Now you've created your own hilarious MAD LIBS® game!

DOGGY DREAMS

ADJECTIVE _____

PART OF THE BODY (PLURAL) _____

ADVERB _____

ADJECTIVE _____

EXCLAMATION _____

VERB ENDING IN "ING" _____

NOUN _____

PART OF THE BODY (PLURAL) _____

EXCLAMATION _____

NOUN _____

SAME NOUN _____

PLURAL NOUN _____

VERB _____

PART OF THE BODY (PLURAL) _____

PLURAL NOUN _____

PERSON IN ROOM _____

PART OF THE BODY _____

ADJECTIVE _____

MAD LIBS®
DOGGY DREAMS

You know what it looks like when your sleeping dog is having a/an __Soft__
ADJECTIVE

dream: Their tail swishes, their __boobies__ twitch, and they
PART OF THE BODY (PLURAL)

bark __hungrly__. But what do dogs dream about? Here's one dog's
ADVERB

__hairy__ dream:
ADJECTIVE

__Oh my__! What's that little flash of white fur __running__
EXCLAMATION   VERB ENDING IN "ING"

in my backyard? It's a bunny __parrot__! I have to chase it! I run, run,
NOUN

run, as fast my __weiner balls__ will carry me. Oh, __daddy pig__!
PART OF THE BODY (PLURAL)   EXCLAMATION

The bunny has hidden in a/an __spoon__! I sniff the __spoon__,
NOUN   SAME NOUN

and sure enough, it's in there with a den of baby __horses__! I want
PLURAL NOUN

to play with them so bad, I could __ridding__! I bark at the top of my
VERB

__bushies__. Come out and play, you fluffy little __curling-irons__!
PART OF THE BODY (PLURAL)   PLURAL NOUN

                                    hole
But before I can, __ms. Potato hol__ scratches my __Butt hole__ and wakes
PERSON IN ROOM   PART OF THE BODY

me up. It was all just a/an __dirty__ dream!
ADJECTIVE

MAD LIBS® is fun to play with friends, but you can also play it by yourself! To begin with, DO NOT look at the story on the page below. Fill in the blanks on this page with the words called for. Then, using the words you have selected, fill in the blank spaces in the story.

Now you've created your own hilarious MAD LIBS® game!

WHO'S THAT DOG?, PART 2

ADJECTIVE _____

VERB _____

ADJECTIVE _____

ADJECTIVE _____

PART OF THE BODY (PLURAL) _____

ADJECTIVE _____

ADJECTIVE _____

PLURAL NOUN _____

ADJECTIVE _____

PLURAL NOUN _____

NOUN _____

NOUN _____

More _____ dog breeds for you to love and _____!
     ADJECTIVE   VERB

Poodle: The curly-haired poodle, best known for its _____ haircut,
                                               ADJECTIVE

is exceptionally smart and _____.
                         ADJECTIVE

Dachshund: Known for its long body and short _____,
                                PART OF THE BODY (PLURAL)

the dachshund has a friendly personality and a/an _____ sense of
                                               ADJECTIVE

smell.

Beagle: This hunting dog is happy-go-_____, friendly, and loves
                                   ADJECTIVE

the company of humans and other _____.
                                 PLURAL NOUN

Great Dane: The gentle Great Dane, famous for its _____ size, is
                                         ADJECTIVE

also known as "the king of _____."
                            PLURAL NOUN

Chihuahua: This sassy little _____, often called a "purse dog," is a
                               NOUN

big dog in a little _____.
                  NOUN

MAD LIBS® is fun to play with friends, but you can also play it by yourself! To begin with, DO NOT look at the story on the page below. Fill in the blanks on this page with the words called for. Then, using the words you have selected, fill in the blank spaces in the story.

Now you've created your own hilarious MAD LIBS® game!

FAMOUS FIDOS: LASSIE

ADJECTIVE _____

ADJECTIVE _____

A PLACE _____

PERSON IN ROOM (MALE) _____

ADJECTIVE _____

ADJECTIVE _____

VERB _____

ADVERB _____

PERSON IN ROOM (MALE) _____

NOUN _____

NOUN _____

NOUN _____

ADJECTIVE _____

NOUN _____

MAD LIBS®
FAMOUS FIDOS: LASSIE

Lassie the collie was famous for her heroics on television and the

_____ screen. On the TV show *Lassie*, the collie lived in
   ADJECTIVE

a/an _____ farming community in (the) _____. Lassie
    ADJECTIVE   A PLACE

belonged to an eleven-year-old boy named _____, as well as
                              PERSON IN ROOM (MALE)

his mother and _____ grandfather. Whenever the _____
               ADJECTIVE   ADJECTIVE

boy got into trouble, Lassie would _____ to the rescue, or she would
                              VERB

run and find help. "BARK, BARK!" Lassie would say _____.
                                         ADVERB

"What's that, girl?" the person would ask. "Little _____ fell
                                PERSON IN ROOM (MALE)

down a/an _____?" Quick as a/an _____, the trapped
          NOUN   NOUN

_____ would be safe and _____. And once again, Lassie
   NOUN   ADJECTIVE

saved the _____!
       NOUN

MAD LIBS® is fun to play with friends, but you can also play it by yourself! To begin with, DO NOT look at the story on the page below. Fill in the blanks on this page with the words called for. Then, using the words you have selected, fill in the blank spaces in the story.

Now you've created your own hilarious MAD LIBS® game!

HAIL TO THE POOCH

PERSON IN ROOM _____

ADJECTIVE _____

ADJECTIVE _____

PLURAL NOUN _____

TYPE OF FOOD _____

NOUN _____

ADJECTIVE _____

ADJECTIVE _____

NOUN _____

NOUN _____

CELEBRITY _____

NOUN _____

MAD LIBS
HAIL TO THE POOCH

From George Washington to _____ to Barack Obama, many
PERSON IN ROOM

United States presidents have been _____ dog lovers. Here's a list of
ADJECTIVE

_____ First Dogs:
ADJECTIVE

- **Laddie Boy:** Warren G. Harding once invited neighborhood _____
  PLURAL NOUN

  to the White House for his Airedale terrier's birthday party, where they ate

  _____ made of dog biscuits!
  TYPE OF FOOD

- **Fala:** Franklin Delano Roosevelt's beloved Scottish terrier was

  named after an Army _____ and had his own _____
  NOUN   ADJECTIVE

  secretary. Fala even starred in a/an _____ movie!
  ADJECTIVE

- **Millie:** George H. W. Bush's springer spaniel published her own book,

  ghostwritten by the First _____, which sold more copies than
  NOUN

  President Bush's _____!
  NOUN

- **Bo and Sunny:** Barack Obama received Bo the Portuguese water dog as a

  gift from _____. A few years later, the First Family got Sunny,
  CELEBRITY

  another Portuguese water _____.
  NOUN

MAD LIBS® is fun to play with friends, but you can also play it by yourself! To begin with, DO NOT look at the story on the page below. Fill in the blanks on this page with the words called for. Then, using the words you have selected, fill in the blank spaces in the story.

Now you've created your own hilarious MAD LIBS® game!

CANINE CAREERS

PLURAL NOUN _____

ADJECTIVE _____

PART OF THE BODY _____

A PLACE _____

A PLACE _____

ADJECTIVE _____

PLURAL NOUN _____

PART OF THE BODY (PLURAL) _____

PLURAL NOUN _____

PLURAL NOUN _____

ADJECTIVE _____

ADJECTIVE _____

PART OF THE BODY (PLURAL) _____

PLURAL NOUN _____

Not all dogs nap and play with their toy ___blocks___ all day. Some dogs

PLURAL NOUN

have ___bushy___ jobs!

ADJECTIVE

- **Guide dogs:** Guide dogs, or Seeing ___crotch___ dogs, help lead

PART OF THE BODY

the blind where they need to go, like to (the) ___disneyland___ or (the)

A PLACE

___Johnny Depps hole___ ♡

A PLACE

- **Military dogs:** These dogs help troops in ___bullhy___ military

ADJECTIVE

missions. They act as guard dogs, looking out for ___boots___, and

PLURAL NOUN

they use their powerful ___weiners___ to sniff out dangerous

PART OF THE BODY (PLURAL)

___bubble blowers___. US Air Force dogs even jump out of flying ___garbage cans___

PLURAL NOUN — PLURAL NOUN

with their airmen!

- **Search-and-rescue dogs:** In a/an ___dancing___ disaster or

ADJECTIVE

in the ___hairy___ wilderness, these dogs use their powerful

ADJECTIVE

___Butt cheevis___ to help track down missing ___christmas trees___

PART OF THE BODY (PLURAL) — PLURAL NOUN

MAD LIBS® is fun to play with friends, but you can also play it by yourself! To begin with, DO NOT look at the story on the page below. Fill in the blanks on this page with the words called for. Then, using the words you have selected, fill in the blank spaces in the story.

Now you've created your own hilarious MAD LIBS® game!

DIVA DOG

ADJECTIVE _____

NOUN _____

PART OF THE BODY _____

SILLY WORD _____

SAME SILLY WORD _____

A PLACE _____

NOUN _____

NOUN _____

NOUN _____

PART OF THE BODY _____

ADJECTIVE _____

VERB ENDING IN "S" _____

ADJECTIVE _____

PART OF THE BODY _____

ADJECTIVE _____

NOUN _____

MAD LIBS
DIVA DOG

Who's that _____ pooch with the fluffy little _____
         ADJECTIVE   NOUN

and the cute _____? Why, that's Little Miss _____!
          PART OF THE BODY   SILLY WORD

Little Miss _____ is famous throughout (the) _____.
         SAME SILLY WORD   A PLACE

Her _____ is splashed all over the Internet, and in books and
     NOUN

magazines like _____ *Weekly* and *Life &* _____. Little
           NOUN   NOUN

Miss can't go anywhere without someone recognizing her _____!
                                         PART OF THE BODY

Luckily, Little Miss likes attention from the _____ pup-parazzi. She
                                   ADJECTIVE

_____ for the cameras, and greets all her _____ fans with
VERB ENDING IN "S"   ADJECTIVE

a smile on her _____. After all, without her _____ fans,
         PART OF THE BODY   ADJECTIVE

Little Miss would be just another cute face in the _____!
                                          NOUN

MAD LIBS® is fun to play with friends, but you can also play it by yourself! To begin with, DO NOT look at the story on the page below. Fill in the blanks on this page with the words called for. Then, using the words you have selected, fill in the blank spaces in the story.

Now you've created your own hilarious MAD LIBS® game!

WHO'S THAT DOG?, PART 3

NOUN _____

ADJECTIVE _____

ANIMAL (PLURAL) _____

NOUN _____

NOUN _____

PART OF THE BODY _____

NOUN _____

PART OF THE BODY _____

NOUN _____

PLURAL NOUN _____

VERB ENDING IN "ING" _____

PLURAL NOUN _____

PART OF THE BODY _____

NOUN _____

PLURAL NOUN _____

A few more dog breeds to brighten your _____!

NOUN

Yorkshire terrier: Yorkies may be small, but they are brave and _____.

ADJECTIVE

Yorkies were originally bred to hunt _____ in _____

ANIMAL (PLURAL) NOUN

factories!

Doberman pinscher: The Doberman is a muscular _____. With

NOUN

its intelligent _____, the Doberman is often trained as a police

PART OF THE BODY

_____.

NOUN

Shih tzu: The shih tzu has a long and luxurious _____. This

PART OF THE BODY

playful _____ is usually friendly toward all _____.

NOUN PLURAL NOUN

Australian shepherd: Aussies are very energetic and require daily

_____ to be happy. They are great at herding crowds of

VERB ENDING IN "ING"

_____ on the farm.

PLURAL NOUN

Pomeranian: The Pomeranian has a big, fluffy _____ to match

PART OF THE BODY

its outgoing _____. This intelligent little dog loves to please its

NOUN

_____.

PLURAL NOUN

MAD LIBS® is fun to play with friends, but you can also play it by yourself! To begin with, DO NOT look at the story on the page below. Fill in the blanks on this page with the words called for. Then, using the words you have selected, fill in the blank spaces in the story.

Now you've created your own hilarious MAD LIBS® game!

POOCH PALACE

ADJECTIVE _____

ANIMAL _____

NOUN _____

TYPE OF LIQUID _____

ADJECTIVE _____

PART OF THE BODY _____

OCCUPATION _____

NOUN _____

SILLY WORD _____

PART OF THE BODY _____

A PLACE _____

PART OF THE BODY _____

NOUN _____

PLURAL NOUN _____

MAD LIBS®
POOCH PALACE

Welcome to the __Succulent__ Pooch Palace, the dog spa for all your
ADJECTIVE

grooming needs! Below is our spa menu. How do you want to pamper your

__lamb whak__ today?
ANIMAL

- **Paw-dicure:** We'll not only trim your __bushy__'s nails, we'll paint
NOUN

them with a coat of __pee__ so your pup looks __obese__
TYPE OF LIQUID   ADJECTIVE

and stylish.

- **Pup massage:** If your dog is in need of some rest and relaxation,

a/an __wener__ massage might be just what the __wener inspekr__
PART OF THE BODY   OCCUPATION

ordered!

- **Doggy 'do:** Is your __bushy__ looking shaggy? Our renowned stylist,
NOUN

Pierre __malarky__, gives the best __booby__-cut this side of
SILLY WORD   PART OF THE BODY

(the) __your moms ass__.
A PLACE

- **Fur dye:** If you've ever wanted your dog's __toe knuckles__ to match the
PART OF THE BODY

color of your favorite __tongue__, look no further. The Pooch Palace
NOUN

will make all your __colonoscopies__ come true!
PLURAL NOUN

MAD LIBS® is fun to play with friends, but you can also play it by yourself! To begin with, DO NOT look at the story on the page below. Fill in the blanks on this page with the words called for. Then, using the words you have selected, fill in the blank spaces in the story.

Now you've created your own hilarious MAD LIBS® game!

HOMEWARD BOUND

A PLACE _____

ADJECTIVE _____

PERSON IN ROOM (FEMALE) _____

NUMBER _____

VERB (PAST TENSE) _____

PERSON IN ROOM _____

PART OF THE BODY (PLURAL) _____

NOUN _____

ADJECTIVE _____

NOUN _____

NOUN _____

PERSON IN ROOM _____

TYPE OF LIQUID _____

ADJECTIVE _____

MAD LIBS
HOMEWARD BOUND

In (the) _____ today, one _____ family was reunited with
 A PLACE   ADJECTIVE

their beloved dog, _____, who made her way home after
                    PERSON IN ROOM (FEMALE)

being missing for _____ days. "She just showed up on our front
                     NUMBER

doorstep this morning and _____," said _____. "We
                           VERB (PAST TENSE)   PERSON IN ROOM

couldn't believe our _____." The family dog disappeared
                      PART OF THE BODY (PLURAL)

after leaving the family's front yard to chase after a wild _____ one
                                                              NOUN

afternoon, and the family has been worried _____ ever since. They
                                             ADJECTIVE

put up "lost _____" posters all over the neighborhood, and even
              NOUN

put a/an _____ in the local newspaper. "We have no idea where
          NOUN

she's been all this time," said _____. "We're just happier than
                                 PERSON IN ROOM

a pig in _____ that she's home again. We can't wait to spoil her
          TYPE OF LIQUID

_____."
 ADJECTIVE

MAD LIBS® is fun to play with friends, but you can also play it by yourself! To begin with, DO NOT look at the story on the page below. Fill in the blanks on this page with the words called for. Then, using the words you have selected, fill in the blank spaces in the story.

Now you've created your own hilarious MAD LIBS® game!

WONDER DOG

VERB _____

ADJECTIVE _____

PART OF THE BODY (PLURAL) _____

ADJECTIVE _____

NOUN _____

PART OF THE BODY _____

VERB ENDING IN "ING" _____

ADJECTIVE _____

PART OF THE BODY (PLURAL) _____

ADVERB _____

NOUN _____

ADJECTIVE _____

PLURAL NOUN _____

ADJECTIVE _____

ADJECTIVE _____

ADVERB _____

VERB _____

MAD LIBS®
WONDER DOG

Lots of dogs can sit, stay, and _____ . But not many can do these
<u>VERB</u>

_____ tricks!
<u>ADJECTIVE</u>

- **Play dead:** When you say, "Bang! Bang!" some dogs will roll onto their

_____ and act _____ . This act is sure to
<u>PART OF THE BODY (PLURAL)</u>   <u>ADJECTIVE</u>

tickle your funny _____ .
<u>NOUN</u>

- **Dance:** Your dog may know how to wag its _____ to the beat,
<u>PART OF THE BODY</u>

but can it dance like nobody's _____? A dog that knows
<u>VERB ENDING IN "ING"</u>

this _____ trick can stand on its hind _____
<u>ADJECTIVE</u>   <u>PART OF THE BODY (PLURAL)</u>

and spin around _____!
<u>ADVERB</u>

- **Bring my slippers:** Feeling lazy and don't want to get out of your

comfy _____? Ask your dog to do it! If your dog knows this
<u>NOUN</u>

_____ trick, say, "Bring my slippers," and your dog will bring
<u>ADJECTIVE</u>

your _____ to you!
<u>PLURAL NOUN</u>

- **Jump rope:** If your dog knows this _____ trick, grab a/an
<u>ADJECTIVE</u>

_____ rope and a partner, swing the rope _____, and
<u>ADJECTIVE</u>   <u>ADVERB</u>

your dog will _____ over it again and again!
<u>VERB</u>

MAD LIBS® is fun to play with friends, but you can also play it by yourself! To begin with, DO NOT look at the story on the page below. Fill in the blanks on this page with the words called for. Then, using the words you have selected, fill in the blank spaces in the story.

Now you've created your own hilarious MAD LIBS® game!

DOG'S DELIGHT

VERB ENDING IN "S" _____

PART OF THE BODY _____

ADJECTIVE _____

PLURAL NOUN _____

ANIMAL _____

VERB _____

VERB _____

PLURAL NOUN _____

NOUN _____

PLURAL NOUN _____

NOUN _____

NOUN _____

NOUN _____

PLURAL NOUN _____

NOUN _____

ADJECTIVE _____

PART OF THE BODY _____

NOUN _____

MAD LIBS
DOG'S DELIGHT

You know your dog is happy when it _____ and wags its
_____ VERB ENDING IN "S" _____

_____ back and forth. If you want your dog to be _____
___ PART OF THE BODY ___ _____ ADJECTIVE _____

as a clam at all times, try any of the following _____. It's a countdown
_____ PLURAL NOUN _____

of your _____'s favorite things!
_____ ANIMAL _____

5. **Walks:** Though some dogs would rather stay home and _____,
_____ VERB _____

most dogs love to go for walks to _____ on fire hydrants and sniff
_____ VERB _____

_____.
___ PLURAL NOUN ___

4. **Naps:** Dogs love to curl up on a/an _____ and dream about
_____ NOUN _____

_____—especially if they're cuddling with their favorite
___ PLURAL NOUN ___

_____.
___ NOUN ___

3. **Playtime:** Fidos love to play fetch with a/an _____ or run around
_____ NOUN _____

chasing a/an _____. Sometimes, _____ just wanna
_____ NOUN _____ _____ PLURAL NOUN _____

have fun!

2. **Food:** Whether it's a can of dog _____ or _____ table
_____ NOUN _____ _____ ADJECTIVE _____

scraps, dogs love to eat. The way to a dog's heart is definitely through its

_____!
___ PART OF THE BODY ___

1. **You!:** After all, a dog is a/an _____'s best friend.
_____ NOUN _____

MAD LIBS® is fun to play with friends, but you can also play it by yourself! To begin with, DO NOT look at the story on the page below. Fill in the blanks on this page with the words called for. Then, using the words you have selected, fill in the blank spaces in the story.

Now you've created your own hilarious MAD LIBS® game!

WHO'S THAT DOG?, PART 4

VERB _____

COLOR _____

NOUN _____

VERB ENDING IN "ING" _____

NOUN _____

PART OF THE BODY _____

VERB _____

PART OF THE BODY (PLURAL) _____

A PLACE _____

NUMBER _____

ADJECTIVE _____

VERB _____

ADJECTIVE _____

PLURAL NOUN _____

A PLACE _____

ADJECTIVE _____

MAD LIBS®
WHO'S THAT DOG?, PART 4

A final few furry dog breeds for you to love and _____ :
                                                    VERB

Collie: The brown and _____ collie is a friendly family _____ ,
                            COLOR   NOUN

known for its grace and elegance when _____ .
                                       VERB ENDING IN "ING"

Dalmation: This black-and-white _____ is the only dog breed
                                     NOUN

with spots on its _____ . They have lots of energy and need to
                   PART OF THE BODY

_____ a lot.
  VERB

Pembroke Welsh corgi: The corgi is known for its very short

_____ and stout body. The queen of (the) _____
PART OF THE BODY (PLURAL)   A PLACE

owns _____ corgis!
        NUMBER

Miniature schnauzer: The miniature schnauzer may be small, but it is

a/an _____ guard dog, and will _____ at the sign of any
      ADJECTIVE   VERB

_____ intruder.
  ADJECTIVE

St. Bernard: The St. Bernard was originally used to hunt for _____
                                                                 PLURAL NOUN

during snowstorms in (the) _____ . They are very gentle and
                           A PLACE

_____ .
  ADJECTIVE

MAD LIBS® is fun to play with friends, but you can also play it by yourself! To begin with, DO NOT look at the story on the page below. Fill in the blanks on this page with the words called for. Then, using the words you have selected, fill in the blank spaces in the story.

Now you've created your own hilarious MAD LIBS® game!

LET'S GO FOR A RIDE!

PERSON IN ROOM _____

PART OF THE BODY (PLURAL) _____

PART OF THE BODY (PLURAL) _____

ADJECTIVE _____

NOUN _____

NOUN _____

PART OF THE BODY _____

PLURAL NOUN _____

PART OF THE BODY (PLURAL) _____

PART OF THE BODY _____

ADJECTIVE _____

ADVERB _____

NOUN _____

PERSON IN ROOM _____

EXCLAMATION _____

NOUN _____

MAD LIBS®
LET'S GO FOR A RIDE!

"_chick fil A weaner head_, come!" I hear my owner call out. My _Bushies_
PERSON IN ROOM · PART OF THE BODY (PLURAL)

perk up—is that the sound of the garage door opening? Suddenly, I am excited

from my head to my _Balls_. Can it be? Am I going
PART OF THE BODY (PLURAL)

for a/an _spicy_ car ride? I bound to the door, where I see my owner
ADJECTIVE

getting into the car. She pats the seat. "Come on, _corn cob_!" she calls.
NOUN

This is the best _juices_ ever! I hop happily into the front seat and
NOUN

immediately stick my _weaner_ out of the car window. We drive
PART OF THE BODY

away down the street, passing houses and mailboxes and _backracks_.
PLURAL NOUN

I can feel the wind in my _Bobbies_ and the sun on my
PART OF THE BODY (PLURAL)

nut sack, and everything smells ~~diddly~~ _spooky_. Where are we
PART OF THE BODY · ADJECTIVE

going? I wonder _diddly_. So you can imagine my _Puddles_ as
ADVERB · NOUN

we pulled into the parking lot of Dr. _sniffer hole_'s office. We're going to
PERSON IN ROOM

the vet? _holy moly_! This is the worst _jolly rancher_ ever!
EXCLAMATION · NOUN

From DOG ATE MY MAD LIBS® • Copyright © 2015 by Penguin Random House LLC.

MAD LIBS® is fun to play with friends, but you can also play it by yourself! To begin with, DO NOT look at the story on the page below. Fill in the blanks on this page with the words called for. Then, using the words you have selected, fill in the blank spaces in the story.

Now you've created your own hilarious MAD LIBS® game!

FAMOUS FIDOS: SCOOBY-DOO

NOUN _____

NOUN _____

PERSON IN ROOM (FEMALE) _____

PERSON IN ROOM (MALE) _____

NOUN _____

ADJECTIVE _____

PLURAL NOUN _____

PLURAL NOUN _____

SAME PLURAL NOUN _____

PLURAL NOUN _____

PLURAL NOUN _____

ADJECTIVE _____

SILLY WORD _____

MAD LIBS

FAMOUS FIDOS: SCOOBY-DOO

Scooby-Doo is the star of the animated television _____ *Scooby-*
                                                    NOUN

Doo, Where Are You! Scooby-Doo, also known as Scooby, is a talking

_____ who solves mysteries along with four teenagers named Shaggy,
    NOUN

Daphne, _____, and _____. Scooby-
        PERSON IN ROOM (FEMALE)   PERSON IN ROOM (MALE)

Doo, a Great _____, belongs to his _____ friend, Shaggy.
                 NOUN   ADJECTIVE

Much like Shaggy, Scooby is scared of _____ and is always hungry
                                         PLURAL NOUN

for cookies called Scooby _____. Luckily, the prospect of eating
                               PLURAL NOUN

Scooby _____ and keeping his friends safe from _____
         SAME PLURAL NOUN   PLURAL NOUN

helps Scooby to be brave and stand up to scary _____. Scooby and
                                                    PLURAL NOUN

his friends always solve the _____ mystery, and Scooby always ends
                                 ADJECTIVE

each episode by saying "_____-dooby-doo!"
                           SILLY WORD

MAD LIBS® is fun to play with friends, but you can also play it by yourself! To begin with, DO NOT look at the story on the page below. Fill in the blanks on this page with the words called for. Then, using the words you have selected, fill in the blank spaces in the story.

Now you've created your own hilarious MAD LIBS® game!

DOGS VERSUS CATS

ADJECTIVE _____

ADJECTIVE _____

PART OF THE BODY _____

NUMBER _____

ADJECTIVE _____

PLURAL NOUN _____

NOUN _____

PLURAL NOUN _____

PART OF THE BODY (PLURAL) _____

NOUN _____

PART OF THE BODY _____

NOUN _____

NOUN _____

NOUN _____

SAME NOUN _____

ADJECTIVE _____

NOUN _____

MAD LIBS
DOGS VERSUS CATS

Which are better, __Spicy__ cats or __glittery__ dogs? Anyone with
ADJECTIVE   ADJECTIVE

half a/an __Boobies__ knows that dogs are __8__ times better
PART OF THE BODY   NUMBER

than cats. Dogs are __firey__ companions, while cats only care about
ADJECTIVE

their own __Plums__. Dogs are loyal to their __hitty__, but cats
PLURAL NOUN   NOUN

will love whoever gives them __easter eggs__ to eat. Dogs like to have their
PLURAL NOUN

__weaners__ rubbed, while cats will bite your __Bushy__
PART OF THE BODY (PLURAL)   NOUN

if you try to put a/an __Butt hole__ on them. Most dogs love going for
PART OF THE BODY

rides in a/an __farts__, but cats just get sick all over your favorite
NOUN

__Sea horse__. Dogs love to play fetch with a/an __Porn bun__, but if
NOUN   NOUN

you throw a/an __Porn bun__ for a cat, it will just look at you like you're
SAME NOUN

__Juicy__. All in all, when it comes to dogs versus cats, only the dog is
ADJECTIVE

truly man's best __Juicy weaners__.
NOUN

From DOG ATE MY MAD LIBS® • Copyright © 2015 by Penguin Random House LLC.

MAD LIBS® is fun to play with friends, but you can also play it by yourself! To begin with, DO NOT look at the story on the page below. Fill in the blanks on this page with the words called for. Then, using the words you have selected, fill in the blank spaces in the story.

Now you've created your own hilarious MAD LIBS® game!

FOREVER HOME

LAST NAME _____

NOUN _____

ADJECTIVE _____

ADJECTIVE _____

PART OF THE BODY (PLURAL) _____

COLOR _____

PART OF THE BODY _____

ADJECTIVE _____

NOUN _____

A PLACE _____

ADJECTIVE _____

PLURAL NOUN _____

ADJECTIVE _____

ADJECTIVE _____

PART OF THE BODY _____

EXCLAMATION _____

ADVERB _____

MAD LIBS®
FOREVER HOME

When the _____ family went to the animal shelter,
                LAST NAME

they never knew they'd find a/an _____ like Rex. The family
                                    NOUN

looked at all the dogs before making this very _____ decision.
                                                  ADJECTIVE

Sure, the puppies were cute and _____, but one older dog stole the
                                  ADJECTIVE

family's _____. His name was Rex, and with his fuzzy
          PART OF THE BODY (PLURAL)

_____ fur, his crooked _____, and his _____
   COLOR   PART OF THE BODY   ADJECTIVE

personality, the family knew they'd found their new _____. Plus, by
                                                       NOUN

bringing Rex back to (the) _____ with them, they saved his life. Now
                            A PLACE

Rex would have a/an _____ place to sleep, _____ to eat, and
                      ADJECTIVE   PLURAL NOUN

a/an _____ family to call his own. And Rex would more than repay
       ADJECTIVE

his family with lots of _____ wet kisses on the _____
                          ADJECTIVE   PART OF THE BODY

and unconditional love. _____! Rex had found his forever home,
                           EXCLAMATION

and they all lived _____ ever after.
                     ADVERB

MAD LIBS®

MUCH ADO ABOUT MAD LIBS

by DW McCann

Mad Libs
An Imprint of Penguin Random House

MAD LIBS®

INSTRUCTIONS

MAD LIBS® is a game for people who don't like games!
It can be played by one, two, three, four, or forty.

• RIDICULOUSLY SIMPLE DIRECTIONS

In this tablet you will find stories containing blank spaces where words are left out.
One player, the READER, selects one of these stories. The READER does not tell anyone
what the story is about. Instead, he/she asks the other players, the WRITERS, to give
him/her words. These words are used to fill in the blank spaces in the story.

• TO PLAY

The READER asks each WRITER in turn to call out a word—an adjective or a noun or
whatever the space calls for—and uses them to fill in the blank spaces in the story. The
result is a MAD LIBS® game.

When the READER then reads the completed MAD LIBS® game to the other players,
they will discover that they have written a story that is fantastic, screamingly funny,
shocking, silly, crazy, or just plain dumb—depending upon which words each WRITER
called out.

• EXAMPLE (*Before* and *After*)

"_____!" he said _____
　　　　EXCLAMATION　　　　　　　　　　　　ADVERB

as he jumped into his convertible _____ and
　　　　　　　　　　　　　　　　　　　NOUN

drove off with his _____ wife.
　　　　　　　ADJECTIVE

"_____OUCH_____!" he said _____STUPIDLY_____
　　　　EXCLAMATION　　　　　　　　　　　　ADVERB

as he jumped into his convertible _____CAT_____ and
　　　　　　　　　　　　　　　　　　　NOUN

drove off with his _____BRAVE_____ wife.
　　　　　　　ADJECTIVE

QUICK REVIEW

In case you have forgotten what adjectives, adverbs, nouns, and verbs are, here is a quick review:

An ADJECTIVE describes something or somebody. *Lumpy, soft, ugly, messy,* and *short* are adjectives.

An ADVERB tells how something is done. It modifies a verb and usually ends in "ly." *Modestly, stupidly, greedily,* and *carefully* are adverbs.

A NOUN is the name of a person, place, or thing. *Sidewalk, umbrella, bridle, bathtub,* and *nose* are nouns.

A VERB is an action word. *Run, pitch, jump,* and *swim* are verbs. Put the verbs in past tense if the directions say PAST TENSE. *Ran, pitched, jumped,* and *swam* are verbs in the past tense.

When we ask for A PLACE, we mean any sort of place: a country or city *(Spain, Cleveland)* or a room *(bathroom, kitchen).*

An EXCLAMATION or SILLY WORD is any sort of funny sound, gasp, grunt, or outcry, like *Wow!, Ouch!, Whomp!, Ick!,* and *Gadzooks!*

When we ask for specific words, like a NUMBER, a COLOR, an ANIMAL, or a PART OF THE BODY, we mean a word that is one of those things, like *seven, blue, horse,* or *head.*

When we ask for a PLURAL, it means more than one. For example, *cat* pluralized is *cats.*

MAD LIBS® is fun to play with friends, but you can also play it by yourself! To begin with, DO NOT look at the story on the page below. Fill in the blanks on this page with the words called for. Then, using the words you have selected, fill in the blank spaces in the story.

Now you've created your own hilarious MAD LIBS® game!

AS YOU LIKE IT
(ACT 2, SCENE 7–PART 1)

NOUN _____

OCCUPATION (PLURAL) _____

VERB ENDING IN "S" _____

NUMBER _____

VERB ENDING IN "ING" _____

VERB ENDING IN "ING" _____

ADJECTIVE _____

ANIMAL _____

NOUN _____

ADJECTIVE _____

PART OF THE BODY _____

ADJECTIVE _____

ADJECTIVE _____

NOUN _____

Jaques: All the world's a/an _____,
_____NOUN_____

And all the men and women merely _____.
_____OCCUPATION (PLURAL)_____

They have their exits and their entrances,

And one man in his time _____ many parts,
_____VERB ENDING IN "S"_____

His acts being _____ ages. At first the infant,
_____NUMBER_____

_____ and puking in the nurse's arms.
_____VERB ENDING IN "ING"_____

Then the _____ schoolboy with his satchel
_____VERB ENDING IN "ING"_____

And _____ morning face, creeping like _____
_____ADJECTIVE_____   _____ANIMAL_____

Unwillingly to school. And then the lover,

Sighing like _____, with a/an _____ ballad
_____NOUN_____   _____ADJECTIVE_____

Made to his mistress' _____. Then a soldier,
_____PART OF THE BODY_____

Full of _____ oaths and bearded like the pard,
_____ADJECTIVE_____

Jealous in honor, sudden and _____ in quarrel,
_____ADJECTIVE_____

Seeking the bubble reputation

Even in the _____'s mouth.
_____NOUN_____

MAD LIBS® is fun to play with friends, but you can also play it by yourself! To begin with, DO NOT look at the story on the page below. Fill in the blanks on this page with the words called for. Then, using the words you have selected, fill in the blank spaces in the story.

Now you've created your own hilarious MAD LIBS® game!

AS YOU LIKE IT
(ACT 2, SCENE 7-PART 2)

TYPE OF FOOD _____

ADJECTIVE _____

ADJECTIVE _____

PLURAL NOUN _____

ADJECTIVE _____

PART OF THE BODY _____

NOUN _____

ADJECTIVE _____

NOUN _____

ADJECTIVE _____

NOUN _____

Jaques: And then the justice,

In fair round belly with good _____ lined,
<u>TYPE OF FOOD</u>

With eyes _____ and beard of _____ cut,
<u>ADJECTIVE</u>   <u>ADJECTIVE</u>

Full of wise _____ and modern instances;
<u>PLURAL NOUN</u>

And so he plays his part. The sixth age shifts

Into the _____ and slippered pantaloon
<u>ADJECTIVE</u>

With spectacles on _____ and pouch on side,
<u>PART OF THE BODY</u>

His youthful hose, well saved, a/an _____ too wide
<u>NOUN</u>

For his shrunk shank, and his _____ manly voice,
<u>ADJECTIVE</u>

Turning again toward childish treble, pipes

And whistles in his _____. Last scene of all,
<u>NOUN</u>

That ends this _____ eventful history,
<u>ADJECTIVE</u>

Is second childishness and mere oblivion,

Sans teeth, sans eyes, sans _____, sans everything.
<u>NOUN</u>

MAD LIBS® is fun to play with friends, but you can also play it by yourself! To begin with, DO NOT look at the story on the page below. Fill in the blanks on this page with the words called for. Then, using the words you have selected, fill in the blank spaces in the story.

Now you've created your own hilarious MAD LIBS® game!

SONNET #5

PLURAL NOUN _____

ADJECTIVE _____

PART OF THE BODY _____

PLURAL NOUN _____

ADJECTIVE _____

VERB ENDING IN "S" _____

ADJECTIVE _____

NOUN _____

ADJECTIVE _____

NOUN _____

NOUN _____

PLURAL NOUN _____

VERB _____

NOUN _____

MAD LIBS®
SONNET #5

Those _____ that with gentle work did frame
       PLURAL NOUN

The _____ gaze where every _____ doth dwell
   ADJECTIVE   PART OF THE BODY

Will play the _____ to the very same
          PLURAL NOUN

And that unfair which fairly doth excel;

For never-resting time leads summer on

To _____ winter and _____ him there,
  ADJECTIVE   VERB ENDING IN "S"

Sap checked with frost and _____ leaves quite gone,
                 ADJECTIVE

Beauty o'er-snowed and bareness everywhere.

Then, were not summer's _____ left
              NOUN

A/An _____ prisoner pent in walls of _____,
   ADJECTIVE   NOUN

Beauty's _____ with beauty were bereft,
      NOUN

Nor it nor no remembrance what it was.

But _____ distilled, though they with winter meet,
   PLURAL NOUN

_____ but their show; their _____ still lives sweet.
  VERB   NOUN

MAD LIBS® is fun to play with friends, but you can also play it by yourself! To begin with, DO NOT look at the story on the page below. Fill in the blanks on this page with the words called for. Then, using the words you have selected, fill in the blank spaces in the story.

Now you've created your own hilarious MAD LIBS® game!

HAMLET
(ACT 5, SCENE 1)

PART OF THE BODY _____

FIRST NAME (MALE) _____

ADJECTIVE _____

PART OF THE BODY _____

PART OF THE BODY (PLURAL) _____

VERB (PAST TENSE) _____

PLURAL NOUN _____

PLURAL NOUN _____

NOUN _____

VERB _____

A PLACE _____

VERB _____

PLURAL NOUN _____

(*Hamlet takes the* _____)
PART OF THE BODY

Alas, poor _____! I knew him, Horatio—a fellow of infinite jest,
FIRST NAME (MALE)

of most _____ fancy. He hath bore me on his _____ a thousand
ADJECTIVE   PART OF THE BODY

times, and now how abhorred in my imagination it is! My gorge rises at it. Here

hung those _____ that I have _____
PART OF THE BODY (PLURAL)   VERB (PAST TENSE)

I know not how oft. Where be your _____ now? your gambols? your
PLURAL NOUN

songs? your _____ of merriment that were wont to set the _____
PLURAL NOUN   NOUN

on a roar? Not one now to _____ your own grinning? Quite chapfallen?
VERB

Now get you to my lady's _____, and tell her, let her _____ an
A PLACE   VERB

inch thick, to this favor she must come. Make her laugh at _____.
PLURAL NOUN

MAD LIBS® is fun to play with friends, but you can also play it by yourself! To begin with, DO NOT look at the story on the page below. Fill in the blanks on this page with the words called for. Then, using the words you have selected, fill in the blank spaces in the story.

Now you've created your own hilarious MAD LIBS® game!

SONNET #18

NOUN _____

ADJECTIVE _____

PLURAL NOUN _____

ADJECTIVE _____

PLURAL NOUN _____

NOUN _____

PART OF THE BODY _____

NOUN _____

NOUN _____

SAME NOUN _____

NOUN _____

VERB _____

CELEBRITY _____

NOUN _____

VERB _____

PART OF THE BODY (PLURAL) _____

SILLY WORD _____

MAD LIBS®
SONNET #18

Shall I compare thee to a/an _____'s day?
<u>NOUN</u>

Thou art more _____ and more temperate.
<u>ADJECTIVE</u>

Rough _____ do shake the _____ _____ of May,
<u>PLURAL NOUN</u>   <u>ADJECTIVE</u>   <u>PLURAL NOUN</u>

And summer's _____ hath all too short a date.
<u>NOUN</u>

Sometime too hot the _____ of heaven shines,
<u>PART OF THE BODY</u>

And often is his gold _____ dimmed;
<u>NOUN</u>

And every _____ from _____ sometime declines,
<u>NOUN</u>   <u>SAME NOUN</u>

By chance or nature's changing _____ untrimmed.
<u>NOUN</u>

But thy eternal summer shall not _____
<u>VERB</u>

Nor lose possession of that fair thou ow'st,

Nor shall _____ brag thou wand'rest in his shade,
<u>CELEBRITY</u>

When in eternal lines to _____ thou grow'st.
<u>NOUN</u>

So long as men can _____ or _____ can see,
<u>VERB</u>   <u>PART OF THE BODY (PLURAL)</u>

So long lives this, and this gives _____ to thee.
<u>SILLY WORD</u>

MAD LIBS® is fun to play with friends, but you can also play it by yourself! To begin with, DO NOT look at the story on the page below. Fill in the blanks on this page with the words called for. Then, using the words you have selected, fill in the blank spaces in the story.

Now you've created your own hilarious MAD LIBS® game!

MACBETH
(ACT 4, SCENE 1)

PLURAL NOUN _____

ADJECTIVE _____

NUMBER _____

NOUN _____

ADJECTIVE _____

VERB _____

PART OF THE BODY _____

ANIMAL _____

NOUN _____

NOUN _____

ADJECTIVE _____

NOUN _____

VERB _____

ADJECTIVE _____

First Witch: Round about the cauldron go;

In the poisoned _____ throw.
PLURAL NOUN

Toad, that under _____ stone
ADJECTIVE

Days and nights has _____-one. . . .
NUMBER

All Three Witches: Double, double toil and trouble;

Fire burn, and _____ bubble.
NOUN

Second Witch: Fillet of a/an _____ snake
ADJECTIVE

In the cauldron _____ and bake.
VERB

_____ of newt and toe of frog,
PART OF THE BODY

Wool of _____ and tongue of dog. . . .
ANIMAL

Third Witch: Scale of dragon, _____ of wolf,
NOUN

Witches' mummy, _____ and gulf
NOUN

Of the _____ salt-sea shark,
ADJECTIVE

_____ of hemlock digged i' th' dark. . . .
NOUN

Second Witch: _____ it with a baboon's blood.
VERB

Then the charm is _____ and good.
ADJECTIVE

MAD LIBS® is fun to play with friends, but you can also play it by yourself! To begin with, DO NOT look at the story on the page below. Fill in the blanks on this page with the words called for. Then, using the words you have selected, fill in the blank spaces in the story.

Now you've created your own hilarious MAD LIBS® game!

SONNET #23

ADJECTIVE _____

NOUN _____

NOUN _____

ADJECTIVE _____

NOUN _____

ADJECTIVE _____

NOUN _____

NOUN _____

PLURAL NOUN _____

PLURAL NOUN _____

VERB ENDING IN "ING" _____

VERB _____

ADJECTIVE _____

VERB _____

MAD LIBS

SONNET #23

As a/an _____ actor on the stage
     ADJECTIVE

Who with his _____ is put beside his _____,
     NOUN   NOUN

Or some _____ thing replete with too much rage,
     ADJECTIVE

Whose strength's abundance weakens his own heart;

So I for fear of _____ forget to say
        NOUN

The _____ _____ of love's rite,
   ADJECTIVE   NOUN

And in mine own love's _____ seem to decay,
         NOUN

O'ercharged with burden of mine own love's might.

O, let my _____ be then the eloquence
    PLURAL NOUN

And dumb _____ of my _____ breast,
    PLURAL NOUN   VERB ENDING IN "ING"

Who _____ for love and look for recompense
   VERB

More than that tongue that more hath more expressed.

O, learn to read what _____ love hath writ.
        ADJECTIVE

To _____ with eyes belongs to love's fine wit.
  VERB

MAD LIBS® is fun to play with friends, but you can also play it by yourself! To begin with, DO NOT look at the story on the page below. Fill in the blanks on this page with the words called for. Then, using the words you have selected, fill in the blank spaces in the story.

Now you've created your own hilarious MAD LIBS® game!

JULIUS CAESAR
(ACT 3, SCENE 2)

PLURAL NOUN _____

PART OF THE BODY (PLURAL) _____

VERB _____

PLURAL NOUN _____

PERSON IN ROOM _____

ADJECTIVE _____

ADVERB _____

PERSON IN ROOM _____

SAME PERSON IN ROOM _____

NOUN _____

NOUN _____

PERSON IN ROOM _____

PLURAL NOUN _____

ADJECTIVE _____

Antony: Friends, Romans, _____, lend me your
PLURAL NOUN

_____.
PART OF THE BODY (PLURAL)

I come to bury Caesar, not to _____ him.
VERB

The evil that men do lives after them;

The good is oft interrèd with their _____.
PLURAL NOUN

So let it be with Caesar. The noble _____
PERSON IN ROOM

Hath told you Caesar was ambitious.

If it were so, it was a/an _____ fault,
ADJECTIVE

And _____ hath Caesar answered it.
ADVERB

Here, under leave of _____ and the rest
PERSON IN ROOM

(For _____ is an honorable _____ . . . .)
SAME PERSON IN ROOM   NOUN

Come I to speak in Caesar's funeral.

He was my _____, faithful and just to me,
NOUN

But _____ says he was ambitious. . . .
PERSON IN ROOM

He hath brought many _____ home to Rome,
PLURAL NOUN

Whose ransoms did the _____ coffers fill.
ADJECTIVE

Did this in Caesar seem ambitious?

MAD LIBS® is fun to play with friends, but you can also play it by yourself! To begin with, DO NOT look at the story on the page below. Fill in the blanks on this page with the words called for. Then, using the words you have selected, fill in the blank spaces in the story.

Now you've created your own hilarious MAD LIBS® game!

HENRY V
(ACT 4, SCENE 3)

NOUN _____

VERB _____

NOUN _____

PLURAL NOUN _____

NOUN _____

PART OF THE BODY _____

PERSON IN ROOM _____

PERSON IN ROOM _____

CELEBRITY _____

ADJECTIVE _____

NOUN _____

NOUN _____

PLURAL NOUN _____

ADJECTIVE _____

PLURAL NOUN _____

MAD LIBS
HENRY V
(ACT 4, SCENE 3)

Henry: This day is called the feast of Crispian.

He that outlives this _____ and comes safe home
NOUN

Will _____ o' tiptoe when this day is nam'd. . . .
VERB

He that shall see this day, and live old _____,
NOUN

Will yearly on the vigil feast his _____
PLURAL NOUN

And say "Tomorrow is Saint Crispian."

Then will he strip his _____ and show his scars . . .
NOUN

Then shall our names,

Familiar in his _____ as household words,
PART OF THE BODY

_____ the King, Bedford and Exeter,
PERSON IN ROOM

Warwick and _____, Salisbury and _____,
PERSON IN ROOM   CELEBRITY

Be in their _____ cups freshly remembered.
ADJECTIVE

This story shall the good _____ teach his son,
NOUN

And Crispin Crispian shall ne'er go by,

From this day to the ending of the _____,
NOUN

But _____ in it shall be rememberèd—
PLURAL NOUN

We few, we _____ few, we band of _____ . . . .
ADJECTIVE   PLURAL NOUN

MAD LIBS® is fun to play with friends, but you can also play it by yourself! To begin with, DO NOT look at the story on the page below. Fill in the blanks on this page with the words called for. Then, using the words you have selected, fill in the blank spaces in the story.

Now you've created your own hilarious MAD LIBS® game!

SONNET #29

PLURAL NOUN _____

ADJECTIVE _____

NOUN _____

VERB _____

PLURAL NOUN _____

NOUN _____

NOUN _____

PLURAL NOUN _____

VERB _____

ANIMAL _____

ADJECTIVE _____

NOUN _____

NOUN _____

MAD LIBS®
SONNET #29

When in disgrace with _____ and men's eyes,
                        PLURAL NOUN

I all alone beweep my _____ state,
                       ADJECTIVE

And trouble deaf heaven with my _____-less cries,
                                NOUN

And _____ upon myself and curse my fate,
     VERB

Wishing me like to one more rich in hope,

Featured like him, like him with _____ possessed,
                                  PLURAL NOUN

Desiring this man's _____ and that man's _____,
                    NOUN   NOUN

With what I most enjoy contented least;

Yet in these _____ myself almost despising,
             PLURAL NOUN

Haply I _____ on thee, and then my state,
        VERB

Like to the _____ at break of day arising
            ANIMAL

From _____ earth, sings hymns at heaven's gate;
     ADJECTIVE

For thy sweet love remembered such _____ brings
                                   NOUN

That then I scorn to change my _____ with kings.
                               NOUN

MAD LIBS® is fun to play with friends, but you can also play it by yourself! To begin with, DO NOT look at the story on the page below. Fill in the blanks on this page with the words called for. Then, using the words you have selected, fill in the blank spaces in the story.

Now you've created your own hilarious MAD LIBS® game!

ROMEO AND JULIET
(ACT 1, SCENE 5)

VERB _____

ADJECTIVE _____

ADJECTIVE _____

NOUN _____

ADJECTIVE _____

PLURAL NOUN _____

PART OF THE BODY _____

SAME PART OF THE BODY _____

PART OF THE BODY (PLURAL) _____

SAME PART OF THE BODY (PLURAL) _____

ADJECTIVE _____

NOUN _____

VERB _____

SAME VERB _____

NOUN _____

ADVERB _____

MAD LIBS
ROMEO AND JULIET
(ACT 1, SCENE 5)

Romeo: If I _____ with my unworthiest hand
<u>VERB</u>

This holy shrine, the _____ fine is this:
<u>ADJECTIVE</u>

My lips, two _____ pilgrims, ready stand
<u>ADJECTIVE</u>

To smooth that rough _____ with a tender kiss.
<u>NOUN</u>

Juliet: _____ pilgrim, you do wrong your hand too much,
<u>ADJECTIVE</u>

Which mannerly devotion shows in this;

For saints have _____ that pilgrims' hands do touch,
<u>PLURAL NOUN</u>

And _____ to _____ is holy palmers' kiss.
<u>PART OF THE BODY</u>   <u>SAME PART OF THE BODY</u>

Romeo: Have not saints _____, and holy palmers too?
<u>PART OF THE BODY (PLURAL)</u>

Juliet: Ay, _____ that they must use in prayer.
<u>SAME PART OF THE BODY (PLURAL)</u>

Romeo: O then, _____ saint, let lips do what hands do.
<u>ADJECTIVE</u>

They pray: grant thou, lest _____ turn to despair.
<u>NOUN</u>

Juliet: Saints do not _____, though grant for prayers' sake.
<u>VERB</u>

Romeo: Then _____ not while my prayer's _____ I take.
<u>SAME VERB</u>   <u>NOUN</u>

(*He kisses her.*) Thus from my lips, by thine, my sin is purged.

Juliet: Then have my lips the sin that they have took.

Romeo: Sin from thy lips? O trespass _____ urged!
<u>ADVERB</u>

MAD LIBS® is fun to play with friends, but you can also play it by yourself! To begin with, DO NOT look at the story on the page below. Fill in the blanks on this page with the words called for. Then, using the words you have selected, fill in the blank spaces in the story.

Now you've created your own hilarious MAD LIBS® game!

SONNET #30

ADJECTIVE _____

NOUN _____

PLURAL NOUN _____

VERB _____

PERSON IN ROOM _____

PERSON IN ROOM _____

NOUN _____

NOUN _____

SAME NOUN _____

ADJECTIVE _____

VERB _____

PLURAL NOUN _____

MAD☺LIBS®
SONNET #30

When to the sessions of sweet _____ thought
ADJECTIVE

I summon up remembrance of things past,

I sigh the lack of many a/an _____ I sought,
NOUN

And with old _____ new wail my dear time's waste;
PLURAL NOUN

Then can I _____ an eye, unused to flow,
VERB

For precious friends hid in _____'s dateless night,
PERSON IN ROOM

And weep afresh _____'s long since canceled woe,
PERSON IN ROOM

And moan th' _____ of many a vanished sight.
NOUN

Then can I grieve at grievances foregone,

And heavily from _____ to _____ tell o'er
NOUN   SAME NOUN

The _____ account of fore-bemoanèd moan,
ADJECTIVE

Which I new pay as if not paid before.

But if the while I _____ on thee, dear friend,
VERB

All _____ are restored and sorrows end.
PLURAL NOUN

MAD LIBS® is fun to play with friends, but you can also play it by yourself! To begin with, DO NOT look at the story on the page below. Fill in the blanks on this page with the words called for. Then, using the words you have selected, fill in the blank spaces in the story.

Now you've created your own hilarious MAD LIBS® game!

MACBETH
(ACT 2, SCENE 1)

NOUN _____

VERB _____

ADJECTIVE _____

ADJECTIVE _____

NOUN _____

PART OF THE BODY _____

ADJECTIVE _____

VERB _____

VERB _____

NOUN _____

PART OF THE BODY (PLURAL) _____

PLURAL NOUN _____

TYPE OF LIQUID _____

ADJECTIVE _____

Macbeth: Is this a/an _____ which I see before me,

NOUN

The handle toward my hand? Come, let me _____ thee.

VERB

I have thee not, and yet I see thee still.

Art thou not, _____ vision, sensible

ADJECTIVE

To feeling as to sight? Or art thou but

A dagger of the mind, a/an _____ _____

ADJECTIVE   NOUN

Proceeding from the heat-oppressèd _____?

PART OF THE BODY

I see thee yet, in form as _____

ADJECTIVE

As this which now I _____. (*He draws his dagger.*)

VERB

Thou _____'st me the way that I was going,

VERB

And such a/an _____ I was to use.

NOUN

Mine _____ are made the fools o' th' other senses

PART OF THE BODY (PLURAL)

Or else worth all the _____. I see thee still,

PLURAL NOUN

And, on thy blade and dudgeon, gouts of _____,

TYPE OF LIQUID

Which was not so before. There's no such thing.

It is the _____ business which informs

ADJECTIVE

Thus to mine eyes.

MAD LIBS® is fun to play with friends, but you can also play it by yourself! To begin with, DO NOT look at the story on the page below. Fill in the blanks on this page with the words called for. Then, using the words you have selected, fill in the blank spaces in the story.

Now you've created your own hilarious MAD LIBS® game!

SONNET #116

ADJECTIVE _____

PLURAL NOUN _____

VERB ENDING IN "S" _____

VERB (PAST TENSE) _____

PLURAL NOUN _____

NOUN _____

NOUN _____

PERSON IN ROOM (MALE) _____

ADJECTIVE _____

VERB ENDING IN "S" _____

NOUN _____

VERB _____

NOUN _____

Let me not to the marriage of _____ minds
                                    ADJECTIVE

Admit _____. Love is not love
            PLURAL NOUN

Which alters when it alteration finds

Or _____ with the remover to remove.
        VERB ENDING IN "S"

O, no, it is an ever-_____ mark
                        VERB (PAST TENSE)

That looks on _____ and is never shaken;
                PLURAL NOUN

It is the _____ to every wand'ring bark,
            NOUN

Whose worth's unknown, although his _____ be taken.
                                        NOUN

Love's not _____'s fool, though _____
            PERSON IN ROOM (MALE)   ADJECTIVE

lips and cheeks

Within his bending sickle's compass come;

Love _____ not with his brief hours and weeks,
        VERB ENDING IN "S"

But bears it out even to the edge of doom.

If this be _____, and upon me proved,
            NOUN

I never _____, nor no _____ ever loved.
            VERB   NOUN

MAD LIBS® is fun to play with friends, but you can also play it by yourself! To begin with, DO NOT look at the story on the page below. Fill in the blanks on this page with the words called for. Then, using the words you have selected, fill in the blank spaces in the story.

Now you've created your own hilarious MAD LIBS® game!

RICHARD III
(ACT 1, SCENE 1)

NOUN _____

ADJECTIVE _____

PLURAL NOUN _____

ADJECTIVE _____

PART OF THE BODY (PLURAL) _____

ADJECTIVE _____

PLURAL NOUN _____

ADJECTIVE _____

PLURAL NOUN _____

NOUN _____

ADJECTIVE _____

VERB _____

ADVERB _____

ADJECTIVE _____

Richard: Now is the _____ of our discontent
NOUN

Made _____ summer by this son of York,
ADJECTIVE

And all the _____ that loured upon our house
PLURAL NOUN

In the _____ bosom of the ocean buried.
ADJECTIVE

Now are our _____ bound with _____ wreaths,
PART OF THE BODY (PLURAL)   ADJECTIVE

Our bruisèd arms hung up for _____,
PLURAL NOUN

Our _____ alarums changed to merry meetings,
ADJECTIVE

Our dreadful marches to delightful _____.
PLURAL NOUN

Grim-visaged war hath smoothed his wrinkled _____;
NOUN

And now, instead of mounting _____ steeds
ADJECTIVE

To _____ the souls of fearful adversaries,
VERB

He capers _____ in a lady's chamber
ADVERB

To the _____ pleasing of a lute.
ADJECTIVE

MAD LIBS® is fun to play with friends, but you can also play it by yourself! To begin with, DO NOT look at the story on the page below. Fill in the blanks on this page with the words called for. Then, using the words you have selected, fill in the blank spaces in the story.

Now you've created your own hilarious MAD LIBS® game!

HAMLET
(ACT 1, SCENE 3)

PART OF THE BODY _____

NOUN _____

NOUN _____

NOUN _____

NOUN _____

ADJECTIVE _____

NOUN _____

A PLACE _____

ADJECTIVE _____

OCCUPATION _____

VERB ENDING IN "S" _____

VERB ENDING IN "ING" _____

NOUN _____

ADJECTIVE _____

MAD LIBS
HAMLET
(ACT 1, SCENE 3)

Polonius: Give thy thoughts no _____,
PART OF THE BODY

Nor any unproportioned thought his _____.
NOUN

Be thou familiar, but by no means vulgar. . . .

Give every _____ thy ear, but few thy voice.
NOUN

Take each man's _____, but reserve thy judgment.
NOUN

Costly thy _____ as thy purse can buy,
NOUN

But not expressed in fancy (_____, not gaudy),
ADJECTIVE

For the _____ oft proclaims the man,
NOUN

And they in (the) _____ of the best rank and station
A PLACE

Are of a most _____ and generous chief in that.
ADJECTIVE

Neither a borrower nor a/an _____ be,
OCCUPATION

For loan oft _____ both itself and friend,
VERB ENDING IN "S"

And _____ dulls the edge of husbandry.
VERB ENDING IN "ING"

This above all: to thine own _____ be true,
NOUN

And it must follow, as the night the day,

Thou canst not then be _____ to any man.
ADJECTIVE

MAD LIBS® is fun to play with friends, but you can also play it by yourself! To begin with, DO NOT look at the story on the page below. Fill in the blanks on this page with the words called for. Then, using the words you have selected, fill in the blank spaces in the story.

Now you've created your own hilarious MAD LIBS® game!

SONNET #126

NOUN _____

CELEBRITY (MALE) _____

VERB ENDING IN "ING" _____

ADJECTIVE _____

NOUN _____

VERB _____

VERB ENDING IN "S" _____

NOUN _____

NOUN _____

VERB _____

NOUN _____

VERB _____

MAD LIBS
SONNET #126

O thou, my lovely _____, who in thy power

NOUN

Dost hold _____'s fickle glass, his sickle hour;

CELEBRITY (MALE)

Who hast by waning grown, and therein show'st

Thy lover's _____ as thy _____ self grow'st.

VERB ENDING IN "ING" ADJECTIVE

If Nature, sovereign mistress over _____,

NOUN

As thou goest onwards still will _____ thee back,

VERB

She _____ thee to this purpose, that her skill

VERB ENDING IN "S"

May _____ disgrace, and wretched minutes kill.

NOUN

Yet fear her, O thou _____ of her pleasure!

NOUN

She may _____, but not still keep, her treasure.

VERB

Her _____, though delayed, answered must be,

NOUN

And her quietus is to _____ thee.

VERB

MAD LIBS® is fun to play with friends, but you can also play it by yourself! To begin with, DO NOT look at the story on the page below. Fill in the blanks on this page with the words called for. Then, using the words you have selected, fill in the blank spaces in the story.

Now you've created your own hilarious MAD LIBS® game!

TWELFTH NIGHT
(ACT 1, SCENE 1)

NOUN _____

VERB _____

NOUN _____

PART OF THE BODY _____

PLURAL NOUN _____

NOUN _____

ADJECTIVE _____

ADJECTIVE _____

VERB _____

NOUN _____

ADJECTIVE _____

PLURAL NOUN _____

ADJECTIVE _____

Orsino: If music be the food of love, play on.

Give me _____ of it, that, surfeiting,
NOUN

The appetite may sicken and so _____.
VERB

That _____ again! It had a dying fall.
NOUN

O, it came o'er my _____ like the sweet sound
PART OF THE BODY

That breathes upon a bank of _____,
PLURAL NOUN

Stealing and giving _____. Enough; no more.
NOUN

'Tis not so _____ now as it was before.
ADJECTIVE

O spirit of love, how _____ and fresh art thou,
ADJECTIVE

That, notwithstanding thy capacity

_____-eth as the sea, naught enters there,
VERB

Of what _____ and pitch soe'er,
NOUN

But falls into abatement and _____ price
ADJECTIVE

Even in a minute. So full of _____ is fancy
PLURAL NOUN

That it alone is _____ fantastical.
ADJECTIVE

MAD LIBS® is fun to play with friends, but you can also play it by yourself! To begin with, DO NOT look at the story on the page below. Fill in the blanks on this page with the words called for. Then, using the words you have selected, fill in the blank spaces in the story.

Now you've created your own hilarious MAD LIBS® game!

SONNET #130

PERSON IN ROOM (FEMALE) _____

PART OF THE BODY (PLURAL) _____

PLURAL NOUN _____

COLOR _____

ADJECTIVE _____

ADJECTIVE _____

NOUN _____

ADJECTIVE _____

SILLY WORD _____

VERB ENDING IN "S" _____

A PLACE _____

NOUN _____

VERB (PAST TENSE) _____

MAD LIBS

SONNET #130

My _____'s eyes are nothing like the sun;
PERSON IN ROOM (FEMALE)

Coral is far more red than her _____' red;
PART OF THE BODY (PLURAL)

If snow be white, why then her _____ are dun;
PLURAL NOUN

If hairs be wires, _____ wires grow on her head.
COLOR

I have seen roses damasked, _____ and white,
ADJECTIVE

But no such roses see I in her cheeks;

And in _____ perfumes is there more delight
ADJECTIVE

Than in the breath that from my _____ reeks.
NOUN

I love to hear her speak, yet well I know

That music hath a far more _____ sound.
ADJECTIVE

I grant I never saw a goddess go;

My _____, when she walks, _____ on the ground.
SILLY WORD   VERB ENDING IN "S"

And yet, by (the) _____, I think my _____ as rare
A PLACE   NOUN

As any she _____ with false compare.
VERB (PAST TENSE)

MAD LIBS® is fun to play with friends, but you can also play it by yourself! To begin with, DO NOT look at the story on the page below. Fill in the blanks on this page with the words called for. Then, using the words you have selected, fill in the blank spaces in the story.

Now you've created your own hilarious MAD LIBS® game!

MACBETH
(ACT 5, SCENE 1)

ADJECTIVE _____

A PLACE _____

OCCUPATION _____

NOUN _____

ADJECTIVE _____

TYPE OF LIQUID _____

NOUN _____

PART OF THE BODY (PLURAL) _____

PLURAL NOUN _____

PART OF THE BODY _____

NOUN _____

CELEBRITY (MALE) _____

NOUN _____

MAD LIBS
MACBETH
(ACT 5, SCENE 1)

Lady Macbeth: Yet here's a spot. . . . Out, _____ spot, out, I say! One.
ADJECTIVE

Two. Why then, 'tis time to do 't. (The) _____ is murky. Fie, my lord,
A PLACE

fie, a/an _____ and afeard? What need we fear who knows it,
OCCUPATION

when none can call our _____ to account? Yet who would have thought
NOUN

the _____ man to have had so much _____ in him? . . .
ADJECTIVE   TYPE OF LIQUID

The _____ of Fife had a wife. Where is she now? What, will these
NOUN

_____ ne'er be clean? No more o' that, my lord, no more
PART OF THE BODY (PLURAL)

o' that. You mar all with this starting. . . . Here's the smell of the blood still. All

the _____ of Arabia will not sweeten this little _____.
PLURAL NOUN   PART OF THE BODY

O, O, O! . . . Wash your hands. Put on your _____. Look not so pale.
NOUN

I tell you yet again, _____'s buried; he cannot come out on 's
CELEBRITY (MALE)

_____.
NOUN

MAD LIBS® is fun to play with friends, but you can also play it by yourself! To begin with, DO NOT look at the story on the page below. Fill in the blanks on this page with the words called for. Then, using the words you have selected, fill in the blank spaces in the story.

Now you've created your own hilarious MAD LIBS® game!

A MIDSUMMER NIGHT'S DREAM (ACT 5, SCENE 1)

PLURAL NOUN _____

VERB _____

VERB (PAST TENSE) _____

PLURAL NOUN _____

ADJECTIVE _____

PLURAL NOUN _____

VERB _____

ADJECTIVE _____

ANIMAL _____

SILLY WORD _____

EXCLAMATION _____

PLURAL NOUN _____

PERSON IN ROOM _____

PLURAL NOUN _____

Puck: If we _____ have offended,
_{PLURAL NOUN}

_____ but this and all is mended:
_{VERB}

That you have but _____ here
_{VERB (PAST TENSE)}

While these _____ did appear.
_{PLURAL NOUN}

And this _____ and idle theme,
_{ADJECTIVE}

No more yielding but a dream,

_____, do not reprehend.
_{PLURAL NOUN}

If you _____, we will mend.
_{VERB}

And, as I am a/an _____ Puck,
_{ADJECTIVE}

If we have unearnèd luck

Now to 'scape the _____'s tongue,
_{ANIMAL}

We will make amends ere long.

Else the Puck a/an _____ call.
_{SILLY WORD}

So _____ unto you all.
_{EXCLAMATION}

Give me your _____, if we be friends,
_{PLURAL NOUN}

And _____ shall restore _____.
_{PERSON IN ROOM} _{PLURAL NOUN}

MAD LIBS®

SHARK ATTACK! MAD LIBS

by Mickie
Matheis

Mad Libs
An Imprint of Penguin Random House

MAD LIBS®

INSTRUCTIONS

MAD LIBS® is a game for people who don't like games!
It can be played by one, two, three, four, or forty.

• RIDICULOUSLY SIMPLE DIRECTIONS

In this tablet you will find stories containing blank spaces where words are left out. One player, the READER, selects one of these stories. The READER does not tell anyone what the story is about. Instead, he/she asks the other players, the WRITERS, to give him/her words. These words are used to fill in the blank spaces in the story.

• TO PLAY

The READER asks each WRITER in turn to call out a word—an adjective or a noun or whatever the space calls for—and uses them to fill in the blank spaces in the story. The result is a MAD LIBS® game.

When the READER then reads the completed MAD LIBS® game to the other players, they will discover that they have written a story that is fantastic, screamingly funny, shocking, silly, crazy, or just plain dumb—depending upon which words each WRITER called out.

• EXAMPLE (*Before* and *After*)

"_____!" he said _____
       EXCLAMATION   ADVERB

as he jumped into his convertible _____ and
                                                      NOUN

drove off with his _____ wife.
                              ADJECTIVE

"_____OUCH_____!" he said _____STUPIDLY_____
       EXCLAMATION   ADVERB

as he jumped into his convertible _____CAT_____ and
                                                      NOUN

drove off with his _____BRAVE_____ wife.
                              ADJECTIVE

MAD LIBS®

QUICK REVIEW

In case you have forgotten what adjectives, adverbs, nouns, and verbs are, here is a quick review:

An ADJECTIVE describes something or somebody. *Lumpy, soft, ugly, messy,* and *short* are adjectives.

An ADVERB tells how something is done. It modifies a verb and usually ends in "ly." *Modestly, stupidly, greedily,* and *carefully* are adverbs.

A NOUN is the name of a person, place, or thing. *Sidewalk, umbrella, bridle, bathtub,* and *nose* are nouns.

A VERB is an action word. *Run, pitch, jump,* and *swim* are verbs. Put the verbs in past tense if the directions say PAST TENSE. *Ran, pitched, jumped,* and *swam* are verbs in the past tense.

When we ask for A PLACE, we mean any sort of place: a country or city *(Spain, Cleveland)* or a room *(bathroom, kitchen).*

An EXCLAMATION or SILLY WORD is any sort of funny sound, gasp, grunt, or outcry, like *Wow!, Ouch!, Whomp!, Ick!,* and *Gadzooks!*

When we ask for specific words, like a NUMBER, a COLOR, an ANIMAL, or a PART OF THE BODY, we mean a word that is one of those things, like *seven, blue, horse,* or *head.*

When we ask for a PLURAL, it means more than one. For example, *cat* pluralized is *cats.*

MAD LIBS® is fun to play with friends, but you can also play it by yourself! To begin with, DO NOT look at the story on the page below. Fill in the blanks on this page with the words called for. Then, using the words you have selected, fill in the blank spaces in the story.

Now you've created your own hilarious MAD LIBS® game!

PREHISTORIC BEGINNINGS

PLURAL NOUN _____

TYPE OF LIQUID _____

A PLACE _____

NUMBER _____

ADJECTIVE _____

NOUN _____

VERB _____

PLURAL NOUN _____

ADJECTIVE _____

ADJECTIVE _____

NOUN _____

PART OF THE BODY (PLURAL) _____

ANIMAL (PLURAL) _____

CELEBRITY _____

PLURAL NOUN _____

NOUN _____

NUMBER _____

PLURAL NOUN _____

MAD LIBS
PREHISTORIC BEGINNINGS

Sharks are among the world's oldest living undersea _____, having
PLURAL NOUN

first appeared in the oceanic _____ of (the) _____
TYPE OF LIQUID   A PLACE

nearly _____ years ago. In fact, sharks are older than the
NUMBER

_____ dinosaurs! Prehistoric sharks were bizarre-looking creatures.
ADJECTIVE

They had _____-like fins that helped them _____ quickly
NOUN   VERB

in the water when dangerous _____ approached. Their skin was
PLURAL NOUN

covered with _____, toothlike scales called denticles. Some had
ADJECTIVE

_____ spikes on their heads that resembled devil horns, while others
ADJECTIVE

sported _____-shaped dorsal fins on their _____.
NOUN   PART OF THE BODY (PLURAL)

Some sharks were as small as miniature _____, while others,
ANIMAL (PLURAL)

such as the legendary megalodon, were bigger than a *Tyrannosaurus rex!* The

megalodon, which literally translates to _____, was one of the most
CELEBRITY

powerful predators in history, with razor-like teeth measuring seven

_____ long! This massive _____ ate _____ pounds
PLURAL NOUN   NOUN   NUMBER

of food every day, including its favorite snack: prehistoric _____.
PLURAL NOUN

MAD LIBS® is fun to play with friends, but you can also play it by yourself! To begin with, DO NOT look at the story on the page below. Fill in the blanks on this page with the words called for. Then, using the words you have selected, fill in the blank spaces in the story.

Now you've created your own hilarious MAD LIBS® game!

FUN FACTS

VERB ENDING IN "ING" _____

NUMBER _____

A PLACE _____

ADJECTIVE _____

PART OF THE BODY (PLURAL) _____

VERB _____

PLURAL NOUN _____

TYPE OF FOOD (PLURAL) _____

PLURAL NOUN _____

ADJECTIVE _____

VERB _____

A PLACE _____

TYPE OF LIQUID _____

A PLACE _____

ADVERB _____

ADJECTIVE _____

MAD LIBS
FUN FACTS

Studies have shown that sharks have been _____ in the
                                          VERB ENDING IN "ING"
oceans for well over four hundred million years. Today, there are more than

_____ known species of sharks throughout (the) _____.
    NUMBER   A PLACE
Young, _____ sharks are called pups. They are born with full sets of
          ADJECTIVE
teeth in their _____, and soon after birth, they leave their
               PART OF THE BODY (PLURAL)
mothers because they are able to feed and _____ on their own. One
                                              VERB
unusual quality about sharks is that they lose teeth on a regular basis, and new

_____ grow in their mouths to replace them. Most shark species eat
  PLURAL NOUN
things like fish, crustaceans, plankton, _____, and
                                          TYPE OF FOOD (PLURAL)
_____. Sharks have exceptionally _____ senses, especially
  PLURAL NOUN   ADJECTIVE
their ability to smell. They live and _____ in a wide range of aquatic
                                          VERB
habitats, such as the warm waters of (the) _____ or the cooler
                                              A PLACE
_____ near (the) _____. Some species are at risk of
  TYPE OF LIQUID   A PLACE
becoming extinct, which would be a/an _____ terrible loss, as sharks
                                          ADVERB
are not just awesome—they're totally _____!
                                        ADJECTIVE

MAD LIBS® is fun to play with friends, but you can also play it by yourself! To begin with, DO NOT look at the story on the page below. Fill in the blanks on this page with the words called for. Then, using the words you have selected, fill in the blank spaces in the story.

Now you've created your own hilarious MAD LIBS® game!

DEEP-SEA DINERS

ADJECTIVE _____

ADVERB _____

NUMBER _____

PART OF THE BODY _____

ANIMAL (PLURAL) _____

VERB _____

ADJECTIVE _____

VERB ENDING IN "ING" _____

ADJECTIVE _____

OCCUPATION (PLURAL) _____

PLURAL NOUN _____

VERB ENDING IN "ING" _____

TYPE OF LIQUID _____

PLURAL NOUN _____

TYPE OF LIQUID _____

A PLACE _____

NOUN _____

MAD LIBS®
DEEP-SEA DINERS

What makes sharks such smart, _____ hunters? Everything about

ADJECTIVE

them! First of all, they have _____ sharp senses, such as their hearing.

ADVERB

Sharks have _____ tiny holes on either side of their _____,

NUMBER ... PART OF THE BODY

which help them to hear other _____ miles away. Their abilities

ANIMAL (PLURAL)

to see, smell, and _____ are also exceptionally _____! Sharks

VERB ... ADJECTIVE

even have a sixth sense called electroreception that alerts them to other living

creatures _____ nearby. When it comes to swimming,

VERB ENDING IN "ING"

sharks are speedy, stealthy, and _____, just like underwater

ADJECTIVE

_____. Some sharks snatch _____ right off the

OCCUPATION (PLURAL) ... PLURAL NOUN

beach while they're _____. Other sharks swim miles below

VERB ENDING IN "ING"

the surface of the _____ to find food. These predators play a very

TYPE OF LIQUID

important role in the ocean's ecosystem. Because they are eating machines, they

help control the numbers of other _____ living in the

PLURAL NOUN

_____ all over (the) _____. After all, very few animals

TYPE OF LIQUID ... A PLACE

can hide from a hungry _____!

NOUN

MAD LIBS® is fun to play with friends, but you can also play it by yourself! To begin with, DO NOT look at the story on the page below. Fill in the blanks on this page with the words called for. Then, using the words you have selected, fill in the blank spaces in the story.

Now you've created your own hilarious MAD LIBS® game!

SHARK SPECIES, PART 1

TYPE OF LIQUID _____

PLURAL NOUN _____

NOUN _____

PART OF THE BODY _____

VERB ENDING IN "ING" _____

NOUN _____

ANIMAL _____

VERB ENDING IN "ING" _____

PLURAL NOUN _____

ADVERB _____

ANIMAL (PLURAL) _____

PART OF THE BODY _____

EXCLAMATION _____

Oceans and other bodies of _____ around the world are populated
TYPE OF LIQUID

with sharks, including these fascinating _____:
PLURAL NOUN

- **Hammerhead Shark:** This weird-looking _____ is best
NOUN
known for its long, narrow _____, which it uses like a
PART OF THE BODY
metal detector to sense food, such as stingrays _____
VERB ENDING IN "ING"
along the ocean floor.

- **Tiger Shark:** This shark gets its name from the vertical stripes and dark
black _____-spots on its body that resemble those of a/an
NOUN
_____. This shark is a lean, mean _____
ANIMAL   VERB ENDING IN "ING"
machine, with a mouthful of sharp _____ shaped like a
PLURAL NOUN
circular saw.

- **Bull Shark:** This stocky shark has a/an _____ aggressive
ADVERB
personality, roughly bumping _____ and other
ANIMAL (PLURAL)
underwater prey with its _____ to make sure they are edible.
PART OF THE BODY
_____, that would hurt!
EXCLAMATION

MAD LIBS® is fun to play with friends, but you can also play it by yourself! To begin with, DO NOT look at the story on the page below. Fill in the blanks on this page with the words called for. Then, using the words you have selected, fill in the blank spaces in the story.

Now you've created your own hilarious MAD LIBS® game!

GREAT WHITES: A TALE ABOUT TEETH

NOUN _____

ADJECTIVE _____

ADJECTIVE _____

PLURAL NOUN _____

NOUN _____

NUMBER _____

PART OF THE BODY _____

VERB ENDING IN "ING" _____

ADJECTIVE _____

TYPE OF FOOD (PLURAL) _____

COLOR _____

ADVERB _____

VERB ENDING IN "ING" _____

MAD LIBS
GREAT WHITES:
A TALE ABOUT TEETH

_____ scientists learn a lot about sharks by studying their
    NOUN

_____ teeth. For example, they can determine if the shark was large,
    ADJECTIVE

small, or _____ and what type of sea-_____ it ate. Did
    ADJECTIVE   PLURAL NOUN

you know that sharks regularly lose their teeth? Luckily, a new _____
                                                NOUN

automatically replaces the lost tooth. Some sharks can lose anywhere from

_____ to thirty thousand teeth in their lifetimes! A shark's teeth are
    NUMBER

arranged in rows inside its massive _____, with the front row
                                       PART OF THE BODY

doing most of the _____ as the shark hunts. Teeth have
                  VERB ENDING IN "ING"

different shapes and uses, depending on the species. For example, sharks that

eat fish have long, _____, needlelike teeth ideal for gripping slippery
              ADJECTIVE

_____. Those that feed on crustaceans have thick teeth that
    TYPE OF FOOD (PLURAL)

resemble dinner plates. Others, such as the great _____ shark, have
                                        COLOR

_____ jagged teeth that cut like knives. Taking a look at a shark's
    ADVERB

teeth is super cool, as long as you're _____ from a distance!
                              VERB ENDING IN "ING"

MAD LIBS® is fun to play with friends, but you can also play it by yourself! To begin with, DO NOT look at the story on the page below. Fill in the blanks on this page with the words called for. Then, using the words you have selected, fill in the blank spaces in the story.

Now you've created your own hilarious MAD LIBS® game!

MYTHS AND MISCONCEPTIONS

PLURAL NOUN _____

NOUN _____

VERB ENDING IN "ING" _____

TYPE OF FOOD (PLURAL) _____

PART OF THE BODY _____

ADJECTIVE _____

SILLY WORD _____

TYPE OF LIQUID _____

NOUN _____

ANIMAL _____

ADJECTIVE _____

NUMBER _____

PART OF THE BODY _____

ADJECTIVE _____

PLURAL NOUN _____

MAD LIBS®
MYTHS
AND MISCONCEPTIONS

The biggest myth about sharks is that they purposely attack human

_____, which is why they have been called "_____-eaters."
PLURAL NOUN   NOUN

But it's far more likely that sharks simply mistake people _____
                                                            VERB ENDING IN "ING"

in the ocean for turtles or other things they like to eat, such as

_____. They will take a test bite with their _____
TYPE OF FOOD (PLURAL)   PART OF THE BODY

because they don't have hands to touch with. When sharks realize humans

don't taste particularly _____, they probably think, "_____,
                          ADJECTIVE   SILLY WORD

yuck!" before swimming away. In reality, people have a better chance of getting

injured by a flying cork from a bottle of _____, a/an _____
                                           TYPE OF LIQUID   NOUN

falling on their head from a coconut tree, or a/an _____ stinging
                                                     ANIMAL

them. It's also not true that every shark is enormously _____. For
                                                          ADJECTIVE

example, the dwarf lantern shark is just _____ inches in length—
                                          NUMBER

roughly the size of a human _____. Sharks have gotten a/an
                             PART OF THE BODY

_____ reputation over the years, but they actually deserve respect
ADJECTIVE

and _____.
     PLURAL NOUN

MAD LIBS® is fun to play with friends, but you can also play it by yourself! To begin with, DO NOT look at the story on the page below. Fill in the blanks on this page with the words called for. Then, using the words you have selected, fill in the blank spaces in the story.

Now you've created your own hilarious MAD LIBS® game!

IF SHARKS COULD FLY

PLURAL NOUN _____

VERB ENDING IN "ING" _____

NOUN _____

ADJECTIVE _____

NOUN _____

ADVERB _____

PART OF THE BODY _____

NUMBER _____

ADJECTIVE _____

TYPE OF LIQUID _____

PART OF THE BODY _____

ADJECTIVE _____

NUMBER _____

NOUN _____

ANIMAL _____

CELEBRITY _____

MAD LIBS®
IF SHARKS COULD FLY

For those adventurous _____ who film sharks _____
                              PLURAL NOUN   VERB ENDING IN "ING"

in the wild, capturing a great white _____ breaching on camera is
                                          NOUN

not only unforgettable, it's downright _____. Breaching is when a
                                           ADJECTIVE

shark launches itself out of the ocean as it's hunting a seal or other fast

_____. Watching a breaching shark in slow motion is _____
    NOUN   ADVERB

epic! The shark leaps, _____-first, anywhere from eight to
                         PART OF THE BODY

_____ feet in the air, twists around like a/an _____ acrobat
    NUMBER   ADJECTIVE

with its prey in its jaws, then drops into the _____ on its
                                                 TYPE OF LIQUID

_____, making a/an _____ splash that can often be
  PART OF THE BODY   ADJECTIVE

heard for miles. While it's hard to imagine a/an _____-pound
                                                    NUMBER

_____ propelling itself almost entirely out of the ocean with the
    NOUN

speed and force of a winged _____, the great white shark does just
                              ANIMAL

that. It's one more reason this species of shark is the _____ of the
                                                          CELEBRITY

shark world!

MAD LIBS® is fun to play with friends, but you can also play it by yourself! To begin with, DO NOT look at the story on the page below. Fill in the blanks on this page with the words called for. Then, using the words you have selected, fill in the blank spaces in the story.

Now you've created your own hilarious MAD LIBS® game!

SHARKS OR DOGS?

ADJECTIVE _____

PLURAL NOUN _____

VERB _____

CELEBRITY _____

SAME CELEBRITY _____

VERB ENDING IN "ING" _____

PART OF THE BODY _____

ADVERB _____

NOUN _____

TYPE OF FOOD _____

TYPE OF LIQUID _____

EXCLAMATION _____

VERB _____

PART OF THE BODY _____

PLURAL NOUN _____

ADJECTIVE _____

MAD LIBS
SHARKS OR DOGS?

Good news! Your family is getting a/an _____ new pet! What should
ADJECTIVE

it be: a dog or a shark? Both of these _____ have their good
PLURAL NOUN

points. For example, dogs are fun to _____ with. You just have to yell,
VERB

"Here, _____! Here, _____!" and they will come
CELEBRITY SAME CELEBRITY

_____. They'll knock you flat on your _____ and
VERB ENDING IN "ING" PART OF THE BODY

_____ lick you all over. That's why dogs are called "man's best
ADVERB

_____." On the other hand, playing fetch with sharks is awesome.
NOUN

Just take a/an _____-covered fish, throw it as far as you can out
TYPE OF FOOD

into the _____, and—_____!—watch that shark
TYPE OF LIQUID EXCLAMATION

_____! Dogs will love you with all their _____, but
VERB PART OF THE BODY

sharks will protect you from menacing _____. Yes, a dog would
PLURAL NOUN

definitely make a great pet. On the other hand, imagine how fantastic it would

be to tell your teacher that your shark ate your _____ homework!
ADJECTIVE

MAD LIBS® is fun to play with friends, but you can also play it by yourself! To begin with, DO NOT look at the story on the page below. Fill in the blanks on this page with the words called for. Then, using the words you have selected, fill in the blank spaces in the story.

Now you've created your own hilarious MAD LIBS® game!

WHAT'S ON THE MENU?

NOUN _____

A PLACE _____

VERB _____

NUMBER _____

ADJECTIVE _____

CELEBRITY _____

NOUN _____

TYPE OF LIQUID _____

PLURAL NOUN _____

ADVERB _____

TYPE OF FOOD (PLURAL) _____

COLOR _____

NOUN _____

A PLACE _____

TYPE OF FOOD (PLURAL) _____

PART OF THE BODY _____

ADJECTIVE _____

ADJECTIVE _____

Welcome to the Shark Fin Grill, the best _____-food restaurant in
NOUN

all of (the) _____! Sit back and _____ in our _____-square-
A PLACE   VERB   NUMBER

foot dining room and enjoy _____ dishes prepared by our world-
ADJECTIVE

class chef, _____. I would suggest starting with our soup of the day,
CELEBRITY

_____ bisque, a steaming _____ broth with flavorful
NOUN   TYPE OF LIQUID

chunks of _____, served with our signature sea-sar salad, a/an
PLURAL NOUN

_____ hearty helping of crisp greens topped with vine-ripened
ADVERB

_____. For your main course, our special tonight is grilled
TYPE OF FOOD (PLURAL)

_____-fish, freshly caught from the pristine waters of the
COLOR

_____ Ocean off the coast of (the) _____. Lightly
NOUN   A PLACE

seasoned with minced _____, this dish will absolutely
TYPE OF FOOD (PLURAL)

melt in your _____. Stop into the Shark Fin Grill soon for
PART OF THE BODY

a/an _____ bite. You'll be _____ you did!
ADJECTIVE   ADJECTIVE

MAD LIBS® is fun to play with friends, but you can also play it by yourself! To begin with, DO NOT look at the story on the page below. Fill in the blanks on this page with the words called for. Then, using the words you have selected, fill in the blank spaces in the story.

Now you've created your own hilarious MAD LIBS® game!

GREATEST SHARK MOVIES OF ALL TIME

PLURAL NOUN _____

ADJECTIVE _____

PERSON IN ROOM _____

VERB ENDING IN "ING" _____

PERSON IN ROOM (MALE) _____

SAME PERSON IN ROOM (MALE) _____

COLOR _____

CELEBRITY (MALE) _____

A PLACE _____

NOUN _____

ADJECTIVE _____

PERSON IN ROOM _____

CELEBRITY _____

ADJECTIVE _____

PLURAL NOUN _____

Grab a bucket of hot buttered _____ and check out these classic
                                    PLURAL NOUN

shark movies:

- **_Kung Fu Shark_**: This animated movie tells the story of a/an

  _____ shark named _____ skilled in the ancient
        ADJECTIVE   PERSON IN ROOM

  art of kung fu _____.
                  VERB ENDING IN "ING"

- **_Finding_** _____: This is the sweet story of
                 PERSON IN ROOM (MALE)

  _____, a little _____ shark whose
   SAME PERSON IN ROOM (MALE)   COLOR

  father, _____, travels to the ends of (the) _____ to
           CELEBRITY (MALE)   A PLACE

  find his son when he goes missing.

- **_Great White and the Seven Sharks_**: A monstrous great white

  _____ roams the ocean with his seven _____
        NOUN   ADJECTIVE

  sidekicks—Bubbles, Coral, Spike, Finn, Crush, _____,
                                                  PERSON IN ROOM

  and _____.
        CELEBRITY

- **_Sea Wars_**: A/An _____ group of aquatic rebels band
                        ADJECTIVE

  together to fight Shark Nader and his dark forces, restoring peace and

  _____ to the ocean.
   PLURAL NOUN

MAD LIBS® is fun to play with friends, but you can also play it by yourself! To begin with, DO NOT look at the story on the page below. Fill in the blanks on this page with the words called for. Then, using the words you have selected, fill in the blank spaces in the story.

Now you've created your own hilarious MAD LIBS® game!

AN UP CLOSE UNDERWATER ENCOUNTER

PART OF THE BODY _____

ADJECTIVE _____

PLURAL NOUN _____

VERB ENDING IN "ING" _____

ANIMAL _____

PLURAL NOUN _____

TYPE OF LIQUID _____

VERB _____

TYPE OF FOOD (PLURAL) _____

NUMBER _____

NOUN _____

PART OF THE BODY _____

COLOR _____

NOUN _____

ADJECTIVE _____

ANIMAL (PLURAL) _____

CELEBRITY _____

PERSON IN ROOM _____

Swimming with sharks is not for the faint of _____! However,
PART OF THE BODY

cage dives are safe, fun, and _____. It's thrilling to see great white
ADJECTIVE

_____ _____ right in front of you! Here's how
PLURAL NOUN   VERB ENDING IN "ING"

the process works. You'll sail out to _____-infested waters and put
ANIMAL

on a wet suit. Then you'll climb into a cage made from galvanized steel

_____, and the crew will slowly lower it into the _____.
PLURAL NOUN   TYPE OF LIQUID

The cage is securely tied to the boat, so if at any time you wish to _____
VERB

or exit, you can. Next, the crew will lure sharks over using chum, which is a

mixture of fish and _____. While it may be terrifying to have a
TYPE OF FOOD (PLURAL)

shark not more than _____ inches from your _____, don't
NUMBER   NOUN

worry, its _____ is too large to fit through the cage bars. You may
PART OF THE BODY

also see dolphins, _____ _____ turtles, and maybe even
COLOR   NOUN

_____ humpback _____. Our satisfied cage-diving
ADJECTIVE   ANIMAL (PLURAL)

clients have included _____ and _____. Won't you be
CELEBRITY   PERSON IN ROOM

next?

MAD LIBS® is fun to play with friends, but you can also play it by yourself! To begin with, DO NOT look at the story on the page below. Fill in the blanks on this page with the words called for. Then, using the words you have selected, fill in the blank spaces in the story.

Now you've created your own hilarious MAD LIBS® game!

SHARK PARTY

NOUN _____

NUMBER _____

PLURAL NOUN _____

ADJECTIVE _____

VERB ENDING IN "ING" _____

ANIMAL (PLURAL) _____

ADJECTIVE _____

NOUN _____

ADVERB _____

PART OF THE BODY _____

VERB _____

NOUN _____

PLURAL NOUN _____

TYPE OF LIQUID _____

ANIMAL _____

VERB _____

The shark-themed party that my mom and <u>crotch pot</u> threw when I
 NOUN
turned <u>30</u> years old was amazing. Ten of my closest
 NUMBER
<u>carrots</u> and I spent the day doing <u>watering</u> shark stuff. We
 PLURAL NOUN ADJECTIVE
played a game in our <u>juicing</u> pool called shark toss. The object
 VERB ENDING IN "ING"
was to throw little plastic <u>monkeys</u> through the center of a floaty.
 ANIMAL (PLURAL)
Whoever got the most in was the <u>stupid</u> winner. And, of course, we
 ADJECTIVE
played pin the fin on the <u>olives</u>. The decorations were
 NOUN
<u>choch grabbingly</u> awesome, too. My parents made this cool cardboard cutout
 ADVERB
of a shark's mouth that you could stick your <u>weaner</u> in for a
 PART OF THE BODY
photo. There were signs all over our lawn that said things such as *Caution:*
<u>cooking</u> *at Your Own Risk* . . . and *Beware!* <u>tonge</u> *-Infested*
 VERB NOUN
Waters . . . and *Do Not Feed the* <u>coolhers</u>. There were fin-shaped ice
 PLURAL NOUN
sculptures floating in the punch bowl to keep the <u>peepee</u> chilled.
 TYPE OF LIQUID
There were gifts, too. My favorite was a giant inflatable pool <u>gerbals</u>.
 ANIMAL
Since I can't <u>licking</u> with real sharks, this was the next best thing!
 VERB

MAD LIBS® is fun to play with friends, but you can also play it by yourself! To begin with, DO NOT look at the story on the page below. Fill in the blanks on this page with the words called for. Then, using the words you have selected, fill in the blank spaces in the story.

Now you've created your own hilarious MAD LIBS® game!

SHARK SPECIES, PART 2

PLURAL NOUN _____

ANIMAL _____

NOUN _____

TYPE OF FOOD (PLURAL) _____

ADJECTIVE _____

PART OF THE BODY _____

VERB _____

TYPE OF LIQUID _____

ADJECTIVE _____

VERB ENDING IN "ING" _____

PART OF THE BODY (PLURAL) _____

ADJECTIVE _____

PLURAL NOUN _____

PLURAL NOUN _____

NOUN _____

Some of the more commonly known species of _____ include:

PLURAL NOUN

- **Whale Shark:** Although this gentle giant is the largest species of aquatic

  _____, it feeds on the tiniest _____ creatures, such

ANIMAL NOUN

  as plankton and microscopic _____. It gets its name

TYPE OF FOOD (PLURAL)

  because of how massively _____ it is. Each whale shark has

ADJECTIVE

  unique spots, like the fingerprints on a human _____.

PART OF THE BODY

- **Mako Shark:** This shark can _____ as fast as a cheetah can

VERB

  run. It shoots through the _____ like a/an _____

TYPE OF LIQUID ADJECTIVE

  torpedo. When it's provoked, the mako will start _____

VERB ENDING IN "ING"

  in a figure eight pattern, lunging at its target with its daggerlike

  _____ bared.

PART OF THE BODY (PLURAL)

- **Great White Shark:** This _____ predator hunts with speed,

ADJECTIVE

  force, and deadly _____. Its mouth contains three hundred

PLURAL NOUN

  large, triangular _____. The only creature capable of taking

PLURAL NOUN

  on a great white is the killer _____!

NOUN

MAD LIBS® is fun to play with friends, but you can also play it by yourself! To begin with, DO NOT look at the story on the page below. Fill in the blanks on this page with the words called for. Then, using the words you have selected, fill in the blank spaces in the story.

Now you've created your own hilarious MAD LIBS® game!

ODE TO THE GREAT WHITE

NOUN _____

COLOR _____

ANIMAL (PLURAL) _____

ADJECTIVE _____

VERB _____

ADJECTIVE _____

PART OF THE BODY _____

NUMBER _____

CELEBRITY _____

VERB ENDING IN "ING" _____

VERB _____

NOUN _____

SILLY WORD _____

ADJECTIVE _____

The great white _____ rules the ocean—
NOUN

he's the king of the deep _____ sea.
COLOR

Schools of fish scatter like spooked _____
ANIMAL (PLURAL)

when they spot His Majesty.

This shark is a/an _____ hunter—
ADJECTIVE

he can _____ with exceptional speed.
VERB

He's known for a/an _____ sense of smell,
ADJECTIVE

and his _____ holds hundreds of teeth.
PART OF THE BODY

He has _____ more muscles than _____—
NUMBER   CELEBRITY

in short, this shark's a beast.

He's a lean, mean _____ machine that
VERB ENDING IN "ING"

lives to _____ and feast.
VERB

You don't ever want to come face-to-face

with this powerful _____-eating shark.
NOUN

Why not? _____! Because it's a fact
SILLY WORD

that his _____ bite is worse than his bark!
ADJECTIVE

MAD LIBS® is fun to play with friends, but you can also play it by yourself! To begin with, DO NOT look at the story on the page below. Fill in the blanks on this page with the words called for. Then, using the words you have selected, fill in the blank spaces in the story.

Now you've created your own hilarious MAD LIBS® game!

HOW TO MAKE A SHARK TOOTH NECKLACE

VERB _____

ADJECTIVE _____

PART OF THE BODY (PLURAL) _____

A PLACE _____

ADJECTIVE _____

NOUN _____

NUMBER _____

ADJECTIVE _____

NOUN _____

PLURAL NOUN _____

NOUN _____

PART OF THE BODY _____

EXCLAMATION _____

PLURAL NOUN _____

PART OF THE BODY (PLURAL) _____

MAD LIBS®
HOW TO MAKE A
SHARK TOOTH NECKLACE

You don't need to _____ with sharks to show your love for them. Try
                        VERB

wearing a fashionably _____ shark tooth necklace instead, made
                        ADJECTIVE

from fossilized _____ found in coastal areas around
                  PART OF THE BODY (PLURAL)

(the) _____. You can make one in a few steps:
       A PLACE

1. Choose a/an _____ tooth, preferably a larger one, such as from
                  ADJECTIVE

   a/an _____ shark.
          NOUN

2. Tie approximately _____ inches of wire around each side of
                        NUMBER

   the _____ tooth and bring the ends together in the shape of
         ADJECTIVE

   a/an _____.
          NOUN

3. Slide a cord made out of leather or _____ through the loop.
                                          PLURAL NOUN

   For extra flair, add a few _____-shaped beads along either side.
                                NOUN

4. Tie the cord around your _____ and—_____!—
                              PART OF THE BODY   EXCLAMATION

   you're done.

See? There's no need to spend a ton of _____ on this cool piece of
                                          PLURAL NOUN

jewelry when you can make one using your own two _____.
                                                    PART OF THE BODY (PLURAL)

MAD LIBS® is fun to play with friends, but you can also play it by yourself! To begin with, DO NOT look at the story on the page below. Fill in the blanks on this page with the words called for. Then, using the words you have selected, fill in the blank spaces in the story.

Now you've created your own hilarious MAD LIBS® game!

SAFETY 101

VERB ENDING IN "ING" _____

NOUN _____

ADJECTIVE _____

VERB _____

TYPE OF LIQUID _____

ADJECTIVE _____

ADVERB _____

PLURAL NOUN _____

PART OF THE BODY _____

SILLY WORD _____

NOUN _____

COLOR _____

ANIMAL _____

NOUN _____

How do you stay safe in the ocean where sharks could be _____?
VERB ENDING IN "ING"
Although encountering a/an _____ while diving can be a thrilling
NOUN
experience, staying _____ is your priority, and here are some ways to
ADJECTIVE
do that:

- First, scan the area where you want to _____. Enter the
VERB
_____ quietly instead of making a/an _____ splash,
TYPE OF LIQUID _ADJECTIVE_
so you don't surprise any sharks.

- Remain _____ alert and aware of your surroundings.
ADVERB

- Stick close to the other _____ you are diving with.
PLURAL NOUN

- Avoid making any sudden or erratic movements with your
_____ or yelling "_____!" especially if you spot
PART OF THE BODY _SILLY WORD_
a/an _____ fin circling the area.
NOUN

The great _____ shark, the bull shark, and the _____
COLOR _ANIMAL_
shark are the most commonly encountered species. Always be respectful of
them. Remember: You are invading their _____, not the other way
NOUN
around!

MAD LIBS® is fun to play with friends, but you can also play it by yourself! To begin with, DO NOT look at the story on the page below. Fill in the blanks on this page with the words called for. Then, using the words you have selected, fill in the blank spaces in the story.

Now you've created your own hilarious MAD LIBS® game!

WANTED: SHARK SCIENTIST

NUMBER _____

ADJECTIVE _____

VERB _____

TYPE OF LIQUID _____

SILLY WORD _____

PLURAL NOUN _____

A PLACE _____

VERB _____

VERB _____

ADJECTIVE _____

NOUN _____

VERB ENDING IN "ING" _____

ARTICLE OF CLOTHING (PLURAL) _____

NUMBER _____

PLURAL NOUN _____

NOUN _____

ADJECTIVE _____

VERB _____

MAD LIBS
WANTED: SHARK SCIENTIST

Do you love sharks? Could you spend _____ hours a day studying
NUMBER

one of the world's most fiercely _____ predators in their natural
ADJECTIVE

habitat? Are you fearless enough to _____ alongside them in
VERB

_____ for research purposes? If you answered "_____"
TYPE OF LIQUID   SILLY WORD

to any of these questions, then we want *YOU* to join our team of

curious-minded _____ here at the Oceanic Observatory in
PLURAL NOUN

(the) _____ as we collect and categorize all types of data on sharks—
A PLACE

what they eat, where they _____, how fast they _____,
VERB   VERB

and more. While _____ experience is not required, priority
ADJECTIVE

consideration will be given to candidates who can expertly use sonar and other

_____ equipment. In addition, preference will be given to those
NOUN

skilled in swimming, scuba diving, and _____. Wet suits and
VERB ENDING IN "ING"

_____ for diving will be provided. Starting salary is
ARTICLE OF CLOTHING (PLURAL)

_____ _____ a month. Think you might be the right
NUMBER   PLURAL NOUN

_____ for the _____ job of a shark scientist? Then
NOUN   ADJECTIVE

_____ today for an application!
VERB

MAD LIBS® is fun to play with friends, but you can also play it by yourself! To begin with, DO NOT look at the story on the page below. Fill in the blanks on this page with the words called for. Then, using the words you have selected, fill in the blank spaces in the story.

Now you've created your own hilarious MAD LIBS® game!

A SHARK-INFESTED STORE

A PLACE _____

ADJECTIVE _____

NOUN _____

VERB _____

PART OF THE BODY (PLURAL) _____

ADJECTIVE _____

ARTICLE OF CLOTHING _____

NOUN _____

PART OF THE BODY _____

TYPE OF LIQUID _____

TYPE OF FOOD _____

NUMBER _____

ADJECTIVE _____

NUMBER _____

PLURAL NOUN _____

PERSON IN ROOM _____

CELEBRITY _____

VERB _____

MAD LIBS®
A SHARK-INFESTED STORE

When I was on vacation in (the) _____, I discovered a/an _____
                                  A PLACE   ADJECTIVE

souvenir place near _____ Beach called the Shark Shop. This was a
                         NOUN

popular place where shark-loving tourists like myself could come to

_____. I couldn't believe my _____ when I saw
     VERB   PART OF THE BODY (PLURAL)

all the _____ shark stuff they stocked. I found a fun _____
         ADJECTIVE   ARTICLE OF CLOTHING

that made you look like a hammerhead _____ when you put it on
                                          NOUN

your _____. Next, I discovered a sporty water bottle that said
       PART OF THE BODY

JAW-SOME! It was perfect for holding my _____. My favorite find
                                         TYPE OF LIQUID

was _____-flavored shark gummies. I bought _____ pounds
     TYPE OF FOOD   NUMBER

of those because they were so deliciously _____! I gave the salesclerk
                                           ADJECTIVE

_____ _____ to pay for my purchases. I couldn't wait to
    NUMBER   PLURAL NOUN

show my cool new stuff to my shark-loving friends, _____ and
                                                    PERSON IN ROOM

_____. And I couldn't wait to come back to the Shark Shop to
   CELEBRITY

_____ again soon!
     VERB

MAD LIBS® is fun to play with friends, but you can also play it by yourself! To begin with, DO NOT look at the story on the page below. Fill in the blanks on this page with the words called for. Then, using the words you have selected, fill in the blank spaces in the story.

Now you've created your own hilarious MAD LIBS® game!

ADOPT A SHARK TODAY

PERSON IN ROOM _____

NUMBER _____

PLURAL NOUN _____

ADJECTIVE _____

CELEBRITY _____

NUMBER _____

NOUN _____

TYPE OF LIQUID _____

A PLACE _____

ANIMAL _____

ARTICLE OF CLOTHING _____

PART OF THE BODY _____

PLURAL NOUN _____

NOUN _____

A PLACE _____

NUMBER _____

ADVERB _____

PERSON IN ROOM _____

MAD LIBS®
ADOPT A SHARK TODAY

Dear __Daddy Depp__ :
 PERSON IN ROOM

Thank you for your generous donation of __2__ __Pots__
 NUMBER PLURAL NOUN

to the Adopt-a-Shark program. Membership to our program earns you these

__Crazy__ benefits:
 ADJECTIVE

• A framed Certificate of Adoption for "__Forrest Gump__,"
 CELEBRITY

a/an __4__-pound __Pillow__ who lives in the __Peepee__
 NUMBER NOUN TYPE OF LIQUID

off the coast of (the) __disneyland__
 A PLACE

• A plush __Lion__ and photo of your adopted pet
 ANIMAL

• A/An __Scarf__ to wear on your __Wiener__
 ARTICLE OF CLOTHING PART OF THE BODY

• A tote bag to carry all your shark-themed __Boobies__
 PLURAL NOUN

• Free admission to any aquarium or other __carrot__ museum in
 NOUN

(the) __TJ maxx__ and a/an __6__ percent discount on
 A PLACE NUMBER

any merchandise in the gift shop

__Slowly__ yours,
 ADVERB

__Amy__, President
 PERSON IN ROOM

MAD LIBS® is fun to play with friends, but you can also play it by yourself! To begin with, DO NOT look at the story on the page below. Fill in the blanks on this page with the words called for. Then, using the words you have selected, fill in the blank spaces in the story.

Now you've created your own hilarious MAD LIBS® game!

SHARK VS. DOLPHIN

PERSON IN ROOM _____

CELEBRITY _____

ADJECTIVE _____

PLURAL NOUN _____

ADJECTIVE _____

NOUN _____

EXCLAMATION _____

VERB _____

VERB _____

ADVERB _____

ADJECTIVE _____

TYPE OF LIQUID _____

PLURAL NOUN _____

VERB ENDING IN "ING" _____

NUMBER _____

PART OF THE BODY (PLURAL) _____

MAD LIBS

SHARK VS. DOLPHIN

This is Ace "Sharkface" McGinnis here with Dr. _____, live from
                                                PERSON IN ROOM

the shark vessel, the _____.
                        CELEBRITY

Ace: Tell me, Doctor, which _____ creature would win in a shark
                                 ADJECTIVE

versus dolphin showdown?

Doctor: Most shark species have the advantage of size, power, and

_____. They are stealthy, _____ hunters, so they can also
 PLURAL NOUN   ADJECTIVE

sneak up on an unsuspecting _____ and—_____!—it's
                             NOUN   EXCLAMATION

game over! But that's not always enough.

Ace: It helps that dolphins can _____ faster than sharks, right?
                                      VERB

Doctor: Yes! Dolphins can usually out-_____ sharks in a chase. They
                                            VERB

are _____ intelligent and use a/an _____ ability called
     ADVERB   ADJECTIVE

echolocation to navigate through _____ and communicate with
                                  TYPE OF LIQUID

their fellow _____ in order to avoid sharks.
              PLURAL NOUN

Ace: It's simple, though. Dolphins should stay away from where sharks are

_____ if they want to keep all _____ of their
 VERB ENDING IN "ING"   NUMBER

_____.
 PART OF THE BODY (PLURAL)

MAD LIBS® is fun to play with friends, but you can also play it by yourself! To begin with, DO NOT look at the story on the page below. Fill in the blanks on this page with the words called for. Then, using the words you have selected, fill in the blank spaces in the story.

Now you've created your own hilarious MAD LIBS® game!

SAVE THE SHARKS

NOUN _____

PLURAL NOUN _____

ADJECTIVE _____

ADJECTIVE _____

NOUN _____

A PLACE _____

VERB ENDING IN "ING" _____

TYPE OF LIQUID _____

PLURAL NOUN _____

ANIMAL (PLURAL) _____

A PLACE _____

VERB _____

ADJECTIVE _____

VERB ENDING IN "ING" _____

A PLACE _____

PLURAL NOUN _____

MAD LIBS®
SAVE THE SHARKS

Sharks need our help! The Worldwide _____ Conservation

NOUN

Organization, which tracks whether _____ should be classified as

PLURAL NOUN

endangered, reports that an alarmingly high number of shark species are close

to becoming _____ . Sharks are hunted for their _____ fins,

ADJECTIVE _ADJECTIVE_

which are used to make _____ soup, considered a delicacy in many

NOUN

parts of (the) _____ . _____ in polluted

A PLACE _VERB ENDING IN "ING"_

_____ harms sharks, too. And sharks are often caught in netted

TYPE OF LIQUID

_____ that are meant to trap other _____ . The increase

PLURAL NOUN _ANIMAL (PLURAL)_

in tourism in parts of (the) _____ is yet another factor. Sharks use

A PLACE

coastal areas to feed, _____ , and give birth to their _____

VERB _ADJECTIVE_

young, but the development of vacation areas is wiping out this space for sharks

to use. Hunting, overfishing, and other _____ activities are

VERB ENDING IN "ING"

badly affecting shark populations. If humans aren't careful, sharks could

disappear from (the) _____ very soon. That wouldn't just be bad for

A PLACE

the oceans, it would affect _____ everywhere!

PLURAL NOUN

MAD LIBS®

PRESIDENTIAL MAD LIBS

by Douglas Yacka

Mad Libs
An Imprint of Penguin Random House

INSTRUCTIONS

MAD LIBS® is a game for people who don't like games!
It can be played by one, two, three, four, or forty.

• RIDICULOUSLY SIMPLE DIRECTIONS

In this tablet you will find stories containing blank spaces where words are left out.
One player, the READER, selects one of these stories. The READER does not tell anyone
what the story is about. Instead, he/she asks the other players, the WRITERS, to give
him/her words. These words are used to fill in the blank spaces in the story.

• TO PLAY

The READER asks each WRITER in turn to call out a word—an adjective or a noun or
whatever the space calls for—and uses them to fill in the blank spaces in the story. The
result is a MAD LIBS® game.

When the READER then reads the completed MAD LIBS® game to the other players,
they will discover that they have written a story that is fantastic, screamingly funny,
shocking, silly, crazy, or just plain dumb—depending upon which words each WRITER
called out.

• EXAMPLE (*Before* and *After*)

"_____!" he said _____
        EXCLAMATION   ADVERB

as he jumped into his convertible _____ and
                                              NOUN

drove off with his _____ wife.
                    ADJECTIVE

"_____OUCH_____!" he said _____STUPIDLY_____
        EXCLAMATION   ADVERB

as he jumped into his convertible _____CAT_____ and
                                              NOUN

drove off with his _____BRAVE_____ wife.
                    ADJECTIVE

QUICK REVIEW

In case you have forgotten what adjectives, adverbs, nouns, and verbs are, here is a quick review:

An ADJECTIVE describes something or somebody. *Lumpy, soft, ugly, messy,* and *short* are adjectives.

An ADVERB tells how something is done. It modifies a verb and usually ends in "ly." *Modestly, stupidly, greedily,* and *carefully* are adverbs.

A NOUN is the name of a person, place, or thing. *Sidewalk, umbrella, bridle, bathtub,* and *nose* are nouns.

A VERB is an action word. *Run, pitch, jump,* and *swim* are verbs. Put the verbs in past tense if the directions say PAST TENSE. *Ran, pitched, jumped,* and *swam* are verbs in the past tense.

When we ask for A PLACE, we mean any sort of place: a country or city *(Spain, Cleveland)* or a room *(bathroom, kitchen).*

An EXCLAMATION or SILLY WORD is any sort of funny sound, gasp, grunt, or outcry, like *Wow!, Ouch!, Whomp!, Ick!,* and *Gadzooks!*

When we ask for specific words, like a NUMBER, a COLOR, an ANIMAL, or a PART OF THE BODY, we mean a word that is one of those things, like *seven, blue, horse,* or *head.*

When we ask for a PLURAL, it means more than one. For example, *cat* pluralized is *cats.*

MAD LIBS® is fun to play with friends, but you can also play it by yourself! To begin with, DO NOT look at the story on the page below. Fill in the blanks on this page with the words called for. Then, using the words you have selected, fill in the blank spaces in the story.

Now you've created your own hilarious MAD LIBS® game!

SO, YOU WANT TO BE PRESIDENT?

NOUN _____

ADJECTIVE _____

A PLACE _____

OCCUPATION _____

PART OF THE BODY (PLURAL) _____

ADJECTIVE _____

PLURAL NOUN _____

NOUN _____

PART OF THE BODY _____

ADJECTIVE _____

VERB (PAST TENSE) _____

ADVERB _____

PART OF THE BODY (PLURAL) _____

VERB ENDING IN "ING" _____

NOUN _____

Do you dream of becoming the next _____ of the United States?
NOUN

You'll probably want to start with a/an _____ position, like a
ADJECTIVE

councilperson or mayor of (the) _____ . Then you could become a
A PLACE

state representative or a/an _____ in order to cut your legislative
OCCUPATION

_____! Just make sure you don't support any _____
PART OF THE BODY (PLURAL)   ADJECTIVE

bills or controversial _____ . When in doubt, always side with the
PLURAL NOUN

everyday _____ . Be sure to keep your _____ clean and
NOUN   PART OF THE BODY

stay free of _____ scandals, which will be sure to surface during
ADJECTIVE

your campaign. Everything you've ever said or _____ will
VERB (PAST TENSE)

come to light. Finally, learn to smile and wave _____ . You'll be
ADVERB

shaking a lot of _____ and _____ a lot of
PART OF THE BODY (PLURAL)   VERB ENDING IN "ING"

babies on the campaign trail! Or you could always start as a reality TV

_____!
NOUN

MAD LIBS® is fun to play with friends, but you can also play it by yourself! To begin with, DO NOT look at the story on the page below. Fill in the blanks on this page with the words called for. Then, using the words you have selected, fill in the blank spaces in the story.

Now you've created your own hilarious MAD LIBS® game!

PRESIDENTIAL FIRSTS

NOUN _____

VERB _____

ARTICLE OF CLOTHING (PLURAL) _____

PART OF THE BODY (PLURAL) _____

NOUN _____

VERB (PAST TENSE) _____

PLURAL NOUN _____

ADJECTIVE _____

PART OF THE BODY (PLURAL) _____

NOUN _____

PLURAL NOUN _____

ADJECTIVE _____

VERB _____

NOUN _____

MAD LIBS®
PRESIDENTIAL FIRSTS

John Adams was the first _____ to live in the White House. James
                             NOUN

Madison was the first to _____ in long pants. Before that, the
                          VERB

gentlemen of the time wore _____ covering their
                           ARTICLE OF CLOTHING (PLURAL)

_____. James Monroe was the first to ride on a/an
PART OF THE BODY (PLURAL)

_____-ship. It is said that he felt queasy and _____
     NOUN   VERB (PAST TENSE)

all over the deck. Rutherford B. Hayes was the first to ban alcoholic

_____ from the White House. The first _____-handed
PLURAL NOUN   ADJECTIVE

president was James A. Garfield, although he learned how to write with both

_____. Benjamin Harrison was the first to have electricity
PART OF THE BODY (PLURAL)

in his _____, but he was afraid to turn the _____ on and
        NOUN   PLURAL NOUN

off. William Howard Taft was the first to throw the ceremonial _____
                                                                ADJECTIVE

pitch at a baseball game. Franklin D. Roosevelt was the first president to

_____ on TV. These days, you can't turn on the _____
   VERB   NOUN

without seeing our president!

MAD LIBS® is fun to play with friends, but you can also play it by yourself! To begin with, DO NOT look at the story on the page below. Fill in the blanks on this page with the words called for. Then, using the words you have selected, fill in the blank spaces in the story.

Now you've created your own hilarious MAD LIBS® game!

AIR FORCE ONE

A PLACE _____

PLURAL NOUN _____

NUMBER _____

VERB ENDING IN "ING" _____

PLURAL NOUN _____

ADJECTIVE _____

VERB ENDING IN "ING" _____

ADJECTIVE _____

ADJECTIVE _____

ADJECTIVE _____

VERB _____

NOUN _____

ADJECTIVE _____

ADJECTIVE _____

OCCUPATION (PLURAL) _____

MAD LIBS®
AIR FORCE ONE

There is no plane in (the) _____ more famous than Air Force One.
                              A PLACE

Many _____ do not realize this, but there are actually _____
        PLURAL NOUN   NUMBER

planes with this designation. "Air Force One" refers to whichever plane the

president is _____ on at the moment. The plane is quite large,
              VERB ENDING IN "ING"

with four thousand square _____, including an office, a bedroom,
                              PLURAL NOUN

two _____ kitchens, and a/an _____ room. Stylish
      ADJECTIVE   VERB ENDING IN "ING"

and _____ décor was added when Jackie Kennedy was First Lady.
      ADJECTIVE

Also on board is a mobile Situation Room in case of a/an _____
                                                            ADJECTIVE

emergency, and even a flying hospital. Security is a/an _____ concern,
                                                          ADJECTIVE

so the plane can _____ enemy signals and deflect weapons. It is
                    VERB

rumored that the plane can act as a/an _____ bunker in case of a/an
                                          NOUN

_____ attack. In addition to the president's staff, members of the
  ADJECTIVE

_____ press are often on board. Even in the air, the president can't
  ADJECTIVE

escape from _____!
              OCCUPATION (PLURAL)

MAD LIBS® is fun to play with friends, but you can also play it by yourself! To begin with, DO NOT look at the story on the page below. Fill in the blanks on this page with the words called for. Then, using the words you have selected, fill in the blank spaces in the story.

Now you've created your own hilarious MAD LIBS® game!

TO TRUMP OR NOT TO TRUMP

VERB _____

ADJECTIVE _____

ARTICLE OF CLOTHING (PLURAL) _____

VERB ENDING IN "ING" _____

NOUN _____

ADJECTIVE _____

TYPE OF BUILDING (PLURAL) _____

PLURAL NOUN _____

VERB ENDING IN "ING" _____

OCCUPATION (PLURAL) _____

PLURAL NOUN _____

CELEBRITY _____

VERB _____

PLURAL NOUN _____

Dan: Did you really ___pooping___ for Trump? I had no idea.
VERB

Joe: Sure. I don't know why everyone acts so ___sloshy___ when I say that.
ADJECTIVE

I even have one of those red ___Speedos___ with his slogan
ARTICLE OF CLOTHING (PLURAL)

on it.

Dan: Doesn't it bother you that he is always ___Crapping___ himself
VERB ENDING IN "ING"

and acts like he's the best ___munch___ in the world?
NOUN

Joe: I think it shows how _____ he is. Remember how successful he
ADJECTIVE

was in building _____ and managing _____?
TYPE OF BUILDING (PLURAL)   *PLURAL NOUN*

Dan: But aren't you worried about him _____ with foreign
VERB ENDING IN "ING"

countries?

Joe: I think foreign _____ will respect his views on
OCCUPATION (PLURAL)

_____. And he's much more persuasive than _____!
PLURAL NOUN   *CELEBRITY*

Dan: Well, we should really _____ back to work
VERB

_____ in his cabinet.
PLURAL NOUN

MAD LIBS® is fun to play with friends, but you [can also]
play it by yourself! To begin with, DO NOT look [at the]
story on the page below. Fill in the blanks on this p[age]
with the words called for. Then, using the words yo[u]
have selected, fill in the blank spaces in the story.

Now you've created your own hilarious MAD LIBS® game!

BAD, BAD BOYS

ADJECTIVE _____

NOUN _____

NOUN _____

TYPE OF EVENT _____

ADJECTIVE _____

PLURAL NOUN _____

TYPE OF LIQUID _____

PLURAL NOUN _____

TYPE OF LIQUID _____

NOUN _____

PLURAL NOUN _____

VERB ENDING IN "ING" _____

CELEBRITY (FEMALE) _____

VERB (PAST TENSE) _____

TYPE OF BUILDING _____

VERB _____

MAD LIBS®
BAD, BAD BOYS

We tend to think of our presidents as upstanding, distinguished, and

_____ figures leading the country. But some have gotten into a/an
   ADJECTIVE

_____ -load of trouble.
   NOUN

Andrew Jackson married a woman who was already married to another

_____ . Also, Jackson's inauguration _____ got so
   NOUN   TYPE OF EVENT

_____ that crowds broke dishes and _____ in the White
   ADJECTIVE   PLURAL NOUN

House. **Ulysses S. Grant's** administration stole taxes from the sale of

_____ , while **Warren G. Harding's** _____ sold the
   TYPE OF LIQUID   PLURAL NOUN

rights to drill for _____ . **Andrew Johnson** was the first _____
                      TYPE OF LIQUID   NOUN

to be impeached for illegally firing his secretary of _____ . **Bill Clinton**
                                                 PLURAL NOUN

was also impeached for _____ under oath about his affair with
                          VERB ENDING IN "ING"

_____ . But the most famous scandal is Watergate, where
   CELEBRITY (FEMALE)

Richard Nixon _____ to cover up a break-in at the Democratic
                  VERB (PAST TENSE)

_____ . He wound up having to _____ in disgrace!
   TYPE OF BUILDING   VERB

MAD LIBS® is fun to play with friends, but you can also play it by yourself! To begin with, DO NOT look at the story on the page below. Fill in the blanks on this page with the words called for. Then, using the words you have selected, fill in the blank spaces in the story.

Now you've created your own hilarious MAD LIBS® game!

HAIL TO THE CHIEF

ADJECTIVE _____

VERB _____

NOUN _____

CELEBRITY (MALE) _____

VERB ENDING IN "ING" _____

ADJECTIVE _____

ADJECTIVE _____

NOUN _____

PERSON IN ROOM _____

NOUN _____

ADJECTIVE _____

PLURAL NOUN _____

A PLACE _____

OCCUPATION _____

NOUN _____

VERB _____

PLURAL NOUN _____

ADJECTIVE _____

MAD LIBS®
HAIL TO THE CHIEF

Imagine having your own _____ anthem that plays almost everywhere
                              ADJECTIVE

you _____! As president, you get to hear it at every _____ you
         VERB   NOUN

attend. Every president since _____ has used the song when
                                CELEBRITY (MALE)

_____ at special occasions, with the exception of Chester A.
VERB ENDING IN "ING"

Arthur, who thought it was _____, and had a different song called
                              ADJECTIVE

" _____ _____ " written just for him. "Hail to the Chief"
   ADJECTIVE   NOUN

was adapted from a poem by _____ called "The _____ of
                            PERSON IN ROOM   NOUN

the Lake." Although the _____ tune is well known, many
                           ADJECTIVE

_____ do not know the lyrics:
PLURAL NOUN

     Hail to the Chief we have chosen for (the) _____,
                                        A PLACE

     Hail to the _____! We salute him, _____ and all.
               OCCUPATION   NOUN

     _____ to the Chief, as we pledge _____,
            VERB   PLURAL NOUN

     In proud fulfillment of a great, _____ call!
                                  ADJECTIVE

MAD LIBS® is fun to play with friends, but you can also play it by yourself! To begin with, DO NOT look at the story on the page below. Fill in the blanks on this page with the words called for. Then, using the words you have selected, fill in the blank spaces in the story.

Now you've created your own hilarious MAD LIBS® game!

PRESIDENTIAL PETS

NOUN _____

NOUN _____

ADJECTIVE _____

ANIMAL _____

VERB ENDING IN "ING" _____

COLOR _____

ADJECTIVE _____

VERB _____

ADJECTIVE _____

VERB (PAST TENSE) _____

ADVERB _____

ADJECTIVE _____

NOUN _____

ADJECTIVE _____

ANIMAL _____

MAD LIBS

PRESIDENTIAL PETS

Even the most powerful _____ in the world likes to snuggle up with
                        NOUN

a cuddly _____ every now and then. The White House has had
          NOUN

many furry, feathered, and _____ pets through the years. Of course,
                            ADJECTIVE

the most popular is man's best friend, the _____. Every president
                                             ANIMAL

since Theodore Roosevelt has had a dog _____ through the
                                        VERB ENDING IN "ING"

halls of the _____ House. Cats are also among the most
               COLOR

_____ of choices. You might _____, though, if you
   ADJECTIVE   VERB

knew some of the more _____ critters on the list. Both Herbert
                       ADJECTIVE

Hoover and John Quincy Adams _____ alligators in the White
                              VERB (PAST TENSE)

House (Adams enjoyed _____ scaring visitors with his gator).
                      ADVERB

Theodore Roosevelt was given a/an _____ bear, and Martin Van
                                   ADJECTIVE

Buren was given two tigers as a gift in place of a/an _____. However,
                                                       NOUN

the most _____ pet owner was probably Calvin Coolidge, who had
          ADJECTIVE

a wallaby, a/an _____, and a hippopotamus!
                 ANIMAL

MAD LIBS® is fun to play with friends, but you can also play it by yourself! To begin with, DO NOT look at the story on the page below. Fill in the blanks on this page with the words called for. Then, using the words you have selected, fill in the blank spaces in the story.

Now you've created your own hilarious MAD LIBS® game!

THE VETO

PLURAL NOUN _____

VERB _____

PLURAL NOUN _____

NOUN _____

VERB _____

A PLACE _____

VERB _____

NUMBER _____

NOUN _____

ADJECTIVE _____

PART OF THE BODY (PLURAL) _____

PLURAL NOUN _____

ADJECTIVE _____

ADJECTIVE _____

MAD LIBS®
THE VETO

One of the special _____ that a president has is the ability to
                    PLURAL NOUN

_____ a bill before it becomes a law. After a bill is approved by the
   VERB

Senate and the House of _____, it makes its way to the president's
                        PLURAL NOUN

_____ to be signed. If the president does not want to _____
   NOUN   VERB

the bill, he or she can use the veto and send it back to (the) _____
                                                               A PLACE

to be reconsidered. Congress can then _____ the president if
                                         VERB

_____ of them vote to override, in which case the _____
   NUMBER   NOUN

becomes law. This will probably make the president _____. In
                                                      ADJECTIVE

certain cases, it's been said that presidents have become so upset that smoke

came out of their _____! The reason for the veto is to keep
                  PART OF THE BODY (PLURAL)

the _____ of the government from having too much
       PLURAL NOUN

_____ power. But by using it, one side will always end up the
   ADJECTIVE

_____ loser!
   ADJECTIVE

MAD LIBS® is fun to play with friends, but you can also play it by yourself! To begin with, DO NOT look at the story on the page below. Fill in the blanks on this page with the words called for. Then, using the words you have selected, fill in the blank spaces in the story.

Now you've created your own hilarious MAD LIBS® game!

HOME SWEET HOME

ADJECTIVE _____

NUMBER _____

NOUN _____

CELEBRITY (MALE) _____

NUMBER _____

NOUN _____

VERB ENDING IN "ING" _____

PLURAL NOUN _____

PART OF THE BODY _____

TYPE OF FOOD _____

TYPE OF FOOD _____

ADJECTIVE _____

ADJECTIVE _____

PLURAL NOUN _____

PLURAL NOUN _____

ADJECTIVE _____

PLURAL NOUN _____

MAD LIBS®
HOME SWEET HOME

Thank you for joining us this morning as we take you on a/an _____
ADJECTIVE

tour of the White House. Over _____ people visit this _____
NUMBER   NOUN

every year. The first president to live here was _____. The
CELEBRITY (MALE)

house itself has 132 rooms, including _____ bathrooms, a movie
NUMBER

theater, a bowling _____, and a/an _____ pool. There
NOUN   VERB ENDING IN "ING"

is a staff of about ninety _____ ready to wait on the president hand
PLURAL NOUN

and _____, including five chefs to cook everything from
PART OF THE BODY

_____ to _____. The most well-known area of the
TYPE OF FOOD   TYPE OF FOOD

building is the _____ Wing, where we find the president's
ADJECTIVE

famous _____ Office. Important _____ are discussed
ADJECTIVE   PLURAL NOUN

here, where many historic _____ have been signed through the years.
PLURAL NOUN

Standing here, you really feel a/an _____ sense of history. Plus, you
ADJECTIVE

can brag about your house to the _____ next door!
PLURAL NOUN

MAD LIBS® is fun to play with friends, but you can also play it by yourself! To begin with, DO NOT look at the story on the page below. Fill in the blanks on this page with the words called for. Then, using the words you have selected, fill in the blank spaces in the story.

Now you've created your own hilarious MAD LIBS® game!

HONEST ABE

PLURAL NOUN _____

ADVERB _____

VERB ENDING IN "ING" _____

PERSON IN ROOM _____

NUMBER _____

PART OF THE BODY (PLURAL) _____

PLURAL NOUN _____

ADJECTIVE _____

OCCUPATION _____

ANIMAL (PLURAL) _____

VERB _____

ADJECTIVE _____

VERB ENDING IN "ING" _____

OCCUPATION (PLURAL) _____

NOUN _____

ADJECTIVE _____

MAD LIBS

HONEST ABE

Few _____ are as revered as Abraham Lincoln, known _____
    PLURAL NOUN   ADVERB

for his honesty. "Honest Abe" earned his nickname when he was a young man

_____ at a general store. When he discovered that he had
VERB ENDING IN "ING"

shorted _____ by _____ pennies, he closed the shop and
         PERSON IN ROOM   NUMBER

ran as fast as his _____ could carry him to return the money!
                    PART OF THE BODY (PLURAL)

Local _____ started asking Abe to settle _____ disputes
       PLURAL NOUN   ADJECTIVE

and contests. Lincoln was interested in the law and became a respected

_____. At the time, most lawyers and politicians were considered
 OCCUPATION

lying _____. When Lincoln would _____ in the
       ANIMAL (PLURAL)   VERB

courthouse, even those who lost to him still respected his _____
                                                            ADJECTIVE

integrity. As president, Lincoln was known for _____ the truth
                                                VERB ENDING IN "ING"

to his generals and _____. His honesty became the
                     OCCUPATION (PLURAL)

_____ of American virtue. And that's the _____ truth!
 NOUN   ADJECTIVE

MAD LIBS® is fun to play with friends, but you can also play it by yourself! To begin with, DO NOT look at the story on the page below. Fill in the blanks on this page with the words called for. Then, using the words you have selected, fill in the blank spaces in the story.

Now you've created your own hilarious MAD LIBS® game!

PRESIDENTIAL PRESS CONFERENCE

NOUN _____

NOUN _____

VERB ENDING IN "ING" _____

NOUN _____

PART OF THE BODY _____

NOUN _____

VERB _____

OCCUPATION (PLURAL) _____

PLURAL NOUN _____

FOREIGN COUNTRY _____

ADJECTIVE _____

CELEBRITY _____

ADJECTIVE _____

EXCLAMATION _____

PLURAL NOUN _____

MAD LIBS®
PRESIDENTIAL PRESS
CONFERENCE

P: I'd now like to open up the _____ for questions.
_____NOUN_____

Q: Can we get your reaction to yesterday's _____?
_____NOUN_____

P: We are _____ into the matter and will release an official
____VERB ENDING IN "ING"____

_____ within the next few days.
_____NOUN_____

Q: Does that mean you've changed your _____?
____PART OF THE BODY____

P: We stand by our current _____, but reserve the right to
_____NOUN_____

_____ if necessary.
_____VERB_____

Q: How do you respond to allegations that _____ in your
____OCCUPATION (PLURAL)____

cabinet traded _____ with _____?
_____PLURAL NOUN_____   ____FOREIGN COUNTRY____

P: I have no comment on this _____ accusation.
_____ADJECTIVE_____

Q: Do you disagree with the statement made by _____, who called
_____CELEBRITY_____

your remarks _____?
_____ADJECTIVE_____

P: _____! I do not need the opinions of Hollywood
____EXCLAMATION____

_____ to run the country. No more questions!
____PLURAL NOUN____

MAD LIBS® is fun to play with friends, but you can also play it by yourself! To begin with, DO NOT look at the story on the page below. Fill in the blanks on this page with the words called for. Then, using the words you have selected, fill in the blank spaces in the story.

Now you've created your own hilarious MAD LIBS® game!

A LETTER FROM GEORGE

PLURAL NOUN _____

OCCUPATION _____

A PLACE _____

NUMBER _____

ADJECTIVE _____

VERB ENDING IN "ING" _____

PLURAL NOUN _____

A PLACE _____

ADJECTIVE _____

PLURAL NOUN _____

VERB ENDING IN "ING" _____

PLURAL NOUN _____

ADJECTIVE _____

NOUN _____

PART OF THE BODY _____

VERB _____

ADJECTIVE _____

PART OF THE BODY _____

Hello, my fellow _____ in 2017, it's me, George Washington, the first
         PLURAL NOUN

_____ . I am writing from (the) _____ , where I have been
   OCCUPATION   A PLACE

secretly living for the past _____ years. I am concerned by the
                                  NUMBER

_____ state of affairs in America these days. It seems that your
   ADJECTIVE

politicians are more concerned with _____ one another than
                                      VERB ENDING IN "ING"

with listening to the _____ of the people. When we declared our
                           PLURAL NOUN

independence from (the) _____ , we set forth on a/an _____
                             A PLACE   ADJECTIVE

path guided by the voices of the everyday _____ . If we're going to
                                              PLURAL NOUN

keep _____ , then we need to learn how to respect all
       VERB ENDING IN "ING"

_____ . Don't get me wrong; we had _____ problems in my
   PLURAL NOUN   ADJECTIVE

day, too. Benjamin Franklin once called me a/an _____ and kicked
                                                    NOUN

me in the _____ . But at the end of the day, we were able to
            PART OF THE BODY

_____ in harmony. Let us find that _____ spirit once again, or
   VERB   ADJECTIVE

else I'm taking my _____ off the quarter!
                     PART OF THE BODY

MAD LIBS® is fun to play with friends, but you can also play it by yourself! To begin with, DO NOT look at the story on the page below. Fill in the blanks on this page with the words called for. Then, using the words you have selected, fill in the blank spaces in the story.

Now you've created your own hilarious MAD LIBS® game!

IN THE IMMORTAL WORDS OF . . .

NOUN _____

ADJECTIVE _____

VERB _____

VERB _____

NOUN _____

NOUN _____

VERB _____

PART OF THE BODY _____

ADVERB _____

NOUN _____

CELEBRITY (MALE) _____

NOUN _____

PART OF THE BODY _____

PART OF THE BODY _____

NOUN _____

- "The only thing we have to fear is _____ itself."
  NOUN
—Franklin D. Roosevelt

- "A president's hardest task is not to do what is _____, but to
  ADJECTIVE
_____ what is right." —Lyndon B. Johnson
  VERB

- "Ask not what your country can _____ for you—ask what
  VERB
you can do for your _____." —John F. Kennedy
  NOUN

- "A/An _____ divided against itself cannot _____."
  NOUN   VERB
—Abraham Lincoln

- "Read my _____: no new taxes." —George H. W. Bush
  PART OF THE BODY

- "Speak _____ and carry a big _____."
  ADVERB   NOUN
—Theodore Roosevelt

- "Mr. _____, tear down this _____!"
  CELEBRITY (MALE)   NOUN
—Ronald Reagan

- "We will extend a/an _____ if you are willing to unclench
  PART OF THE BODY
your _____." —Barack Obama
  PART OF THE BODY

- "I'm not a/an _____!" —Richard Nixon
  NOUN

MAD LIBS® is fun to play with friends, but you can also play it by yourself! To begin with, DO NOT look at the story on the page below. Fill in the blanks on this page with the words called for. Then, using the words you have selected, fill in the blank spaces in the story.

Now you've created your own hilarious MAD LIBS® game!

EXCERPT FROM TRUMP'S DIARY

ADJECTIVE _____

VERB ENDING IN "ING" _____

ADJECTIVE _____

OCCUPATION _____

PLURAL NOUN _____

NOUN _____

ADVERB _____

ADJECTIVE _____

VERB _____

ADJECTIVE _____

VERB _____

VERB _____

PART OF THE BODY _____

A PLACE _____

VERB ENDING IN "ING" _____

PLURAL NOUN _____

NOUN _____

Dear Diary,

Today was yet another _____ day at the White House. Who knew
                            ADJECTIVE

_____ the country would be so _____? When I was
VERB ENDING IN "ING"   ADJECTIVE

a/an _____, I had tremendous success in building _____.
        OCCUPATION   PLURAL NOUN

I also liked being a reality TV _____, but this is _____
                                    NOUN   ADVERB

different. There are all of these _____ rules, and everyone seems to
                                      ADJECTIVE

_____ them except me. To make matters worse, I am surrounded by
     VERB

a million _____ people telling me to _____ one moment
              ADJECTIVE   VERB

and then _____ the next. I feel like my _____ is spinning.
             VERB   PART OF THE BODY

And finally, I wish the press would go to (the) _____ and leave me
                                                    A PLACE

alone. They are constantly _____ my every move and asking
                            VERB ENDING IN "ING"

me about my _____. What kind of _____ have I gotten
                PLURAL NOUN   NOUN

myself into?!

Proudly yours,

Donald

MAD LIBS® is fun to play with friends, but you can also play it by yourself! To begin with, DO NOT look at the story on the page below. Fill in the blanks on this page with the words called for. Then, using the words you have selected, fill in the blank spaces in the story.

Now you've created your own hilarious MAD LIBS® game!

SECOND TO NONE

ADJECTIVE _____

ADJECTIVE _____

PART OF THE BODY _____

NOUN _____

OCCUPATION _____

VERB ENDING IN "ING" _____

PLURAL NOUN _____

VERB _____

VERB ENDING IN "ING" _____

NOUN _____

ADJECTIVE _____

PLURAL NOUN _____

PLURAL NOUN _____

VERB ENDING IN "ING" _____

TYPE OF FOOD _____

ADJECTIVE _____

America's First Ladies have been as _____ as the presidents themselves.
<u>ADJECTIVE</u>

Martha Washington was so _____ that they put her _____
<u>ADJECTIVE</u> <u>PART OF THE BODY</u>

on the one-dollar bill briefly. Abigail Adams, no less of a/an _____,
<u>NOUN</u>

was referred to as Mrs. _____. Some of these ladies liked
<u>OCCUPATION</u>

_____ parties. John Tyler's wife, Julia, was fond of lavish
<u>VERB ENDING IN "ING"</u>

_____. She was even known to _____ a polka dance!
<u>PLURAL NOUN</u> <u>VERB</u>

Florence Harding was known for _____ strong cocktails, and
<u>VERB ENDING IN "ING"</u>

Lucy Hayes started the annual Easter _____ hunt on the White
<u>NOUN</u>

House lawn. Many championed _____ causes. Abigail Fillmore
<u>ADJECTIVE</u>

loved to read _____ and created the White House library. Lucretia
<u>PLURAL NOUN</u>

Garfield campaigned for women to be paid the same as _____.
<u>PLURAL NOUN</u>

Laura Bush believed in _____ for education, and Michelle
<u>VERB ENDING IN "ING"</u>

Obama taught kids to eat their _____ instead of cookies. As the
<u>TYPE OF FOOD</u>

saying goes, behind every _____ man is a great woman!
<u>ADJECTIVE</u>

MAD LIBS® is fun to play with friends, but you can also play it by yourself! To begin with, DO NOT look at the story on the page below. Fill in the blanks on this page with the words called for. Then, using the words you have selected, fill in the blank spaces in the story.

Now you've created your own hilarious MAD LIBS® game!

ROOSEVELT VS. ROOSEVELT

PLURAL NOUN _____

ADJECTIVE _____

NUMBER _____

PLURAL NOUN _____

VERB ENDING IN "ING" _____

ADJECTIVE _____

OCCUPATION (PLURAL) _____

ADVERB _____

ANIMAL _____

NUMBER _____

ADJECTIVE _____

ADJECTIVE _____

ADJECTIVE _____

PART OF THE BODY _____

PERSON IN ROOM _____

Theodore "Teddy" Roosevelt: Many _____ confuse us, but Franklin
                                     PLURAL NOUN

and I couldn't be more _____ .
                          ADJECTIVE

Franklin D. Roosevelt: True. For starters, our presidencies were _____
                                                                        NUMBER

years apart.

Teddy: I liked to be outside, enjoying the _____ of nature, while
                                                 PLURAL NOUN

you were always _____ indoors.
                    VERB ENDING IN "ING"

FDR: I brought America out of the _____ Depression. Let's not
                                         ADJECTIVE

forget how many _____ I put back to work.
                   OCCUPATION (PLURAL)

Teddy: Well, I fought _____ against big businesses, so you can get
                             ADVERB

off your high _____ !
                 ANIMAL

FDR: I also had to deal with World War _____ . Do you think that
                                               NUMBER

was a/an _____ task?
            ADJECTIVE

Teddy: I wouldn't know. I kept the world a much more _____ place as
                                                            ADJECTIVE

president.

FDR: Don't be _____ . They put my _____ on the dime.
                    ADJECTIVE   _PART OF THE BODY_

Teddy: Dimes are small. My giant face is on the side of Mt. _____ .
                                                                  PERSON IN ROOM

Looks like I win!

MAD LIBS® is fun to play with friends, but you can also play it by yourself! To begin with, DO NOT look at the story on the page below. Fill in the blanks on this page with the words called for. Then, using the words you have selected, fill in the blank spaces in the story.

Now you've created your own hilarious MAD LIBS® game!

TWEETS FROM THE TOP

A PLACE _____

TYPE OF EVENT _____

NOUN _____

ADJECTIVE _____

EXCLAMATION _____

NOUN _____

OCCUPATION (PLURAL) _____

PLURAL NOUN _____

CELEBRITY (MALE) _____

ADJECTIVE _____

PART OF THE BODY _____

PLURAL NOUN _____

ADJECTIVE _____

MAD LIBS
TWEETS FROM THE TOP

Donald J. Trump @surrealDonaldTrump • 6m

Holding a big rally in (the) _____ this afternoon. Biggest crowd since
A PLACE

the presidential _____ !
TYPE OF EVENT

Donald J. Trump @surrealDonaldTrump • 7m

Reports of a/an _____ scandal totally untrue. Everything here at
NOUN

the White House is totally _____ . #_____ !
ADJECTIVE   _EXCLAMATION_

Donald J. Trump @surrealDonaldTrump • 5h

_____ growth is the biggest it's been in a decade,
NOUN

_____ say. Bringing _____ back to America!
OCCUPATION (PLURAL)   _PLURAL NOUN_

Donald J. Trump @surrealDonaldTrump • 7h

Comments by @ _____ totally _____ ! He is losing his
CELEBRITY (MALE)   _ADJECTIVE_

_____ . #canttouchthis
PART OF THE BODY

Donald J. Trump @surrealDonaldTrump • 9h

Don't believe the _____ . We are making America _____
PLURAL NOUN   _ADJECTIVE_

again!

MAD LIBS® is fun to play with friends, but you can also play it by yourself! To begin with, DO NOT look at the story on the page below. Fill in the blanks on this page with the words called for. Then, using the words you have selected, fill in the blank spaces in the story.

Now you've created your own hilarious MAD LIBS® game!

DID YOU KNOW...?

NUMBER _____

NOUN _____

NOUN _____

ADJECTIVE _____

VERB ENDING IN "ING" _____

NOUN _____

NOUN _____

NOUN _____

TYPE OF LIQUID _____

ADJECTIVE _____

MAD LIBS®
DID YOU KNOW . . . ?

- James Madison was our shortest president, at only five feet _____ inches tall.
  NUMBER

- Barack Obama was a collector of _____ books, such as *Conan*
  NOUN

  the _____ and *Spider-Man*.
  NOUN

- William Howard Taft was so _____ that he got stuck in the
  ADJECTIVE

  White House bathtub.

- The record for _____ to other countries belongs to Bill
  VERB ENDING IN "ING"

  Clinton.

- Chester A. Arthur was known as " _____ Arthur" because
  NOUN

  of his sense of fashion.

- Four presidents have received the Nobel _____ Prize.
  NOUN

- William Henry Harrison died exactly one month after taking the

  _____ of office.
  NOUN

- George Washington owned a/an _____ distillery. That
  TYPE OF LIQUID

  explains why his portraits look so _____!
  ADJECTIVE

MAD LIBS® is fun to play with friends, but you can also play it by yourself! To begin with, DO NOT look at the story on the page below. Fill in the blanks on this page with the words called for. Then, using the words you have selected, fill in the blank spaces in the story.

Now you've created your own hilarious MAD LIBS® game!

THOSE ARE THE PERKS

NOUN _____

ADJECTIVE _____

VEHICLE _____

NOUN _____

NUMBER _____

ADJECTIVE _____

TYPE OF FOOD _____

TYPE OF FOOD (PLURAL) _____

OCCUPATION _____

ADJECTIVE _____

PART OF THE BODY _____

PERSON IN ROOM _____

VERB _____

PLURAL NOUN _____

PLURAL NOUN _____

Aside from being the most powerful _____ in the world, you also get
_____NOUN_____

a/an _____ number of perks as president. Your _____,
_____ADJECTIVE_____   _____VEHICLE_____

nicknamed "The _____," is the safest there is. You are also surrounded
_____NOUN_____

by _____ Secret Service agents at any given time, so you should feel
_____NUMBER_____

_____ going anywhere. You get your own personal chef, who will
____ADJECTIVE____

make you _____ every day if you want, and prepares special
_____TYPE OF FOOD_____

_____ for important guests. Fresh flowers are provided daily
TYPE OF FOOD (PLURAL)

by a/an _____, and a personal valet makes sure you look
_____OCCUPATION_____

_____ from head to _____. A vacation home called
____ADJECTIVE____   ____PART OF THE BODY____

Camp _____ is your place to privately _____ when you
___PERSON IN ROOM___   _____VERB_____

need to get away from the _____ in DC. And best of all, after you
_____PLURAL NOUN_____

leave your job, you still get paid two hundred thousand _____ a year
_____PLURAL NOUN_____

for the rest of your life!

MAD LIBS® is fun to play with friends, but you can also play it by yourself! To begin with, DO NOT look at the story on the page below. Fill in the blanks on this page with the words called for. Then, using the words you have selected, fill in the blank spaces in the story.

Now you've created your own hilarious MAD LIBS® game!

STATE OF THE UNION

NOUN _____

ADJECTIVE _____

NUMBER _____

OCCUPATION (PLURAL) _____

PLURAL NOUN _____

NOUN _____

PLURAL NOUN _____

PLURAL NOUN _____

ADVERB _____

VERB ENDING IN "ING" _____

PLURAL NOUN _____

VERB ENDING IN "ING" _____

PART OF THE BODY _____

NOUN _____

ADJECTIVE _____

EXCLAMATION _____

MAD LIBS®
STATE OF THE UNION

My fellow Americans, as the new _____ begins, I am _____
NOUN   ADJECTIVE

to say how much we've accomplished. _____ new jobs have been
NUMBER

created. Our _____ are earning more _____ than
OCCUPATION (PLURAL)   PLURAL NOUN

ever before. We have finally reformed our _____ care system. Millions
NOUN

of _____ now have access to _____ that they
PLURAL NOUN   PLURAL NOUN

_____ need. Across the globe, America is _____ to
ADVERB   VERB ENDING IN "ING"

ensure our safety and to ensure that _____ are protected. But we
PLURAL NOUN

have to keep _____ if we are going to continue to flourish. I
VERB ENDING IN "ING"

am certain we can, if we work hand in _____ to achieve our
PART OF THE BODY

goals. The state of our _____ has never been more _____.
NOUN   ADJECTIVE

I think we can all collectively shout, " _____ !"
EXCLAMATION

MAD LIBS® is fun to play with friends, but you can also play it by yourself! To begin with, DO NOT look at the story on the page below. Fill in the blanks on this page with the words called for. Then, using the words you have selected, fill in the blank spaces in the story.

Now you've created your own hilarious MAD LIBS® game!

ALL THE PRESIDENT'S

_____
PLURAL NOUN

VERB _____

NOUN _____

PLURAL NOUN _____

VERB _____

FOREIGN COUNTRY _____

FOREIGN COUNTRY _____

PLURAL NOUN _____

ADJECTIVE _____

VERB _____

NUMBER _____

PLURAL NOUN _____

VERB ENDING IN "ING" _____

TYPE OF FOOD _____

PLURAL NOUN _____

NOUN _____

VERB _____

MAD LIBS
ALL THE PRESIDENT'S
PLURAL NOUN

The **president** is constantly surrounded by advisors who _____ for

VERB

him or her every day. For example . . .

The **chief of staff** coordinates every _____ between the president

NOUN

and other _____.

PLURAL NOUN

The **secretary of state's** job is to _____ all around the world to

VERB

places like _____ and _____.

FOREIGN COUNTRY   FOREIGN COUNTRY

The **attorney general** oversees enforcement of all our _____. He or

PLURAL NOUN

she is the most _____ legal officer in the United States.

ADJECTIVE

The **secretary of defense** must _____ all _____ branches

VERB   NUMBER

of the military.

The **secretary of education** makes certain we educate our _____ properly

PLURAL NOUN

by _____ on behalf of our schools.

VERB ENDING IN "ING"

The **secretary of agriculture** oversees farming, and the safety of your favorite

foods, like _____.

TYPE OF FOOD

And the **secretary of** _____ might be the most important, making

PLURAL NOUN

sure that every _____ can _____!

NOUN   VERB

Download Mad Libs today!

Join the millions of Mad Libs fans
creating wacky and wonderful
stories on our apps!